# CHURCH AND
# STATE IN THE NEW
# MILLENNIUM

# CHURCH AND STATE IN THE NEW MILLENNIUM

## ISSUES OF BELIEF AND MORALITY

### FOR THE 21ST CENTURY

## DAVID HOLLOWAY

HarperCollins*Publishers*

HarperCollins*Publishers*
77–85 Fulham Palace Road, London W6 8JB
www.fireandwater.com

First published in Great Britain in 2000
by HarperCollins*Publishers*
This edition 2000

1 3 5 7 9 10 8 6 4 2

Unless otherwise stated, Scripture quotations are taken
from the HOLY BIBLE, NEW INTERNATIONAL VERSION.
Copyright © 1973, 1978, 1984 by International Bible Society.
Used by permission.

In Chapter 7, Hugh Montefiore's book review of *Darwin on Trial*
by Philip E. Johnson is quoted with the kind permission of the
Editor of the *Church Times*

David Holloway asserts the moral right
to be identified as the author of this work

A catalogue record for this book
is available from the British Library

ISBN 0 00 274060 5

Printed and bound in Great Britain by
Omnia Books Ltd, Glasgow

# CONTENTS

# INTRODUCTION

As the twenty-first century begins one thing is certain. The intellectuals who predicted the end of religion under the acids of modernity have been proved wrong. Europe did see a great loss of belief and a weakening of the Christian faith during the twentieth century. That, however, is not the case in the rest of the world. The most 'modern' of all nations, the United States, is significantly religious. Four out of 10 people are in church in America every Sunday. It is not true that economic and social modernization and faith in God are incompatible.

At the start of the twenty-first century there is also a growing awareness that the big issues for public life are no longer 'political' but 'cultural'. Issues to do with the quality and 'the good' of public life are taking centre stage. Debates in the UK Parliament over religious and moral issues now generate an interest that other debates do not. The Education Reform Act 1988 and the Broadcasting Act 1990 (which mandated the teaching of Christianity and religious programming respectively), the Criminal Justice and Public Order Act 1994 (which reduced the age of homosexual consent from 21 to 18, but failed to lower the age to 16), the Family Law Act 1996 (which sought – and ultimately failed – to bring in 'no fault divorce'), the Human Rights Act 1998 (which means courts must have special regard to religious rights), the Crime and Disorder Act 1998 (which again failed to reduce the age of homosexual consent to 16) and the Sexual Offences Bill 1999 (which, yet again, failed to reduce the age of consent) all attracted great media attention and took up a considerable amount of Parliamentary enthusiasm and time.

There is what is called a 'culture war' going on. As James Davison Hunter describes it, 'a culture war emerges over fundamentally different conceptions of moral authority, over different ideas and beliefs about truth, the good, obligation to one another, the nature of community and so on.'[1] There is political and social conflict rooted in different belief systems and moral codes. That is why it is impossible to base a system of public order on a pluralistic view of religion, morals and ethics. No culture and no society can cohere without some shared beliefs and values, and the West is beginning to learn that lesson.

The way we understand the State and politics is changing. The fact that so few people voted in the European elections in June 1999 is symptomatic of a growing indifference to old-fashioned politics and political debate.

In October 1998 a Lord Chancellor's Department Consultation Paper indicated a concern over 'political balance in the lay magistracy'. This was because the notions of 'left' and 'right' are now becoming irrelevant: 'It has been argued that recent trends in society indicate that politics is becoming more cultural or value based ... Party loyalties, it is said, have become weakened where traditional left/right supporters have become more volatile and are voting according to issue or value priorities.'[2] According to the paper, research is now focusing on 'a variety of issues including sex, homosexuality, education, religion, drugs and single parents' as key 'post-material non-economic concerns' for public life.

As we start out on the twenty-first century the issues we have to debate in terms of the Church, State and public life are therefore 'cultural' issues. They look very different from, and more interesting than, those we would have been debating at the start of the twentieth century.

This shift, however, has its dangers. It means that the current 'two-party' system of government cannot give leadership in respect

---

[1] James Davison Hunter, *Culture Wars – The Struggle to Define America*, New York, Basic Books, 1991, p. 49.

[2] 'Political Balance in the Lay Magistracy', a Lord Chancellor's Department Consultation Paper, October 1998.

of these significant issues. This is true not just in the UK but also, and especially, in the US. The problem comes from the divisions within the political parties which mean they cannot handle these issues effectively. At the risk of oversimplifying, we can analyse the two main UK parties at the start of the new millennium following the classification of Norman Dennis of Newcastle University.[3]

In the UK Labour party there are on the one hand 'ethical socialists'. Sadly their numbers are declining, but they used to include traditional Roman Catholics and Methodists with a strong sense of personal responsibility, strong social conscience and strong working-class roots. On the other hand there are 'egoistic socialists'. These are often university educated, middle class, former student protesters who may have tried drugs, most likely support cohabitation and most seem to vote in favour of homosexual sex. They are, according to Dennis, socialist only in that they call for the State – which means other people – to pick up the bill for their folly.[4]

In the UK Conservative party there are on the one hand 'ethical capitalists', or classical liberals. For them, the heart of a free society is personal responsibility guided by conscience. They have a strong attachment to marriage and the family, and a good number have allegiance to the (orthodox) Church of England. On the other hand there are 'egoistic capitalists', or libertarians. Some of these can be brutal, paying little attention to human need and morally decadent, therefore supporting the immoral agenda as much as the 'egoistic socialists'.

On the issues that the public now think important, ethical socialists and ethical capitalists have more in common with each other than either group has with the other section of its own political party. That is why the party system is now dangerous. Inevitably pluralism *within* the parties means that the parties have to develop 'lowest common denominator' policies on moral issues to embrace all their members. The 'immoralists' win every time.

What is the duty of the Church in this new political scenario? Surely, one thing it must do is to look at these issues and problems

[3] See David Green, 'Foreword' to Norman Dennis and George Erdos, *Families without Fatherhood*, London, IEA Health and Welfare Unit, 1993, p. vii.
[4] Ibid.

from a biblical perspective. That is the way we reach the mind of Christ and his apostles today. And that is what I have attempted to do in the pages which follow.

Over the last 10 years I have addressed the issues covered in this book on more than one occasion. Every month, or nearly every month, I write a 'Coloured Supplement' in the *Jesmond Parish Church Newsletter* (in the pulpit we believe we should be expounding the Bible directly). I have looked back at, and 'refreshed', some of that material. I also give lectures for the Newcastle-based Christian Institute (which remarkably influenced legislation over the last decade of the twentieth century) and I write papers for Reform (the Anglican campaigning group) from time to time. I have included some of that material as well. Most of it has been rewritten. My editor suggested that I should personalize the discussion from my own experience, so there is also some autobiography. I hope this will be helpful and not self-advertising!

There is one omission: I have not discussed the politics of the media. Andrew and Juliet Quicke's book *Hidden Agendas – the politics of religious broadcasting in Britain 1987–1991* gives a factual and full account of the campaign in which I was involved over the Broadcasting Act 1990.[5] For me to have written adequately on the media would have required a disproportionate amount of space.

[5] Andrew and Juliet Quicke, *Hidden Agendas – The Politics of Religious Broadcasting in Britain 1987–1991*, Virginia Beach, Dominion Kings Grant Publications, 1992.

# CHAPTER ONE

# BENEFITS OF BELIEF

## A Spiritual and Psychological Slum

Inflation was high and all was not well with the economy. 'The state of the nation' was being debated in the General Synod of the Church of England. I was invited to speak. We had just heard some words from the Old Testament book of Amos during the opening prayers. The prophet had said there was 'a famine through the land – not a famine of food, or a thirst for water, but a famine of hearing the words of the LORD' (Amos 8:11). I tried to argue that those words were highly relevant to our present condition and ended by saying, 'As one distinguished non-Christian commentator has recently put it, "We live now in this nation in relative physical and economic splendour, but in a spiritual and psychological slum."'[1]

This quotation from my first speech in the General Synod is, I believe, still a challenge as we enter the twenty-first century. It is perhaps even more true now than it was in 1976, the year of the debate. The reason I say this will, I trust, become clear.

One half of our subject is the Church. That will be understood in the widest sense of the totality of Christian believers and their faith, but we must also bear in mind the 'God-fearers' or well-wishers. These people may still have questions about the Christian faith, but they prefer the way of Christ to the way that leads to the spiritual

---

[1] General Synod February Group of Sessions 1976, *Report of Proceedings*, London, Church Information Office, pp. 428–9.

slums. They often appear in the opinion polls as 'Christian' but not as regular churchgoers.

The other half of our subject is the State. That also will be understood in the widest sense – namely human society united both geographically and under a system of enforceable rules and regulations.

The thesis of the book is that when the Church fails to influence society and its rules and regulations so that they conform as much as possible to God's will, the result is not a happy neutrality. Rather the result is a nasty and unpleasant 'spiritual and psychological slum'. The discussion will be wide ranging, covering areas where the Church should be having an input as we move into the new millennium. For the moment, however, we must go back to the 1970s.

In 1973, three years before that General Synod debate, having been teaching doctrine and ethics at Wycliffe Hall theological college in Oxford, I moved to Newcastle upon Tyne in the Northeast of England. I was to be vicar of Jesmond, an evangelical Church of England parish in the centre of the city, where I have been ever since. It has been a great privilege to see the church grow over the years. At the time of writing, 900 different people will be present on a Sunday, half of them under 30 years of age, many being students.

This move to Newcastle upon Tyne unwittingly led to my involvement in synodical government for the 15 years from 1975 to 1990. For most of that period Robert Runcie was the Archbishop of Canterbury (and so the leader not only of the Church of England but also of the worldwide Anglican Communion); Mrs Thatcher was Prime Minister of the UK; and evangelicalism in Britain was growing in all the denominations, as it was growing worldwide.

## A WATERSHED

This period was a watershed in the history of the Church of England and the churches in the West generally. For many faithful people, no doubt, much of it passed over their heads. In reality, however, the mainline churches saw the development (as the title of a recent book puts it) of *Two Religions – One Church*.[2] This is seen most clearly in the US and Canada, but the problem is also present in the UK. One religion is identifiable with the apostolic faith of the Bible and the Western reformed catholic tradition. The other religion seems heretical, Gnostic or even pagan.

How much these changes in England were accelerated by the introduction of synodical government, we may never know. However, for good or ill the first General Synod of the Church of England was convened in 1970, and in 1975 I was elected to the second.

On 11 November 1975 I found myself in Westminster Abbey in London for the opening service of this new General Synod. I was soon listening to Her Majesty Queen Elizabeth II telling us in her opening speech that we would 'take thought for the ordering and government of the Church and the further development of its liturgy. But you will also, I am sure, think how the unchanging message of our faith can be proclaimed and brought to bear on the lives of people and the nation.'[3]

At the second session of that General Synod in February 1976 we held our debate on 'the state of the nation'. So there was I, a younger person in a relatively elderly assembly with its array of bishops and archbishops, called to speak on issues of Church and State.

The debate was on a report submitted for discussion by a distinguished clergyman, David Edwards, formerly Dean of King's College, Cambridge, Dean of Norwich and then Provost of Southwark. He had made his name in the 1960s as the publisher of a paperback, *Honest to God*, written by the radical Bishop John Robinson.[4] The book was a bestseller and in that respect a success. The trade-off, however, was that it eroded faith in the God of the Bible, in the Jesus of traditional understanding and in Christian morality. It was a key element in the deconstruction of Christian belief in the 1960s. Along with other similar writings it ushered in the permissive culture that validated recreational sex, drugs, divorce, violence, pornography, abortion and, therefore, misery for millions.

[2] George R. Eves, *Two Religions – One Church*, New Brunswick, V.O.I.C.E, 1998.
[3] General Synod November Group of Sessions 1975, *Report of Proceedings*, London, Church Information Office, p. 2.
[4] John A.T. Robinson, *Honest to God*, London, SCM Press, 1963.

After speaking as I did, I was immediately drafted onto the Board for Social Responsibility of the General Synod. For the next 10 years, as a Board member, I was required to address a wide range of political and ethical issues, many arising out of the traumas, tragedies and hedonism of those permissive years. Ominously, during this period the Church had to address publicly for the first time the controversial issue of homosexual relationships and 'gay' activism – something that in the last quarter of the twentieth century was to become the motor for a revision of our entire sexual culture.

## A THREE-LEGGED STOOL

As we start out on the twenty-first century we are not just facing a calendar change. There is a 'culture war' being waged for the soul of the West. Too many are unaware of this. Unless there is a reaffirmation and reacceptance of key truths and insights that relate to both Church and State, much of what is treasured in the West could be lost. Systems of social cohesion and shared values take centuries to build, but they can be destroyed easily in a short space of time. I hope to reaffirm and argue for some of these fundamentals in what follows. For clarity, however, I must start with some basic assumptions.

The *first* assumption is very simple: the State – any State – is to be viewed like a three-legged stool. If one leg is missing it cannot stand up. What does that mean? Simply that, for a society to function in a healthy way, there needs to be, first, a sound political order; secondly, a good economic order; and thirdly, a true and correct moral and spiritual order. All three elements are necessary. Problems in one area cause problems in the others.

The *second* assumption is that currently there is a problem with our moral and spiritual order. For over 200 years in the West some have been trying to exclude the spiritual dimension of life. Also, since the 1960s and the days of Bishop John Robinson (whom most people have now forgotten) there has been an erosion of the Christian faith. This erosion has been caused by a number of theologically liberal conformists within the Church. In this they have had greater good fortune than is safe for our public life.

Further, the Marxist project of analysing public life in terms of economics has had huge success with both the Left *and* the Right. The collapse of the Soviet Empire in 1989 underlined that this analysis is palpably flawed. Nonetheless, its assumption that public life is grounded in economics is now a de facto axiom of modern materialism.

Even Christian people can be unwittingly tempted to elevate the economic and marginalize the spiritual. In the 1980s in the Church of England there was a report by an Archbishops' Commission on Urban Priority Areas called *Faith in the City*. It provided helpful information, but it was immediately rubbished by the Thatcher Government of the day as 'Marxist'. That was not wise. It was heard as an accusation of *intentional* Marxism when there was none.

For all the excellent fact-finding and its proper challenge to face the problems of the inner city, however, much of the Commission's analysis was inadequate. The report *did* seem to suggest that economic arrangements were all-important and that lack of money was not *just one* but *the ultimate* problem behind urban social needs. There was a practical ignoring of Jesus' words when he spoke about social problems and said, 'from within, out of men's hearts, come evil thoughts, sexual immorality, theft, murder, adultery, greed, malice, deceit, lewdness, envy, slander, arrogance and folly' (Mark 7:20).

The report concentrated instead on 'Marx's perception that evil is to be found, not just in the human heart, but in the very structures of economic and social relationships'.[5] The Commission had not done its homework on the social condition of some urban poor ghettos around the world. Sometimes the best and only way out of poverty, deprivation and underclass despair can be to join a Pentecostal church! As Régis Debray put it, religion is not 'the opium of the people, but the vitamin of the weak'.[6] The Commission had failed to articulate a fundamental Christian insight – namely that the root of human problems is essentially not social or environmental but individual and personal. That is true for rich and poor alike.

[5] Archbishops' Commission, *Faith in the City*, London, Church House Publishing, 1985, p. 51.
[6] Régis Debray, 'God and the Political Planet', *New Perspectives Quarterly*, 11, Spring 1994, p. 15.

To put the primary stress on external problems and not on the human heart and its sinful disobedience is a classic heresy – Pelagianism. True, sinful individuals then distort and disfigure the environment, whether political, economic or cultural. But to address external problems without addressing the problems of the human soul is like trying to mend a puncture by washing the wheel. And this disobedience, either through defiance or through ignoring God, *does* have actual social consequences.

## THE WAGES OF SIN

This leads to the *third* assumption. The wages of sin are not just for eternity but also for now – there are actual *contemporary* social consequences. It is worth spending some time on this. Too few people are aware of the facts.

In the last part of the twentieth century a new range of social research was carried out. Most of it – though not all – came from the US. It related to the social and civic consequences of being an active Christian in contrast to being an unbeliever not involved in a church. The findings show that *on average* living according to God's will is beneficial. That is not to say that Christian believers do not suffer. Indeed they do, and in many ways. Undoubtedly there are also the 'pleasures of sin'. On average, however – though not always – there appears to be an advantage even in this life from obeying God. 'The pleasures of sin' are real, but as the Bible says, they are only 'for a short time' (Hebrews 11:25).

### SOCIAL STABILITY

In an important study entitled 'Why Religion Matters: the Impact of Religious Practice on Social Stability', Patrick Fagan has reported a wide range of findings.[7] I will draw attention to some of these, plus some other research as well.

---

[7] Patrick F. Fagan, 'Why Religion Matters: the Impact of Religious Practice on Social Stability', *Backgrounder No. 1064*, Washington, The Heritage Foundation, 1996.

Take general well-being first. In the *Journal of Social Psychology* in 1994 there was a report of a survey of 1,481 adults aged 18–89. It showed that religious commitment and regular church attendance indicate who is most likely to have a sense of 'well-being'.[8] Parallel studies have found that the religiously committed generally experience much less psychological distress than the uncommitted.[9]

Then take family stability. There is now seen to be a powerful relationship between religious commitment and stability in the family. One classic research project – 'Middletown' – studied the lives of the inhabitants of a typical town from the 1920s to the 1980s. It concluded that 'there is a relationship between family solidarity – family health if you will – and church affiliation and activity.'[10]

It has also been found that marital stability and church attendance are related. And with regard to the primary modern value of sexual satisfaction, studies in the 1970s noted that religiously committed women achieve greater satisfaction in sexual intercourse with their husbands than do moderately religious or non-religious women. These findings were confirmed in a very public way by the comprehensive *Sex in America* survey, published in 1995 and parallel to the British *Sexual Attitudes and Lifestyles* survey of 1994.[11]

This blew the minds of some secular journalists. 'The women most likely to achieve orgasm each and every time (32 per cent),' said *Time* magazine on 17 October 1994, 'are, believe it or not, conservative Protestants.' No longer could such journalists laugh off the research that shows that women who follow the Christian

---

[8] Harsha N. Mookherjee, 'Effects of Religiosity and Selected Variables on the Perception of Well-Being', *The Journal of Social Psychology*, vol. 134, no. 3, June 1994, pp. 403–5.

[9] Rodney Stark, 'Psychopathology and Religious Commitment', *Review of Religious Research*, vol. 12, 1971, pp. 165–79; and R.W. Williams, D.B. Larson, R.E. Buckler, R.C. Heckmand and C.M. Pyle, 'Religion and Psychological Distress in a Community Sample', *Social Science Medicine*, vol. 32, 1991, pp. 1257–62.

[10] Howard M. Bahr and Bruce A. Chadwick, 'Religion and Family in Middletown, USA', *Journal of Marriage and the Family*, vol. 47, May 1985, pp. 407–14.

[11] Robert T. Michael (ed.) et al., *The Social Organization of Sexuality: Sexual Practices in the United States*, University of Chicago Press, 1994; Anne M. Johnson, J. Wadsworth, K. Wellings, Julia Field, *Sexual Attitudes and Lifestyles*, Oxford, Blackwell, 1994.

ethic are, on average, better in bed than those who do not; and that women who have sex only with their husbands are twice as responsive sexually as women with multiple partners.[12] Generally the findings of the *Sex in America* survey were not unique to the US: 'The findings were pretty much in line with recent studies conducted in England and France ... that found low rates of homosexuality and high rates of marital fidelity.'[13]

Other research has found that church attendance leads to less divorce or cohabitation (and cohabitation goes with high divorce rates after marriage). So church attenders are less likely to suffer significant financial, social and health problems through marriage breakdown. If true, this is vitally relevant to us in the UK today. According to the UK Government the annual 'costs to the public purse of marital breakdown' are a staggering £5 billion, and that excludes all hidden costs.[14]

## RELIGION, HEALTH AND CRIME

There is now an established relationship between faith and health. Education and income are not the only factors in determining health levels. In the last quarter of the twentieth century it was discovered that religious practice is also important. As long ago as 1972 it was found that cardiovascular diseases were reduced significantly in early old age by a lifetime of regular church attendance. By contrast, nonattenders had higher mortality rates from cirrhosis of the liver, emphysema and arteriosclerosis.[15] Research on mortality rates among the poor in 1984 confirmed that regular church attenders live longer.[16] In 1991 an article in the *Journal for the Scientific Study of Religion* reported two national surveys. These

[12] Richard John Neuhaus, 'Sex, Religion, Virtue and Reward', *First Things*, no. 43, May 1994, pp. 63–76.

[13] *Time*, 17 October 1994.

[14] Helena Jeffs, Home Affairs Section, *Research Paper 96/42*, House of Commons Library, 21 March 1996, p. 74.

[15] George W. Comstock and Kay B. Partridge, 'Church Attendance and Health', *Journal of Chronic Disease*, vol. 25, 1972, pp. 665–72.

[16] D.M. Zuckerman, S.V. Kasl and S.V. Osterfield, 'Psychosocial Predictors of Mortality among the Elderly Poor', *American Journal of Epidemiology*, vol. 119, 1984, pp. 410–23.

indicated that the health status of people who prayed and were active at church was significantly affected, regardless of age.[17]

A 1998 study in the *American Journal of Public Health* also found that long life and churchgoing were connected. For nearly five years, 2,025 over-55s were followed and their death rates tracked. Over that period 454 of these people died. A host of factors were recorded that might contribute to keeping healthy and living longer. Attending religious services was the most significant factor. 'For each sex, weekly attendees had the lowest mortality and non-attendees had the highest mortality,' wrote the researchers. 'Only attending church was significantly associated with mortality [delaying death], although attending museums or art galleries was marginally protective ... Even after controlling for six classes of potential confounding and intervening variables, we were unable to explain the protection against mortality offered by religious attendance.'

The researchers noted how their findings supported other research which showed that attending religious services was linked with lower blood pressure, fewer deaths from cardiovascular disease, less depression, and less earlier death from all causes.[18] With the British Health Service budget costing billions of pounds, health service managers, senior and junior doctors, general practitioners and other health professionals cannot ignore these findings.

A clear relationship has also been discovered between problematic adolescent sexual behaviour and an absence of religious commitment. Higher levels of churchgoing are correlated with lower levels of teenage pregnancy. Religious practice results in a sharp reduction of premarital sex, and a lack of Christian commitment results in an increase in sexual permissiveness.[19] To reduce teenage pregnancy, it is now being said, 'you don't want a condom

[17] K.F. Ferraro and C.M. Albrecht-Jensen, 'Does Religion Influence Adult Health?', *Journal for the Scientific Study of Religion*, vol. 30, 1991, pp. 193–202.

[18] Douglas Oman and Dwayne Reed, 'Religion and Mortality among the Community-Dwelling Elderly', *American Journal of Public Health*, vol. 88, no. 10, 1988, pp. 1469–75.

[19] See Scott H. Beck, Bettie S. Cole and Judith A. Hammond, 'Religious Heritage and Premarital Sex: Evidence from a National Sample of Young Adults', *Journal for the Scientific Study of Religion*, vol. 30, no. 2, 1991, pp. 173–80.

culture but a Christian culture'. Similar findings to the above relate to alcohol, drug abuse and suicide.

Then there is the effect of the Christian faith on crime and delinquency. In 1975 a four-year longitudinal, stratified, random sample (i.e. a representative group of people followed up long term) of secondary school pupils showed that religious involvement significantly decreased drug use, premarital sex *and* delinquency.[20] A 1995 study published in *Criminology* found that religious behaviour – that is, *participation* in religious activities, not simply holding religious beliefs or values – had a significant relationship to lower levels of crime.[21] And a 1997 study in *Justice Quarterly* found that once in prison, participation in a prison Bible study group was related significantly to a lower likelihood of arrest during the follow-up period than in the case of matched nonparticipants.[22]

ACTION NEEDED

Finally, in this random sample of studies, there is the question of poverty. The US National Longitudinal Survey of Youth shows the development of young people from the late 1970s. This survey plots the difference which regular religious practice makes for those who grew up in similar poverty in the 1970s and 1980s. Among those who attended church weekly in both 1979 and 1982, average family income in 1993 was $37,021. Among those who never attended church in 1979 and 1982, average family income in 1993 was $24,361 – one-third lower.[23] This does not permit the development of a 'prosperity gospel' – 'pray and you will get rich' – but it does underline the truth of the general biblical principle that, *on average*, obeying God leads to a good life and disobeying him to a

[20] John Rohrbaugh and Richard Jessor, 'Religiosity in Youth: A Personal Control against Deviant Behaviour', *Journal of Personality*, vol. 43, no. 1, 1975, pp. 136–55.

[21] D.T. Evans, F.T. Cullen, R.G. Dunaway and V.S. Burton, Jr, 'Religion and Crime Re-examined: The Impact of Religion, Secular Controls and Social Ecology on Adult Criminology', *Criminology*, vol. 33, no. 2, 1995, pp. 195–217.

[22] Press release from National Institute for Healthcare Research, 31 March 1997. The results were published in the March 1997 edition of *Justice Quarterly*.

[23] Analysis of the National Longitudinal Survey of Youth by the Heritage Foundation analyst Christine Olson, see Fagan, 'Why Religion Matters: the Impact of Religious Practice on Social Stability', op. cit.

less good life (see, for example, Psalm 1). Of course, sometimes the wicked do prosper and the righteous are in distress. That is why there is a 'problem of suffering'.

One implication of this third assumption, in the light of these and similar findings, is that it is urgent that Christian citizens work for the defeat of secular humanist attitudes and policies in education, health care, social services and government – particularly those which work against the Christian faith. This is not to imply a desire for a theocracy. It is simply to say that for the well-being of the State it is now time for committed Christians to speak out. That is the way to exhibit genuine love and concern in the public arena.

There needs to be a national debate on the role of Christianity in public life. And very practically (and immediately), it is imperative that in social surveys in the UK reasonable data is gathered on religious beliefs and practice, plus family and marriage patterns. Hostile 'ethics' committees which claim that religion is private must not be allowed to block such research. In the national census there should be questions not only on religious affiliation but also on frequency of attendance at a place of worship. We need new UK studies into the relationship between regular church attendance and social issues such as crime, drug abuse, health, births outside marriage and poverty.

Stephen Carter, Professor of Law at Yale University, writes in his book *The Culture of Disbelief*:

> One sees a trend in our political and legal cultures toward treating religious beliefs as arbitrary and unimportant, a trend supported by rhetoric that implies that there is something wrong with religious devotion. More and more, our culture seems to take the position that believing deeply in the tenets of one's faith represents a kind of mystical irrationality, something that thoughtful, public-spirited ... citizens would be better to avoid.[24]

Our third assumption, and the details of the surveys given above, show why this trend is pernicious and false: positive social

[24] Stephen L. Carter, *Culture of Disbelief*, New York, Anchor, 1994, pp. 6–7.

consequences arise from Christian obedience and faith in God and negative ones from disbelief and disobedience.

## ABSURDITY AND THE NEW 'BAALISM'

The *fourth* assumption is that the last century, or a major part of it, has rightly been described as 'absurd'. In the mid-twentieth-century period there was, some may remember, the Theatre of the Absurd. This reflected the collapse of belief and the ensuing disillusionment. Here is Martin Esslin:

> *The social and spiritual reasons for such a sense of loss of meaning are manifold and complex; the waning of religious faith that had started with the [European] Enlightenment and led Nietzsche to speak of the 'death of God' by the eighteen-eighties; the breakdown of the liberal faith in inevitable social progress in the wake of the First World War; the disillusionment with the hopes of radical social revolution as predicted by Marx after Stalin had turned the Soviet Union into a totalitarian tyranny; the relapse into barbarism, mass murder, and genocide in the course of Hitler's brief rule over Europe during the Second World War; and, in the aftermath of that war, the spread of spiritual emptiness in the outwardly prosperous and affluent societies of western Europe and the United States. There can be no doubt: for many intelligent and sensitive human beings the world of the mid-twentieth century had lost its meaning and simply ceased to make sense.*[25]

The *fifth* assumption is that the new 'Baalism' which emerged in the second half of the twentieth century has failed to give meaning and make sense. Esslin was writing in the mid-1960s. What actually followed? An immersion in the stream of nature, whether through sexual arousal and release or through violence and killing. That was not so unlike the practices and style of the ancient Canaanite religions – Baalism – inveighed against by Old Testament prophets. In those days, as now, this failed to reveal life's meaning. The

---

[25] Martin Esslin (ed.), *The Absurd Drama*, London, Penguin Books, 1965, p. 13.

Hebrew prophets, indeed, pitted the full weight of their preaching and ire against God's people when they followed the Baals. They warned strongly against abandonment of the true God, child sacrifice, female and male prostitution, divorce, violence and the ill treatment of the poor.

Since the 1960s we have come to approve this prophetic indictment against violence and injustice. But we now think that godlessness, child sacrifice through abortion, sexual licence and divorce are legitimate options. The prophets, however, argued a linkage between religious, moral and social distress. Your long-term quality of public life, they said, depends on your personal beliefs and private behaviour. If you cheat on your wife, why should you not cheat in your business, in your school, or in your government department? The consequences for society are clear.

## Necessary Beliefs and Tolerance

The *sixth* assumption is that underlying beliefs are necessary for moral behaviour. You cannot just exhort people to goodness. The human animal is made in such a way that we do not instinctively do what is right. It is a truism that 'no culture can appear or develop except in relation to a religion.'[26] Some may regret that, but it is an observation of social fact. In the West we are rooted in the Judaeo-Christian spiritual tradition along with the best of the Graeco-Roman political traditions. You can cut a plant off from its roots, but you cannot then expect it to survive for long.

The *seventh* assumption relates to tolerance – something necessary where there are strong beliefs. Since the Reformation the West has developed an important tradition of religious tolerance. This must be preserved. The assumption is that tolerance is not the same as indifference. Tolerance means that you allow to continue without legal interference beliefs or practices of which you personally disapprove and think wrong. Indifference means that you do not mind or care what other people believe or do.

[26] T.S. Eliot, *Notes towards the Definition of Culture*, London, Faber and Faber, 1948, p. 15.

In the religious and moral sphere, tolerance in society is only possible where there is a dominant religious and moral tradition. Tolerance is the friend of religion; indifference is the enemy. It is certainly the enemy of religious liberty, defined by Lord Acton as 'the right of all religious communities to the practice of their own duties, the enjoyment of their own constitution, and the protection of the law, which equally secures to all the possession of their own independence'.[27]

Professor John McIntyre of Edinburgh has pointed out that religious minorities fare better when there is a dominant religious tradition that is tolerant of others than when there is an attempted neutrality or indifference towards all religions. McIntyre has worked this out in regard to modern educational theory. He has described the 'religious rake's progress'. First, there is 'neutrality', where each religion of the world is presented neutrally. That slides into 'subjectivism', where choice is emphasized and religion is seen as purely a matter for subjective preference. Finally there is 'indifferentism', where it is a matter of pure indifference which religion you choose.

He argues that members of other faiths fare as badly as Christians under a cult of openness. Paradoxically, they are better off when Christianity is presented as a matter of 'truth' or even '*the* truth'. Other faiths stand a better chance of being taken seriously when one faith at least is being treated this way, than when all are treated neutrally. McIntyre's conclusion is this: 'Even for the sake of the subordinate cultures and the other faiths which sustain them, we have to ensure the continuance of the dominant culture and the values, ideas, concepts and beliefs which are its inspiration.'

The point is that if all religions are treated on the 'supermarket' principle, a positive, not a neutral, philosophy is in fact being promulgated – i.e. 'truth claims' are not only unimportant, but also to be denied in respect of any particular faith. That, in McIntyre's judgement, is 'the final emasculation' of religion.[28] It is a view also held by the Chief Rabbi, who says that 'giving many religions equal

[27] Quoted in Alec R. Vidler, *The Orb and the Cross*, London, SPCK, 1945, p. 115.

[28] John McIntyre, *Farmington Institute Occasional Paper No. 3*, Oxford, Farmington Institute for Christian Studies, 1978.

weight is not supportive of each but instead tends rapidly to relativize them all.'[29]

## A DOMINANT CULTURE

The *eighth* assumption is that we do have a dominant culture. Sane government cannot ignore what the majority think and believe. Here we must distinguish between public articulation and private conviction. Britain, most of Europe and the US are secular *theistic* societies. They are not secular *atheistic* societies.

If 'secular' is defined by an absence of public reference to God, we are secular. There is little said about God, Jesus Christ and his purposes for the world (apart from blasphemously) in the mainstream media or education (both key areas for public expression). Nonetheless, surveys find that the majority of people in the West still believe in God and huge percentages consider themselves 'Christian'. Social surveys would seem to indicate that around 70 per cent of the British public regard themselves as Christian, while under 4 per cent regard themselves as belonging to another faith, and around 20 per cent claim to be 'nothing' (see Chapter 3).

In the US there is considerably more churchgoing than in Europe, but even Britain is not as 'non-churchgoing' as some think. Only just over 10 per cent of the population go to church weekly in the UK. Excluding such special occasions as weddings, funerals and baptisms, however, 20 per cent go monthly, 30 per cent go every six months, and nearly 40 per cent go annually.[30]

With the number of all other religionists (Hindu, Jewish, Muslim, Sikh, Buddhist) being only 3 or 4 per cent, Britain is hardly a multifaith society. It is the same in the US. A million Muslims in Britain would still only mean 2 per cent of the population. Of course, there is a substantial *ethnic* minority, but many from that minority are positively Christian and more so than much of the white population – witness the growth of Afro-Caribbean churches.

[29] Jonathan Sacks, '1990 Reith Lectures (4), Paradoxes of Pluralism', *The Listener*, 6 December 1990, p. 18.
[30] R. Jowel, L. Brook, G. Prior and B. Taylor, *British Social Attitudes, The 9th Report*, Aldershot, Dartmouth, 1992, p. 269.

Multifaith pockets of the UK such as parts of London, the Midlands and Yorkshire must not mislead us when it comes to seeing the whole picture.

There *is* a dominant Christian culture and religion, therefore, and that needs sustaining. There is also a subordinate religious pluralism of small minority groups who have rights to be respected. That does not make the UK pluralist in terms of religion or morality, however. The danger, as Richard Neuhaus says, is that 'pluralism' is a buzz word used 'to argue that no normative ethic even of the vaguest and most tentative sort, can be "imposed" in our public life. In practice it means that public policy decisions reflect a surrender of the normal to the abnormal, of the dominant to the deviant.'[31]

In the second half of the twentieth century public policy decisions were taken against 'the dominant' ethic that effected wholesale changes to our Christian culture. But there was no democratic vote. Instead, individuals with influence in public life unilaterally took personal decisions that de-moralized society. To take one example, this happened in the UK in the area of broadcasting.

The Director-General of the BBC in 1948, Sir William Haley, told the British Council of Churches:

> *There are many demands of impartiality laid on the Corporation, but this [about Christian values] is not one of them. We are citizens of a Christian country and the BBC – an institution set up by the State – bases its policy upon a positive attitude towards Christian values. It seeks to safeguard those values and to foster acceptance of them. The whole preponderant weight of its programmes is directed towards this end.*[32]

Just over a decade later, things were quite different. In the mid-1960s the new Director-General, Hugh Greene – an arch-secularist and permissive – told a conference in Rome: 'I believe we have a duty ... to be ahead of public opinion rather than always to wait upon it ... relevance is the key – relevance to the audience and to

[31] Richard John Neuhaus, *The Naked Public Square*, Grand Rapids, Eerdmans, 1984, p. 146.

[32] Quoted in Malcolm Muggeridge, *Christ and the Media*, London, Hodder and Stoughton, 1977, p. 64.

the tide of opinion in society. Outrage is impermissible. Shock is not always so. Provocation may be healthy and indeed socially imperative.'[33]

It is understandable why the Chairman at the time thought that Greene had 'an excessive attachment to libertarianism'. It is understandable, too, why Greene then wrote to the lady who was to become his third wife that he 'was not very fond of' the Chairman.[34]

## SIGNS OF HOPE

So much for our assumptions. But are there any signs of hope? There is some evidence as we enter the new millennium that there is change in the wind. The linkage of irreligion, immorality and social distress is now being noted again in the US – not by the leaders in the media or in Washington but by social scientists, as we have just seen. Also in the US there has been a significant pushing of moral issues to the centre of the public agenda. These include the reinstitutionalizing of the married family, no abortion, no pornography, school choice and 'zero tolerance' policing. If Talcott Parsons, the American sociologist, is correct and the US is 'the lead society', we should expect a similar change to reach Britain at some point. Perhaps the House of Lords, in the dying years of the twentieth century, twice voting against lowering the age of consent for homosexual sex, in spite of massive lobbying by gay groups in the media and in Parliament, was more important than many recognized.[35]

There is more than just academic research and discussion going on in the US, however. Some things *are* happening. In 1999 Karl Zinsmeister wrote, 'Some remarkable and encouraging developments have taken place. Many of the social trend lines that turned ugly in the sixties and seventies have begun to level off and even retreat, in many cases to their lowest levels in two or three decades.'[36]

[33] Quoted in Andrew Quicke, *Tomorrow's Television*, Berkhampstead, 1976, p. 173.
[34] *The Observer*, 14 August 1983.
[35] The votes took place on 22 July 1998 and 13 April 1999.
[36] Karl Zinsmeister, 'Chin Up: Some Ugly Trends Grow Lovelier', *The American Enterprise*, vol. 10, no. 1, January/February 1999, p. 5.

There is also, allegedly, a change in attitude. Many in the US are now edging their way back to what has been described as 'tradition, moderation and sanity'. Importantly, strong majorities now place 'reversing moral decline' as their highest priority for the nation, higher than any economic, foreign or other domestic issue. In all, 62 per cent think that 'a let-down in moral values' is one of the 'major causes of our problems today'. And to the question: 'Which worries you more – that the country will become too tolerant of behaviours that are bad for society or that the country will become too intolerant of behaviours that don't do any real harm to society?' – while 6 per cent have no opinion, 66 per cent say they are more worried by too much tolerance, and only 28 per cent by too much intolerance. Furthermore, as the century turns, in the US the divorce rate is down 19 per cent since 1981; the birthrate for unmarried teenagers is down 7.5 per cent since 1994; abortion is down 15.3 per cent since 1990; and even the crime rate is down.[37]

It was General Douglas MacArthur who once wrote, 'History fails to record a single precedent in which nations subject to moral decay have not passed into a political and economic decline. There has either been a spiritual awakening to overcome the moral lapse, or a progressive deterioration to ultimate national disaster.'[38] That is fairly apocalyptic. But if it is true, how urgently there needs to be a spiritual awakening in the West, and in Britain in particular, in the twenty-first century.

---

[37] K. Zinsmeister, S. Moore and K. Bowerman, 'Is America Turning a Corner?', ibid., pp. 36–51.

[38] Quoted in Zinsmeister, 'Chin Up: Some Ugly Trends Grow Lovelier', op. cit.

# CHAPTER TWO

# ADULT PLEASURE AND DAMAGED CHILDREN

## LESBIAN ADOPTION

I was asked in 1998 to conduct the funeral of an elderly lady, and in preparation for the service I contacted her daughter. In a conversation on the telephone the daughter said, 'By the way, I know your wife.'

'Oh! How's that?' I asked.

'Do you remember "the lesbian adoption case"?' she replied.

'Yes, indeed I do.'

'Well, I'm the foster mother who adopted the little boy.'

On visiting the family, never having met the foster mother before, I found a remarkable woman together with her son, no longer the 'little boy' of the press reports but now growing up, integrated in what seemed a happy family and with normal life chances. It could have been so very different. Thereby hangs a moral tale, indeed it provides a cameo of the moral and social environment we have inherited at the start of the twenty-first century.

The story began in Newcastle upon Tyne, in the autumn of 1990. Brian Roycroft, a top social worker with a national reputation, was the Director of Social Services for Newcastle. Just before his retirement in 1993 he was questioned on Tyne-Tees TV about some of the most difficult times he had had to face in his long career. The first case mentioned was the Mary Bell tragedy of 1968, when a disturbed Tyneside child had brutally murdered two other young children. At the time it shook the whole of Britain. The second was the lesbian adoption scandal of 1990.

The scandal started quite innocently. An article in the *Sunday Express* on 30 September 1990 reported that eight local authorities admitted to placing children for foster care with homosexual couples. The paper had contacted 133 authorities and found that, in addition to the eight, a further 91 local authorities said they would not rule out homosexual placements. Only five claimed they would rule them out (29 refused to comment or did not reply). Almost in passing, the article then stated that two lesbians were adopting (not just fostering) a boy under the age of 10 in Newcastle.

The following day the local Newcastle press picked up the story and made it headline news. How did the Director of Social Services, Brian Roycroft, respond? According to the *Evening Chronicle*, he said that 'the decision to place the child with the lesbian couple was only made after a nationwide search'. He added that his department 'would always act in the best interests of the child'.[1] According to *The Journal*, the then Chairman of Newcastle Social Services Committee said that the boy was handicapped and that the only alternative to the placement with the lesbian couple 'was long-term care in a hospital or institution'.[2] In the same paper Bryan Roycroft himself was also quoted as saying that the child would have 'a quality of life he would never experience in a hospital or institution'. Another journalist was told that the Director of Social Services had 'sought the views of a High Court judge, a child psychiatrist, and an adult psychiatrist before deciding'.

Then on 6 October 1990 *The Times* newspaper reported that the lesbian couple had been approved (and so promoted) by the famous charity Barnardo's, something that shook many Christian people. Thomas Barnardo, the founder, was a great evangelical philanthropist of the nineteenth century who had worked with destitute children.

This is what the public were told, and people therefore believed that the little boy had been placed for adoption with a lesbian couple as an alternative to life in an institution or a hospital. Then came the bombshell.

[1] *Evening Chronicle*, 1 October 1990.
[2] *The Journal*, 2 October 1990.

## EXPOSURE

On 8 October an irate foster mother told the press that she had fostered the boy for two and a half years, since he was a tiny baby. Not only that, she had applied to adopt him herself after learning that another couple had applied to adopt the child. Her application, however, had been turned down and the boy had been taken away and placed for adoption with this lesbian couple. It was believed that one of the lesbians was a social worker herself and the other had worked for Newcastle City Council. It was also discovered that the foster mother had had considerable experience, fostering a total of 30 children over a period of 19 years.

The public could not believe what it was hearing. The *Evening Chronicle* said, 'the stories don't add up'. The comments made by the foster mother called into question the 'claim that but for the willingness of the lesbian couple to provide him with a home, this toddler would have faced a life of institutional care'.[3]

Further controversy was generated when one of the two Medical Advisers to the Newcastle Adoption and Fostering Unit – my wife, Dr Joy Holloway, a paediatrician who specializes in the field of adoption and fostering – wrote to a local newspaper stating that, as a matter of policy, 'accepting practising lesbian or male homosexuals as foster or adoptive parents' was not 'appropriate' and it was 'not only morally wrong but unkind'. Furthermore, she wrote, 'I have expressed this opinion strongly to the Chief Executive and to the Director of Social Services over the past six months, saying that I believe such a policy should not be introduced without an open airing in the full City Council.'

I only learnt about this case from the press, however, through the chance but thorough investigative work of a *Sunday Express* journalist. At that point I took action and decided to fight the case publicly along with the Newcastle-based Christian Institute with which I was (and still am) involved. But I could learn nothing at all from my wife, who is the model of discretion and a believer in proper

---

[3] *Evening Chronicle*, 8 October 1990.

confidentiality. There was, however, no problem in finding out the facts from many friendly local and national journalists. What I learnt day by day, in my judgement, was disgraceful. What became clear was this: once you set out on a course of action that involves respecting, rewarding and so validating sexual immorality, soon in its wake come misinformation, half-truths and bad decisions.

How was the dispute resolved? In January 1991 the case reached the High Court, which ordered the little boy to be returned to the foster mother. What went on behind those closed doors we do not know. The public had only the thinnest of press statements to go on, agreed by the court and Newcastle Social Services. It revealed nothing about the judge's views on lesbian adoption and fostering, one way or the other.

## THE ISSUES

Sadly, the debate has still not ended. In his pre-retirement interview, Bryan Roycroft said the real problem with the Newcastle case was that the public were not ready for lesbian adoption 'yet'. This case was simply one of the first shots in a major campaign to legitimize lesbian adoption and fostering that had been orchestrated by gay pressure groups.

In the light of our experience in Newcastle, my wife and I were asked by a senior MP to meet the British Secretary of State for Health who was consulting over these issues. We discussed the dangers of lesbian adoption and fostering and how it was not in the best interests of the child. The Secretary of State seemed genuinely pleased to see us. We discovered that in the period of consultation (now ending), we were the only people who in face-to-face discussion had represented the common-sense, traditional and Christian position – the one that the polls said was held by the overwhelming majority of the British public. The other representations had been from gay activists or their sympathizers.

No one, therefore, had detailed the problems children experience in lesbian households – the problem of secrecy; of other children responding negatively; of a sense of difference; of not being close to other children; of girls thinking of turning to other women sexually after boyfriend trouble; of a lack of peer support;

of boys having anger towards the female lover and saying the mother's lover had become 'a threat to my sense of family', or simply identifying the major problem as the lover – 'she sleeps with my mother'.[4] Nor had it been detailed how one study found that in lesbian households 'older boys were significantly less confident about their popularity with other boys', and 'older girls' were more 'masculine'. They 'were more likely to mention a man as someone they would like to be like when grown'.[5]

The agenda of homosexual adoption and fostering is being vigorously pursued as we enter the new millennium. It must be stopped. Children in care do need families, some desperately – but not *any* family. And if potential carers are excluded because they hold to the Christian ethic – for example, that homosexual adoption and fostering is wrong – no wonder there is a childcare problem. It may be that on some measurements two educated, middle-class lesbians score better in parenting skills than a less educated single mother. But the problems in lesbian fostering and adoption are not so much the lack of parenting skills: they are in the relationship of the child to the outside world. The problem is summed up in one clinical study as follows: 'Even under the best of circumstances, children in gay step-families may experience difficulty since it is not easy for them to grow up in a family that is disapproved of by society and to be labelled as pathological or undesirable by association.'[6]

To read the paper summarizing existing research by the pro-gay Saralie Pennington, 'Children of Lesbian Mothers', leads to the only conclusion that it is cruel placing children with lesbian couples. She reports that children 'commonly fear that other children will find out that their mother is a lesbian. This awareness

[4] Karen Gail Lewis, 'Children of Lesbians: their Point of View', *Social Work 1980*: 25, pp. 198–203.

[5] R. Green, J.B. Mandel, M.E. Hotvedt, J. Gray and L. Smith, 'Lesbian Mothers and their Children: a Comparison with Solo Parent Heterosexual Mothers and their Children', *Archives of Sexual Behaviour*, vol. 15, no. 2, 1986, pp. 167–85.

[6] D. Baptiste, 'Psychotherapy with gay/lesbian couples and their children in "Stepfamilies": a challenge for marriage and family therapists', *Journal of Homosexuality*, vol. 14, no. 1–2, 1987, pp. 217–32.

frequently occurs after seven years of age and intensifies during pubescence and the early teenage years.'[7]

A fostered or adopted child would therefore be forced to live with these fears for six or seven years. We are also told that 'children may fear being ostracized and isolated if their mothers' sexual orientation becomes known ... Girls, more than boys, commonly fear that they, too, will be gay or that people will think they are gay.' And then she says, 'Out of fear of discovery of their mothers' homosexuality, these children can become anxious, withdrawn, hypervigilant, or secretive, and may attempt to control their mothers' behaviour. Some children, particularly as they approach their teens, shy away from friends and refuse to bring them home out of concern that someone will "find out".'[8]

All this is put down – by gay propaganda and commentators like Saralie Pennington – to 'dysfunctionality', not from homosexual behaviours (which are axiomatically held to be healthy and normal) but from other aspects of family dynamics and especially from the 'profound impact of a homophobic culture'.[9] The communal wisdom of human society as it has evolved over the centuries is not entertained as even possibly correct. Such traditional communal wisdom says that it is in the best interests of a child to have a mother and a father, not two mothers or two fathers who are in a sexual relationship.

## THE 1983 STUDY

It is difficult to know what would ever count as 'proof positive'. In the UK one academic survey was often quoted in the 1980s and 1990s to claim that children could happily be reared in lesbian households. It was a 1983 study by Susan Golombok and others, called 'Children in Lesbian and Single-parent Households'. It was claimed the study proved that 'rearing in a lesbian household per

[7] Saralie Bisnovich Pennington, 'Children of Lesbian Mothers', in Frederick W. Bozett (ed.), *Gay and Lesbian Parents*, New York, Praeger, 1987, p. 62.
[8] Ibid., p. 63.
[9] Ibid., p. 61.

se did not lead to atypical psycho-sexual development or constitute a psychiatric risk factor'.[10]

This study and its conclusion was cited regularly on television and in various debates as watertight evidence. For many in the UK it undoubtedly legitimized homosexual parenting. However, it was not commonly pointed out that the conclusions and deductions from the study, if true, would mean only that children in lesbian households did no worse than children in father-absent, single-parent households. Nor was it pointed out that the mean age of the children in this study was 9.5 years old. This is far too young to see long-term emotional and psychiatric effects, or to see how the children coped with puberty. Nor was it pointed out that the lesbian mothers were more educated and 'professional' than the control group. Nor was it pointed out that both groups of children had much higher rates of emotional and behavioural problems than those in the general population.

Golombok's 1996 follow-up study on these children as young adults – such as it was – showed that one quarter of the young adults from her lesbian households became involved 'in same-gender sexual relationships', whereas none of the participants from the heterosexual single-parent backgrounds did so – 'a significant difference'. That compares with only 2 per cent of this age group in the general population who have ever had a homosexual relationship.[11] The study also reported that two-thirds of the daughters from lesbian households and over half the sons 'significantly ... stated that they had previously considered, or thought it a future possibility, that they might experience same-gender attraction or have a same-gender sexual relationship or both'. That compared with only one-sixth of all the young adults from the heterosexual control group. The results of this study, therefore, suggest that the homosexuality of two lesbian parents *is* associated with homosexuality in the children – something many deny.[12]

[10] S. Golombok, A. Spencer and M. Rutter, 'Children in Lesbian and Single-parent Households: Psychosexual and Psychiatric Appraisal', *Journal of Child Psychology & Psychiatry*, vol. 24, no. 4, 1983, pp. 551–72.

[11] Johnson, Wadsworth, Wellings, Field, *Sexual Attitudes and Lifestyles*, op. cit., p 191.

[12] Susan Golombok and Fiona Tasker, 'Do Parents Influence the Sexual Orientation of Their Children? Findings from a Longitudinal Study of Lesbian Families', *Developmental Psychology*, vol. 32, no. 1, 1996, p. 7.

There must be protection for vulnerable children. The public must know what is done in its name and with its taxes. A significant number of children may not yet have been adopted by such 'alternative families'. We can assume, however, that many are being fostered, some long term, by homosexual couples. There is nothing in law to stop such fostering. But we have no clear picture of the true situation. Parties interested in pushing or helping the gay agenda hide behind a screen of 'confidentiality', manipulated to cover not particulars (the proper area for confidentiality) but principles (a very improper area for it). Children will be suffering. It is urgent that we know what is happening in this adoption and foster-care underworld. Many will not be so fortunate as the boy in the Newcastle case. They are suffering from the paganizing of our culture and a new anti-Christian ethic.

## ANTI-CHRISTIAN DRIFT

Significant attempts, some of them successful, are being made to exclude the Christian faith from our public culture – and not least by those working with the young.

Dr Jim Howe was Tony Bland's consultant neurologist. Tony Bland had been injured during the Hillsborough football stadium disaster in 1989 and it resulted in him being in a 'persistent vegetative state'. The British Law Lords made a controversial ruling to allow the withdrawal of food and water on the basis that this was 'medical treatment' and not a normal right – in this case. Tony Bland was then allowed to die. Jim Howe reckoned he was not 'a person', for a person is someone with 'the capacity to value their life'.[13] The case was complex, but there were certainly problems with Jim Howe and *his* views. When he was asked, 'Does a young baby have value as a person?' he replied:

*A new-born baby probably doesn't … One of the things that irritates me about people who believe in the sanctity of life is that they don't extend that sanctity of life to higher primates and dolphins and so on*

[13] Andrew Dunnett, *Euthanasia*, London, Hodder and Stoughton, 1999, p. 79.

*– or maybe they do – because I think they should. They think that we have a God-given sanctity of life. Well, I don't believe in God so I don't see any divine imprint.*[14]

This is dangerous territory. The concept of the divine image (or imprint) on all human beings is a core principle behind Western systems of justice and protection. It comes from those famous words in Genesis 9:6, 'Whoever sheds the blood of man, by man shall his blood be shed; for in the image of God has God made man.'

There is no evidence that the public at large believes, as Jim Howe does, that 'chimpanzees and gorillas are persons' while newborn babies are not. Nonetheless, to allow such thinking to influence life-or-death decisions is frightening.

The state educational system in the UK over the last part of the twentieth century, as well as the state health service, has also been subject to a programme of de-Christianization. We have seen, for example, the attempted exclusion of a positive Christian content from school assemblies and in religious education.[15] There is no evidence that this is generally wanted. The reverse seems to be the case. Where there is a school like Emmanuel College, Gateshead (on Tyneside), a *Christian* City Technology College – a full state school but privately sponsored, with 1,250 pupils and an overt Christian philosophy – it is greatly oversubscribed. The school's intake is 196 places a year. Sadly for many parents and pupils, there are over 600 applications annually.

The school resulted from an initial vision of Colin Hart, the director of the Christian Institute, who saw the possibilities; the drive, energy and financial competence of Peter Vardy, a Northeast Christian businessman who turned possibilities into reality; and the professionalism of John Burn, Lay Reader of Jesmond Parish Church and already a brilliant head teacher.

Not only is there a strong Christian ethos giving pupils a sense of value and significance, but the academic results are among the best in the country – and that is when the school is serving an inner-city

[14] Ibid., p. 84.
[15] Richard Dyter, *School Assemblies Need You!*, Crowborough, Monarch, 1997, p. 16.

area and is truly comprehensive. It is required to have 'equal numbers of children above and below the average score of 95–105', according to John Burn, now Vice-Chair of the school board after retiring as the school's headmaster at Christmas 1998. In his last year as head the school's GCSE results were twice the national average. According to the Newcastle *Journal,* 'the average points score achieved by each pupil put it in the national top 20, including independent schools.'[16] It is no wonder that parents – working-class parents – are desperate to get their children enrolled. Most parents want their children at least to have the option of rejecting the Christian faith. And most parents, as one pupil was heard to say, prefer a school where the girls do not get pregnant and the boys are not on drugs. For many 'guardians' of our public culture, however, parents' wishes do not matter. These 'guardians' arrogantly pursue an agenda of de-Christianization.

This problem is not peculiar to Britain: it is the same in the US. There may be change in the air as we have seen, but much more has to happen before there is a real turnaround. A best-selling book by William Strauss and Neil Howe entitled *The Fourth Turning* argues that the US 'feels like it's unravelling'. The authors go on:

> *Though we live in an era of relative peace and comfort, we have settled into a mood of pessimism about the long-term future, fearful that our superpower nation is somehow rotting from within.*
>
> *Neither an epic victory over Communism nor an extended upswing of the business cycle can buoy our public spirit … We yearn for civic character but satisfy ourselves with symbolic gestures and celebrity circuses. We perceive no greatness in our leaders, a new meanness in ourselves. Small wonder that each new election brings a new jolt, its aftermath a new disappointment.*[17]

Britain is often a mirror image of the US. While we have different traditions, where America goes first, Britain goes also in the end.

'But isn't this all alarmism?' someone may ask. 'Isn't it unfair to see the eccentricity of lesbian parenting as a symptom of a wider

[16] *The Journal,* 17 March 1999.
[17] William Strauss and Neil Howe, *The Fourth Turning,* New York, Broadway, 1997, p. 1.

dysfunction in society?' An answer requires us to be more specific. We must look further at the case of children and young people. That case in Newcastle will then, indeed, be seen as a symptom and not an eccentricity.

## PSYCHOSOCIAL DISORDERS IN YOUNG PEOPLE

In 1995 Sir Michael Rutter, a Professor of Child and Adolescent Psychiatry in London (who had been involved with Susan Golombok in her 1983 study of lesbian parenting), and David Smith, a Professor of Criminology in Edinburgh, proved there were serious issues regarding young people that we ignore to our peril. They showed that what common sense knows, serious study now confirms. In their publication entitled *Psychosocial Disorders in Young People* (a massive, 843-page book), they edited a multinational collection of papers on young people's problems researched by a group of leading European and American scholars.[18] The authors focus on disorders that are increasing in the teenage years: crime, suicide, suicidal behaviour, depression, anorexia and bulimia, alcohol and drug abuse. The findings are frightening.

At the launch of the book, Sir Michael Rutter claimed that 'this is the first major study to highlight the upward trend in psychosocial disorders of youth since the Second World War across the most developed countries.' He went on to say, 'It is striking that this increase in psychosocial disorders happened at a time when physical health was improving.'

David Smith added, 'It is also striking that a major increase in psychosocial disorders happened in the "golden era" of low unemployment and rising living standards between 1950 and 1973. Increasing psychosocial disorders are not related to deprivation or to increasing affluence in any simple way.'[19]

The key findings were as follows.

---

[18] M. Rutter and David J. Smith, *Psychosocial Disorders in Young People*, Chichester, John Wiley, 1995.

[19] Comments made at the press conference to launch the book, 26 May 1995.

1 In Britain the rate of recorded crime, mostly committed by young people, increased tenfold from 1950 to 1993; and over that period there were substantial increases in the psychosocial disorders of young people (this is also true in nearly all developed countries). But these increases of the past 50 years were sudden increases. There had been no similar increases earlier in the century. And, very importantly, as psychosocial disorders were increasing, physical health was improving.

2 In most countries alcohol consumption increased greatly among the young between 1950 and 1980, with deaths from cirrhosis of the liver increasing in a similar way, as did alcohol-related problem behaviours.

3 With regard to drugs, national surveys in the US show that the illicit use of drugs and drug dependency were very low for those born in 1940, but increased for each successive birth cohort afterwards. Western European countries have similarly experienced a massive increase in drug use and abuse since 1950.

4 In Europe rates of suicide have increased over the whole of the twentieth century, but the most striking increase was among young males between 1970 and 1990.

5 There has been a substantial increase in the proportion of those suffering from depressive disorders, as shown by a wide range of studies carried out in the US, Canada, New Zealand and Britain.

What do the authors think are the causes of these increased problems? Rutter and Smith note that the poor, the unemployed, and people living on 'sink estates' are more likely to be criminal, depressed, suicidal and addicted to drugs than those in more comfortable circumstances. Yet, they argue, worsening living conditions *cannot* account for rising levels of crime, suicide, depression, alcohol and drug abuse in young people. This is because the rise was most marked during a period of two to three decades in which living conditions improved. Between 1950 and 1973 there was a 'golden era' of economic growth, low unemployment and improving living conditions throughout the developed world. But this coincided with the post-war rise in psychological disorders. Also, the high unemployment in the 1930s was not associated with rises in crime, suicide or drug abuse.

## THE CAUSES

So what are the causes? Many are now attempting to give answers. Rutter and Smith suggest as one answer that the level of family discord and break-up can play a role in the rise of psychosocial disorders.

Norman Dennis, a social scientist from Newcastle University (politically socialist and *not* of the far right), has shown how significant this factor is.[20] He argues that the crime and social disorder of our inner cities are not to be analysed primarily in terms of poverty but in terms of family breakdown. This is the breakdown of the traditional pattern of a married father and mother providing security and stability for their developing young and being committed to each other for life.

Another factor is sexual experimentation. Alongside adolescent 'isolation' and a desire for independence, young people, say Rutter and Smith, 'may be more stressed by early sexual experiences and the break-up of love relationships'.[21] This is the damage caused by sexual promiscuity and experimentation. It is not really clever – it is emotionally damaging. And it does not lead, long term, to sexual satisfaction. As we saw earlier, other research confirms that those most satisfied with their sexual lives and the most sexually adjusted are those who keep to biblical standards of sexual morality.

All this is common sense. Common sense is now being confirmed by academic child psychiatrists, criminologists and social scientists. A number are now saying that the serious problems they identify among young people are *fundamentally moral.*

How do you change moral behaviour? The tragedy is that many simply urge new moral effort. That will not work. If the Bible is right, the reality is that men and women do not do what is right by nature. That is the result of the Fall: we all sin. If you believe nothing else in the Bible, you have to believe that. The evidence is all around today and down the centuries of history. You cannot, however, simply tell people to pull themselves up by their moral

---

[20] Dennis and Erdos, *Families without Fatherhood,* op. cit.; and Norman Dennis, *Rising Crime and the Dismembered Family,* London, IEA Health and Welfare Unit, 1993.

[21] Official press handout; and Rutter and Smith, *Psychosocial Disorders in Young People,* op. cit., p. 807.

bootlaces. It does not work. People need the love of God the Father, the forgiveness of Jesus Christ the crucified Saviour and the power of the Holy Spirit for new life. That is the Christian analysis and solution in a nutshell.

To reject the Fatherhood of God, as people are doing today, is to lose before long the brotherhood of man. There will be social consequences. A recent UK study by Christie Davies, Professor of Sociology at Reading University, entitled 'Moralization and Demoralization: A Moral Explanation for Changes in Crime, Disorder and Social Problems' shows how this works.[22] He has studied not just the last 50 years, like Rutter and Smith, but the last 150 years. He has charted the same rise in crime and social disorder over the last 50 years which Rutter and Smith highlight, but he has also charted the *fall* in crime and disorder at the end of the nineteenth century.

He, too, shows that the current slide into lawlessness cannot be blamed on bad housing, poverty or unemployment. There were far more of all three in the earlier part of the twentieth century, but there was little crime. In fact, there has been a U-curve. The overall incidence of serious offences recorded by the police in the 1890s was about 60 per cent of what it had been in the 1850s – and the efficiency of reporting and recording crime was improving at this time. The real fall in the crime rate was therefore probably far greater. What this means is that by 1900 Britain was not only a less violent and less dishonest country than it is today. It was also less violent and less dishonest than it had been in the earlier part of the nineteenth century. There must be a cause for this. But what is it?

## THE KEY TO CHANGE

The most persuasive answer seems to be the religious revival which took place in the nineteenth century and the related remoralization of society. These two things led to a heightening of conscience

---

[22] Christie Davies, 'Moralization and Demoralization: A Moral Explanation for Changes in Crime, Disorder and Social Problems', in Digby Anderson (ed.), *The Loss of Virtue*, London, Social Affairs Unit, 1992, pp. 3–13.

and an increase of self-control (something relevant for the twenty-first century). The basic problem is the sinfulness of men and women. This is the teaching of the Old Testament, the New Testament and now social science. Christie Davies has this comment to make on common false perceptions: 'For the Left the villain is capitalism and for the Right it is welfare; both are ways of avoiding the conclusion that wicked and irresponsible choices are made by wicked and irresponsible individuals.'[23]

As I argued earlier, for the West the turning point or watershed became evident in the 1960s when there was a new theology and a new morality. People then claimed that 'God is dead'; homosexual behaviour was legalized; pornography was no longer 'pornography' but 'adult expression' and regular fare in the cinema and on television; and society began to fall apart. Things *were* different before the 1960s. In 1955 Geoffrey Gorer commented in his *Exploring English Character*: 'In public life today, the English are certainly among the most peaceful, gentle, courteous and orderly populations that the civilized world has ever seen.'[24]

What, then, were the roots of that 'peaceful, gentle' life? Answer: the Christian faith, and foremost was the Sunday school, 'whose enrolments,' says Davies, 'rose as the incidence of deviant behaviour fell in the late 19th century. Significantly, the numbers enrolled in and the influence of this institution then fell in the years prior to the reversal of the U-curve of deviance which has produced Britain's present high level of moral problems.'[25]

By 1888 about three out of every four children in England and Wales attended Sunday school, 'a remarkable proportion when it is remembered that parents of the higher social groups did not particularly favour attendance'.[26] Wales, which had been one of the more violent and lawless parts of Britain, became in the later nineteenth century an especially peaceful and law-abiding country. And it was in Wales that Sunday schools organized by Nonconformist chapels were at their strongest. Professor Christie Davies summarizes:

[23] Ibid., p. 7.
[24] Quoted in ibid., p. 6.
[25] Ibid., p. 10.
[26] Alan Wilkinson, *The Church of England and the First World War*, London, SPCK, 1978, p. 7.

*It is pointless to ask whether children became moral and respectable as a result of the teaching they received in Sunday school, or whether the key factor was the pre-existing aspirations of their parents who sent them there. What is important is that these reinforced one another and that any potential delinquents were confronted on all sides and from all sources with the consistent moral view that forms of antisocial behaviour with clear and direct harmful consequences such as violence, theft, illegitimacy and drunkenness were quite simply wrong.*[27]

At some point we have to say, 'Enough is enough.' Fathers and mothers must ensure something better for their children in the twenty-first century. In some quarters there is little opposition to the new moral decadence. There is little opposition from our elected representatives in government, where many now validate immorality. There is little opposition from radio or television, where many are often the first to support immoral behaviour. There is no opposition – or little opposition – in our schools or universities. As George Will has said, 'There is nothing so vulgar left in our experience for which we cannot transport some professor from somewhere to justify it.'[28] There is little opposition from social workers who have to interface with suffering children: they now regularly endorse sexual deviancy.

Sadly, there is often also little opposition from leaders in the Church – both bishops and clergy. Of course, there is forgiveness for every sin. Jesus forgave an adulteress – but he then said, 'Go and sin no more.' He did not say, 'Go and change the law to fit your behaviour.' We are becoming insensitive to sin and evil. What would John the Baptist say if he was alive today? It was because of his outspoken condemnation of Herod's immoralities that John was beheaded.

Not so long ago I was taking part in a BBC *Heart of the Matter* television debate. Among others, I was arguing with someone who, along with his homosexual lover, was trying to find a surrogate

---

[27] Davies, 'Moralization and Demoralization', op. cit., p. 12.
[28] Quoted in Ravi Zacharias, *Can Man Live without God?*, Milton Keynes, Word, 1995, p. 17.

mother to have a baby for them. In an interview he expressed his views: 'We feel that the love and respect that a child brings would complete our lives. *We all have the right to have children.*'[29] We do not!

Our treatment of children and their well-being is an indicator of social health. On present showing there is serious social disease. We are not only sick; we are evil. Children are being treated as commodities. They can be acquired or dispensed with according to adult requirements. They are now being seen by many as a means to adult happiness.

Alexander Pope once wrote these lines – and they need to be repeated at the beginning of the twenty-first century:

*Vice is a monster of so frightful mien,*
*As, to be hated, needs but to be seen;*
*Yet seen too oft, familiar with her face,*
*We first endure, then pity, then embrace.*[30]

[29] Press Association, 27 May 1997.
[30] Alexander Pope, *An Essay on Man*, Epistle 2, 1733, l. 217.

# CHAPTER THREE

# POLITICS, MORALITY
# AND THE LAW

## THE MORAL MAZE

Every new diplomat in the British Foreign and Commonwealth
Office undergoes a process of induction. In the early 1980s every
graduate entrant was told in clear terms that 'adultery represented
a potential security risk as well as being damaging to one's professional credibility, particularly in smaller overseas posts'. So said
Simon Brocklebank-Fowler in a letter to *The Times* on 6 August 1997,
writing as a former member of the Foreign Office. He then went on
to say that 'broadly these views still prevail within the Office'.

The following day I was asked to take part in a BBC Radio 4
programme called *The Moral Maze*. Why?

The tabloid *News of the World* had flushed out an adulterous affair
between the British Foreign Secretary in the New Labour
Government and his secretary. Only a few years previously this
would have meant instant resignation for the head of the Foreign
and Commonwealth Office. Despite the fact that such behaviour
was deemed by the Foreign Office to be 'damaging to one's professional credibility', however, Robin Cook and the Labour spin
machine decided to weather the storm.

Robin Cook and New Labour were claiming to promote an
'ethical' foreign policy. But in a matter of weeks here was Mr Cook
violating an old, tried-and-tested ethical marriage policy. This
sparked a great debate on the relationship between public and
private morality. *The Moral Maze* decided to pursue the subject.

First a panel of four set out the issues. Then in the main part of the programme the panel interrogated five witnesses. In conclusion there was a brief comment from each of the panellists to wind up the programme.

The panellists were Janet Daley of the *Daily Telegraph*, someone with conservative views; Dr David Starkey of the London School of Economics, who, as a campaigning homosexual, had once opposed me in a formal debate at London University; Dr David Cook, a medical ethicist and theologian from Oxford, whom I knew personally; and Geoffrey Robinson QC, a non-traditionalist lawyer.

The first witness was Steven Norris, the former Transport Minister, who proved that moral decadence is not the prerogative of New Labour. He retained his job in the former Tory Government, as was said on the programme, 'despite and, come to think of it, maybe because of cheerfully having five mistresses while still being married'. Then came David Banks, the Editor in Chief of the *Sunday Mirror* – a paper, like the *News of the World*, which did things like 'spying on Robin Cook's private life', or so it was implied on the programme. He was followed by Jonathan Friedland, the Policy Editor of the *Guardian* – one of the main vehicles for New Labour ideas; then by myself and, finally, by Anthony Howard, a distinguished political commentator from a previous generation.

When my turn came I was introduced as 'vicar of Jesmond and a founder member of Reform'. Michael Buerk asked me a straight question about the relationship between private and public morality. It will be instructive to follow some of the discussion by way of a transcript,[1] as it shows the level of public debate over these critical issues as we begin the new millennium. I started by stating the obvious point that 'when we talk about private morality in this context, let's face it, we are talking about sexual morality'. And I pointed out that the previous month Lord Nolan, the Chairman of the Committee on Standards in Public Life, had said that you cannot separate the private from the public because adultery *does* affect your public performance. I then added that this 'separation' goes back to the 1950s:

---

[1] This is my own transcript of the programme, made with permission.

*David Holloway: It started with the Wolfenden Committee … That was when formally there was a separation, or a theoretical separation, between private morality and public morality on the assumption there were no harms associated with private sexual morality. Well, 30 [or 40] years later we see there's a vast amount of harm publicly, following on from the sexual revolution, in terms of marriage break-down and so forth.*

*Michael Buerk: But shouldn't our only interest be, in the case of – I don't want to keep harping on Robin Cook, but in the case of a Government Minister, the way in which he performs his public office, not what happens in his private life? That's our only legitimate interest, surely.*

*David Holloway: Yes, but, if your marriage of 23 years (or whatever it was) is disrupting and you've got children you've got obligations to, if you don't feel that, if you're not emotionally involved, you're clearly abnormal; and I don't think you would be an adequate person to conduct the affairs of State. Let's face it, the very day Robin Cook's marriage, it was revealed – or the day after – his marriage had broken down, he was having to deal with critical negotiations with the Bosnian Muslims; and huge judgements were having to be made. Well, if all the time you're thinking about 'what's happening to my wife?' 'what's happening to my children?' and 'how are they feeling?' you, clearly, cannot think clearly.*

*Michael Buerk: But everybody goes through – has things in their private lives, even if they aren't, in quotes, 'immoral'. But I mustn't hog you. David Starkey.*

## CONFRONTATION

It was then David Starkey's turn to interrogate me.

*David Starkey: I'll do my best to hog you! Mr Holloway, you have very strong feelings, do you not, on Prince Charles and his possible role as Monarch, as an adulterer and as supreme Governor of the Church of England – as an un-reformed adulterer?*

*David Holloway: Yes, those feelings are related not to the private and public issue, so much as he, as Monarch, has to swear, as part of the Constitutional arrangements that are so vital to our own country, 'to maintain and preserve' and, I quote, 'to maintain and preserve the laws of God and the true profession of the gospel'; and then 'the doctrine, worship, discipline and Government of the Church of England'. And you clearly cannot do that with integrity when you are keeping a mistress.*

**David Starkey:** *Can I ask you to scrape the depths of your memory? You've been quite good on adulterers. Can we actually look at the decisions of the Synod of the Church of England. Do you recall a Measure, passed in 1990, called the 'Divorce Ordinands Measure'?*

**David Holloway:** *No, that was the Clergy (Ordination) Measure, the one which—*

**David Starkey:** *Indeed – well tell us about it. What did it allow?*

**David Holloway:** *I may say, I certainly voted against it—*

**David Starkey:** *Ah, but can we find out what it does? It allows clergy to be divorced and keep their cures, to be remarried—*

**David Holloway:** *The argument was—*

**David Starkey:** *No, no, Mr Holloway. Let me! The listeners are less familiar with it than you are. This measure allows clergy of the Church of England to be divorced and to keep their cures, to be remarried and keep their cures; and indeed in one case of an actual bishop at the moment, to marry a divorcee – exactly the position that Charles would be in if he married Camilla – and be a bishop. If you can be a bishop and divorced and remarried to a divorcee, why can't you be Supreme Governor?*

**David Holloway:** *Why do you think I'm a member of Reform? Because there are certain areas in the Church of England that at the moment many of us are quite appalled about. But these are not, I may say, majority positions—*

**David Starkey:** *I'm sorry, Mr Holloway, I'm not going to let you slip away … You represent a minority within the Church of England. The Church of England has decided, out of convenience, its own clergy can do what you would forbid to the Supreme Governor. I submit you are a case of absolute fundamental institutional—*

**David Holloway:** *With respect—*

**David Starkey** *[shouting]: There's no need for you to respect me, I don't respect you … a case of fundamental institutional hypocrisy.*

At that point Michael Buerk called a halt to David Starkey's questioning. But that discussion highlighted significant issues.

### 'THINGS THAT REALLY MATTER'

The wrongness of the Robin Cook affair, and the truth of my proposition on the programme – that private sexual morality could indeed be relevant to public performance – seemed to be proved as more sordid details emerged. In January 1999 the ex-Mrs Cook gave her side of the story in a book that was serialized in the *Sunday Times*.[2] It did not make happy reading.

Was that not all 'private' and intrusive, though? Tony Blair, the Prime Minister, obviously thought so. He thought that the new revelations about Robin Cook were no real problem. He immediately sprang to the defence of his Foreign Secretary after his former wife's allegations. The Prime Minister appeared on the BBC's *Breakfast with Frost* programme on 10 January 1999. He defended his Cabinet colleague as 'the most respected foreign minister in the rest of Europe that we've had for years and years and years'. He also said, 'If you go through any big corporation, employees had problems in their private lives that did not affect the way they carried out their jobs.' Speaking on behalf of himself and his colleague, he asked to be judged not on 'scandal, gossip and trivia' but 'on the things that really matter'.

So what about 'the things that really matter'? In January 1999 President Milosevic of Yugoslavia was bringing to fruition his evil policy of the 'ethnic cleansing' of Albanians in Kosovo. The response of NATO, spearheaded by Britain and the US, was to conduct an aerial bombing war against Serbia. This, however, accelerated the humanitarian crisis it was aimed to prevent. With no NATO ground troops present in Kosovo, appalling atrocities could be, and were, committed. NATO provided an excuse for the Serbs.

This response by NATO was being worked out at the very time Britain's Foreign Secretary was having to cover for his sexual misbehaviour; at the very time the American President was also having to

[2] *Sunday Times*, 10, 17 and 24 January 1999.

cover for his sexual misbehaviour; and at the very time the British Prime Minister was having to cover for his Foreign Secretary. The stakes were high. What would have happened if Robin Cook and Bill Clinton had both done the honourable thing and resigned? Had their successors a greater grip on private morality, might there have been a better solution for the Balkans and, later in the year, for East Timor?

It is not an unfair question in the light of a comment made by Lord Nolan, the Chairman of the Committee on Standards in Public Life. When interviewed soon after Tony Blair took office, he said, 'Of all the behaviour which in my personal experience has caused the greatest misery to other human beings, I would put adultery pretty high on the list. I don't actually think you can expect a man with the strains of public life to perform adequately unless he has got a good home life to go back to.'[3]

## PAUL

What would the apostle Paul have thought about all this? What view would he have taken of the relationship between private and public morality? There may be a clue in what he told his young friend Timothy. He told him that he should pray 'for kings and all those in authority, that we may live peaceful and quiet lives in all godliness and holiness' (1 Timothy 2.2).

The implications are significant. Paul was saying that politics should not only be concerned with the protection of life, limb and property (peaceful and quiet lives) but also with so structuring public life that religion (godliness) as well as morality (holiness) are helped rather than hindered.

Such sentiments are unthinkable for some today. Definitely religion and probably morality, they say, must be kept away from the 'public square'. If they are to exist at all, they should exist in private. Not surprisingly some Christians show signs of extreme timidity. Christians are still good at standing alongside people in their moral confusions, but less good at saying, 'This is right,' and 'That is

---

[3] *Daily Mail*, 14 July 1997, reporting a GMTV interview with Lord Nolan.

wrong.' While no doubt believing them to be wrong, some Christian leaders now find it hard to say positively and definitely, 'Adultery is wrong,' or 'Homosexual relations are wrong.'

The irony is that most citizens of the UK think that both adultery and homosexual relations *are* morally wrong; and most citizens of the UK think of themselves as Christian. There is no need for reticence. The massive 1994 national British survey *Sexual Attitudes and Lifestyles* found that 79 per cent of men thought adultery was always or mostly wrong, and 70 per cent thought the same about male homosexual acts.[4]

The same year the most recent survey from the religious broadcasting department of the ITC (the Independent Television Commission), published under the title *Seeing is Believing*, found that 71 per cent of our population still identify as Christian. Only 22 per cent claim to be nothing, while under 4 per cent are of other faiths – some just 'don't know'.[5] The dominant tradition is, therefore, Christian. We are not a pluralist, multifaith society as is frequently claimed. Why, then, is the Christian and moral majority so self-effacing?

One answer is that the plausibility structure of modern Britain, within which beliefs are nurtured or destroyed, is being shaped by that one-fifth of the population without belief. Such nonbelievers, who now include a significant group of 'anti-Christians', seem to crop up disproportionately in education, the media and various therapeutic agencies such as social work departments – areas or agencies which are modern carriers of values. In this environment Christians are losing confidence both in their faith and in their morals.

We are in a bizarre situation. The majority believe in the rightness of traditional Christian moral behaviour, but they have also been conditioned to think it is wrong to say so publicly. The vacuum allows unrepresentative, immoral minorities, who have no such reticence, to erode even further our public moral culture.

[4] Johnson, Wadsworth, Wellings and Field, *Sexual Attitudes and Lifestyles*, op. cit., pp. 471, 475.
[5] Barrie Gunter and Rachel Viney, *Seeing is Believing: Religion and Television in the 1990s*, London, John Libbey, 1994, p. 13.

## LIBERTY AND BLOOMSBURY

The assault on Christian faith and morality is serious. Unless the moral fabric is restored, with the prior restoration of faith in Jesus Christ, the long-term future of the so-called Christian nations as free societies must be in question. A free society needs not only a commitment to the ideal of liberty but also a commitment to the common good. As it forged the political traditions of the West, classical liberalism was – unlike much contemporary libertarianism – quite hostile to denials of the Christian faith and to immorality. It saw the loss of faith and the loss of morals as destructive of the common good. A great political philosopher of that classical liberal tradition, Alexis de Tocqueville, said, 'Liberty requires religion as its companion in all its battles and its triumphs ... It considers religion as the safeguard of morality, and morality as the best security of law and the surest pledge of the duration of freedom.'[6]

The erosion in Britain of that common-sense view has been due in no small part to the Victorian philosopher and economist John Stuart Mill and his modern heirs. Mill argued that religion and morality must be privatized in a free society, and if they were to be privatized then they could be no business of the State. The State could only intervene through the law to protect against measurable harms. It could not intervene to uphold the common good. Even Nietzsche, the anti-Christian German philosopher, saw through Mill's liberal moralism. He unambiguously referred to 'that flat-head Mill'. Nietzsche saw that beneath the 'insipid and cowardly concept "man"', there is the 'cult of Christian morality'. These 'moral fanatics', he said, do not realize how dependent their morality is on the religion they want to discard.[7]

Nietzsche also foresaw that morality would have problems. It did. In the early years of the twentieth century morality was eviscerated. True, this was initially limited to intellectual circles and the upper reaches of British society. Before the advent of television, the development of other mass media and also the 1944 UK Education Act, there could be considerable insulation and

[6] Quoted in Gertrude Himmelfarb, *On Looking into the Abyss*, New York, Alfred A. Knopf, 1994, p. 100.
[7] Ibid., p. 86.

isolation of the different stratas of society. This afforded the elite circles both protection and greater scope for their 'new' ways of behaving as human beings (which often meant behaving as animals).

Adherents to this new morality, or nonmorality, centred on Bloomsbury in London. Few outside their own circle knew about the depravity and depression that went on behind the walls of those grand terraces. It was all masked by great literary skill. The damage done by this group to the moral fabric of Britain was not immediate in its effect, but their ideas were taken up by lesser intellects later on in the century. We are still suffering from the fallout. Lord Acton once wrote, 'Ideas have a radiation and development, an ancestry and posterity of their own, in which men play the part of godfathers and godmothers more than that of legitimate parents.'[8]

Ideas take on a life of their own. This is especially so when they are seen to validate desires and practices which should normally generate guilt but which some people want to justify. They also take on a life of their own in the various liberal arts faculties that have spawned in colleges and universities since the 1960s. They can likewise take on a life of their own in the pre-college, school classroom. C.S. Lewis once spoke of the danger of people like 'the Bloomsberries', as they called themselves – the 'Cultured', to use Lewis's phrase – forming a new ruling class, a 'charientocracy' who 'use the social term *vulgar* of those who disagree with them'.[9] In the vacuum left by the loss of a Christian culture, he feared people schooled in this new 'religion of poetry and art' and sexual decadence would use the education machine to shape future generations. They would find, he said, that 'the modern pupil is the ideal patient ... helpless Plasticine'.[10]

How right he was. He saw how morals and values are transmitted. 'The young people today are un-Christian because their teachers have been either unwilling or unable to transmit Christianity to them,' he wrote. It had nothing to do with the merits or demerits of the faith. 'The school masters of today are, for the most part,' he said, 'the undergraduates of 20 years ago.'[11]

[8] Quoted in ibid., p. 82.
[9] C.S. Lewis, *Christian Reunion and Other Essays*, London, Fount, 1990, p. 33.
[10] Ibid., p. 35.
[11] C.S. Lewis, *First and Second Things*, London, Fount, 1985, p. 64.

The Bloomsbury set generated the myth that the modern world was very different from anything that had gone before. Virginia Woolf claimed a new world order had begun in 1910. The modern age, they said, is quite unlike any other age. That is why we have to remake our own individual morality. But Bloomsbury was a pathetic and sad charade. Leonard Woolf claimed that they were 'the builders of a new society which should be free, rational, civilized'.[12] But behind the bedroom doors there was anything but freedom, reasonableness and civility. Take homosexuality – just one of their ways of having sex. As we have already seen and will see again, this is a common and important thread running through the decadence of the twentieth century. They believed in the 'higher sodomy', which in reality was promiscuous sodomy. We now know that in 1907 Lytton Strachey discovered that his lover (and cousin) Duncan Grant was also having an affair with Arthur Hobhouse, who was having an affair with Maynard Keynes (the Bloomsbury economist), who distressed Strachey the following year when Strachey found out that Grant was now having an affair with Keynes as well.[13]

Why, however, should they not be allowed to do what they liked? Some might find it offensive and immoral, but in a free society is it reasonable for the law and the courts to intervene in questions of morality, and private morality at that? This was a debate which opened up in a new way in the late 1950s – and the focus was homosexuality.

## WOLFENDEN

In 1955 the British Government set up a Committee under Sir John Wolfenden to publish a report on prostitution and homosexuality. It did so in 1957. The basic issue which had to be discussed was this: 'What is the connection between crime and sin and to what extent, if at all, should the Criminal Law of England concern itself with the enforcement of morals and punish sin, or immorality as such?'[14]

[12] Quoted in Gertrude Himmelfarb, *Marriage and Morals among the Victorians*, London, Faber and Faber, 1986, p. 46.

[13] Ibid., p. 43ff.

[14] Patrick Devlin, *The Enforcement of Morals*, London, Oxford University Press, 1965, p. 2.

The Committee's conclusion was as follows. They said that the function of the criminal law was

> *to preserve public order and decency, to protect the citizen from what is offensive or injurious, and to provide sufficient safeguards against exploitation and corruption of others … It is not, in our view, the function of the law to intervene in the private lives of citizens, or to seek to enforce any particular pattern of behaviour, further than is necessary to carry out the purposes we have outlined.*[15]

Their recommendation was that 'homosexual behaviour between consenting adults should no longer be a criminal offence'. This, the Committee said, was because of

> *the importance which society and the law ought to give to individual freedom of choice and action in matters of private morality. Unless a deliberate attempt is to be made by society, acting through the agency of the law, to equate the sphere of crime with that of sin, there must remain a realm of private morality which is, in brief and crude terms, not the law's business. To say this is not to condone or encourage private immorality.*[16]

This seemed so reasonable at the time. It was, of course, pure John Stuart Mill. Today, however, the Wolfenden Report seems far less reasonable than in those heady years of the late 1950s and early 1960s. Its fallacy was to think that what is legal can easily be distinguished from what is moral and what is private easily distinguished from what is public. It cannot.

## THE LEGAL AND MORAL, THE PRIVATE AND PUBLIC

Logically one can distinguish between the legal and the moral. But in the practical life of public affairs this is not always possible. With the decline of the Church and the break-up of the family (both

[15] *The Report of the Committee on Homosexual Offences and Prostitution 1957*, London, HMSO, 1957, para. 13.
[16] Ibid., para. 62.

traditional carriers of values and moral authority), it is hard to maintain that something is immoral and to act accordingly when the law says it is legal.

After Wolfenden, it is a fact that we now have in Britain a range of laws and regulations which have legislated a new morality. These are laws that condone sexual promiscuity, undermine family values and sanction, through a removal of restraints, alternative lifestyles. The result of Wolfenden has not been a separating of law from morality and of the criminal from the sinful. Rather, the Committee's proposals have led to Parliament legislating for a *new* morality and for a *new* political correctness which has generated a *new* set of sins. This has certainly interfered with private lives. At a stroke it justified an attack on the rights of individuals to have legal support for their moral endeavours, a support they had grown to expect as part of the social contract.

In addition to this, Wolfenden had assumed that what you do in private – by which he meant the privacy of the bedroom – could be quite separate from public life. This was following the notion, born of Bloomsbury, that the arguments against a sexual free-for-all were not related to empirical realities but simply to the squeamishness of the moralistic. It was a shibboleth that disjoined morality from social consequences. 'Harm', it was said, was a category entirely inappropriate in respect of sexual preferences and practices.

We have now learnt from social studies how false that is. Wolfenden was quite wrong. The private and the public are *not* separated in matters of sex and sexuality. The law must therefore intervene when necessary.

Private sin has public consequences. In his book *The Rising Price of Love*, Dr Patrick Dixon documents the cash price of the sexual revolution. In terms of AIDS, other sexual diseases and other health charges, the cost to the public purse is over £1 billion a year; the annual cost of divorce is £5 billion a year; the costs of other support for family disintegration is £600 million; related youth crime £1.5 billion; and single parenting £1 billion. This makes a grand total of £9 billion pounds in costs to the public purse.[17] At the time of

---

[17] Patrick Dixon, *The Rising Price of Love*, London, Hodder and Stoughton, 1995, p. 190.

Patrick Dixon's writing it approximated to a quarter of the entire Health Service budget or a quarter of the entire Education budget.

When the public behaviour of others destroys or diminishes my property, I have a recourse to the law. If you are drunk and crash into my car, you should be, and in all likelihood will be, punished at law or at least forced to make reparation through your insurers. It will be a cost to you. But when the social or medical consequences of the *chosen* sexual behaviour of others is a cost to me (through National Insurance or various taxes), I have no recourse to the law. That is to say, when the private sexual behaviour of others affects my property, the law will not intervene. That is clearly unjust. Surely the time has come for the law to act again as a restraining force. After all, it has been successful in respect of drinking and driving. This is now recognized as antisocial and so is properly penalized and stigmatized.

For all of us legislation, in a free society, should be a last resort. At times, however, legislation is necessary as a restraining force. It was Edmund Burke who said, 'Society cannot exist unless a controlling power upon will and appetite be placed somewhere, and the less of it there is within, the more there must be without.'[18] There is, simply, a necessary trade-off.

[18] Quoted in Gertrude Himmelfarb, 'Preface' to Digby Anderson (ed.), *This Will Hurt*, London, Social Affairs Unit, 1995, p. x.

# CHAPTER FOUR

# THE MONARCH,
# THE PRESIDENT
# AND LYING

## NATURAL JUSTICE AND MORALITY

The establishment of the Church of England means it is entitled to propose 'Measures' for the UK Parliament. After being agreed by the Ecclesiastical Committee of Parliament (who can merely veto a Measure wholesale), they have the same status as Acts of Parliament.

One of my duties in the 1980s as a General Synod member was to be a member of the Steering Committee for the Patronage (Benefices) Measure 1986. Assisted by a senior parliamentary draftsman, we had to review the proposed Measure clause by clause in the light of Synod debates and members' submissions. The details of the Measure need not detain us here, but at one point we were discussing ancient trusts established in the last century and still of financial benefit. It was proposed by someone on our committee that these be abolished.

I replied by instinct, saying in my naïveté, 'You can't do that.'

'Oh yes, you can!' I was told. 'Parliament can do anything.' And, of course, it can.

This brought home to me how fragile is the nature of Western democracy and how much it needs moral support. Unless that moral support is firm, constitutional democracy degenerates into a form of ochlocracy – the rule of the mob or, in its more sophisticated form, rule where large majorities can do as they please. But it was not for such systems of government that people fought Hitler in the Second World War, or stood up to Stalin in the period that followed, or took issue with Iraq or the Balkans at the end of the twentieth century. It was for democracy, moral good and justice. According to J. Budziszewski, 'Constitutional democracy – which is really more like what Aristotle called "polity", mixed government, but ennobled (today) by the biblical understanding that human beings bear the image of God – means that many groups share power on principles of equal dignity, institutional balance, and natural justice.'[1]

But 'institutional balance and natural justice' are coming under threat, certainly in the US and the UK. This is serious, because if a majority acts or legislates immorally or unjustly, it raises the stakes. It invites civil disobedience.

In the past influential elements of the State have been moral 'props'. They have acted as moral reinforcers and restrainers. Notably these have been the universities, the responsible end of the press and, particularly in Britain, the BBC. But with these institutions now often being in the forefront of de-moralization, the core constitutional elements have to bear even greater weight. In the US these elements are the American Constitution itself, together with the Presidency. In the UK it is the 'Establishment', and that establishment is royal and religious. Moral support in Britain, until the last part of the twentieth century, has been given constitutionally by the Establishment of the Church of England and the Church of Scotland on the one hand, and on the other hand by the monarchy.

## THE MONARCHY

The monarch is both supreme in the State and Supreme Governor of the Church of England, at the same time and equally. This puts Parliament under a Christian head. That is why non-Christian belief or behaviour on the part of a monarch has constitutional consequences both for the Church and the State.

[1] J. Budziszewski, 'The Future of the End of Democracy', *First Things*, no. 91, March 1999, p. 19.

In her 1992 City of London speech, Queen Elizabeth II spoke of the questioning that needs to go on regarding the monarchy, as indeed questioning is needed in any institution. She seemed to be encouraging a public debate.

The issues for the Church at the start of the twenty-first century are relatively simple. Whether we like it or not, the Crown and the Church of England play – or should play – a key role in maintaining the spiritual tradition of the nation. As part of our British Constitution, this is enshrined in law. That is why the Church of England must take seriously the issue of Prince Charles, the heir to the throne. He is a tragic figure, having lived through a sad marriage marred by adultery. There are genuinely confused emotions in the UK regarding the Prince (and his late wife). There are feelings of deep sympathy for both Prince Charles and his sons. Christian people know that they must pray for them all. But they also know that Prince Charles cannot, *as things stand*, be the Supreme Governor of the Church of England.

The problem is the Coronation Oath. Among other things, Prince Charles would have to swear to 'maintain and preserve the laws of God and the true profession of the gospel [and] the doctrine, worship, discipline and government [of the Church of England].'[2] At the moment, if he was called upon to be king immediately, how can he swear that oath in such a way that it would remain credible?

First, he seems to support a pluralistic, multifaith position and has said publicly on television that he wants to be 'Defender of Faith' not 'Defender of *the* Faith'. But Article XVIII (of the Thirty-nine Articles setting out the doctrine of the Church of England) makes it clear that the Church of England is *not* multifaith. It says, 'Holy Scripture doth set out to us only the name of Jesus Christ, whereby men must be saved.'

Of course, being fully committed to the Christian faith does not mean that the monarch has no duty to be concerned for the rights and liberties of those of other faiths or none within the nation. In a tolerant society there are rights and liberties for those holding

[2] From *The Music with the Form and Order of the Service to be performed at the Coronation of Her Most Excellent Majesty Queen Elizabeth II*, London, Novello, 1953, p. 14ff.

beliefs that the dominant religious culture will consider wrong. Toleration is not indifference, as we saw earlier. You can only tolerate what you believe *is* wrong. The monarch therefore has to ensure the rights and liberties of those having beliefs with which he or she *will* disagree. But the monarch does not need a multifaith indifference as a condition of upholding these rights and liberties.

Secondly, the Prince's relationship with Mrs Parker Bowles seems to be continuing. That is incompatible with maintaining the true profession of the gospel and the discipline of the Church of England to which he has to swear.

## THE CONSTITUTION

It is as simple as that. Nor is this a matter just for the royals. Since 1689 we have had a *constitutional* monarchy. That is to say, it is a conferred monarchy – conferred by Parliament. Key decisions about the monarchy must be Parliament's in the first instance.

The Queen rules not by simple hereditary right, as did James II, but because of the agreement of William and Mary to accept the Declaration of Rights set out in an Act of 1689. Normal succession in the monarchy is by primogeniture (the right to the throne of the eldest son). But a failure to live by Christian moral principles, which he would have had to swear to in the Coronation Oath, led to the abdication of Edward VIII. His younger brother, George VI, succeeded him to the throne.

In addition to members of Parliament, there are others with a direct interest in the constitutional questions relating to Prince Charles. There are judges and magistrates, for example. There are also the clergy of the Church of England. The clergy have to swear an oath of allegiance on being ordained or on being licensed. They have to swear as follows: 'I, AB, do swear that I will be faithful and bear true allegiance to Her Majesty Queen Elizabeth II, her heirs and successors, *according to law.* So help me God.'[3]

But *if* Prince Charles continues to hold new age or multifaith beliefs and also continues to have an illicit relationship with Mrs

[3] Canon C 13, 'Of the Oath of Allegiance', *The Canons of the Church of England*, London, Church House Publishing, 1988, p. 72.

Parker Bowles, he forfeits the right to that allegiance. All this calls into question his succession 'according to law'. Were he to swear *his* oath without a clear change of mind and heart, many clergy would find it difficult to swear *their* oath of allegiance to a 'King Charles III'. They would know that he was not 'maintaining the true profession of the gospel'. As Vernon Bogdanor of Oxford puts it, 'Allegiance to the sovereign is not unconditional but dependent upon the sovereign's keeping to the terms of the oath.'[4]

With regard to immorality, some will say that there have been many monarchs before who have misbehaved. That is true, but there *were* consequences. The monarchy was often barely tolerated before Queen Victoria. Some of her predecessors had been little respected for the very reason that their private lives were scandalous. Sir Robert Peel declared that the monarchy had become so unpopular that only a miracle could save it.[5] Had mass communication, universal education and the full franchise been available in his day, that miracle might not have happened. It is no good quoting immoral former monarchs to justify immoral contemporary royalty. Our goal today is to repair the moral fabric of the nation and that must be at every level, from pauper to prince.

## THE WAY AHEAD

As things stand, Prince Charles cannot be the Supreme Governor of the Church of England *and* secure the support necessary for his own good, the good of the Church of England or the good of the nation. There would be major conflict right at the start of his reign. This could only damage the Crown as an institution. This is a hard and painful fact to be faced. It is not an easy conclusion. So what follows? The Church must continue to pray, but in addition plans must be made soon for the future.

A proposal which is often made is for the separation of the Crown from the Church of England.[6] It is believed that this would

[4] Vernon Bogdanor, *The Monarchy and the Constitution*, Oxford, Clarendon Press, 1995, p. 8.

[5] Ibid., p. 36ff.

[6] Tim Hames and Mark Leonard, *Modernizing the Monarchy*, London, Demos, 1998, pp. 29–30.

solve the problem overnight. Such a suggestion, according to the press, has even come from the royal 'Way Ahead Group'.

How could that be done, however, without separating the Crown from the Christian faith? To make that separation would mean that many would lose respect for the monarchy. They would not want the Crown, the symbol of our national identity and unity, to be associated with persons whose claim to their position would be seen only as wealth and birth. At present it is the moral dimension, secured through the monarch's attachment to the Christian faith, that warrants respect. The abdication crisis of the 1930s did great good to the monarchy. The Crown was seen to be morally serious and worthy of allegiance. A separation of the Crown from the Church would have consequences unforeseen by many, including a possible demise, in time, of the monarchy. For many that would be a great loss. There does not seem to be a general desire for a republic in Britain.

There are also immediate constitutional reasons why the Crown and the Church should not part company. We have no written constitution in Britain. European legislation now has some external control over the country, but Parliament is still supreme and would be frighteningly so if there were no moral check. The courts are also becoming loose cannons, with judges sometimes 'creatively' reinterpreting the law while they gain new independent power under the Human Rights Act 1998. And the Cabinet has more power than ever. Public accountability is not good in our society. The monarch, however, although wielding little power, has influence through encouragement and advice. Swearing to uphold *at one and the same time* the laws of God and the laws of Parliament, the monarch in his or her person acts as a 'reminder' – a reminder that Parliament, the Cabinet, the courts and the British nation as a whole must acknowledge that there is a higher authority, and that is God. His law is over all. He is on the ultimate throne.

It was King George V who summarized the value of the monarchy as follows:

a  it makes government intelligible to the masses,
b  it makes government interesting to the masses, and

c  it strengthens government with the religious tradition connected with the crown.[7]

That last point is still vital. That is why to disconnect the Crown from the religious tradition, as has been well argued by various people, would 'mean a further dissociation between religion and public culture and would intensify the dangers of a collapse in our moral ecology'.

Prince Charles, of course, is his own man and his convictions and choices are his alone. There should certainly be no improper intrusion into his private life. But information volunteered by himself (and his late wife) over beliefs and relationships has affected his ability to be the Supreme Governor.[8] If the Crown and the Church should not separate, the monarch must remain the Supreme Governor of the Church of England, and if Prince Charles cannot be that Supreme Governor, the sad conclusion – a conclusion reached only with deep regret – must inevitably be that *as things stand, Prince Charles cannot become King.*

That means difficult decisions will have to be made. A clean break now, however, would allow time for careful discussion and consultation over the way forward. The Queen would be able to conduct any negotiations in a wise and statesmanlike way on behalf of the royal family.

A Succession Committee, under the Prime Minister together with the Archbishops of Canterbury and York, would need to meet to discuss the options and the way ahead. Provision would need to be made for someone else, Prince William presumably, to succeed. The British nation prays and hopes for long life for the Queen, but wisdom dictates that provisional plans should be made at the earliest opportunity. This is a far more modest suggestion than some reformists are making.[9] Something must happen soon, however.

If such a committee and discussions were set up, the Archbishop of Canterbury would need to play a leading role. He has to crown

[7] Ted Harrison, *Defender of the Faith*, London, Fount, 1996, p. 39.

[8] See, for example, Jonathan Dimbleby, *The Prince of Wales*, London, Warner Books, 1995, pp. 480–81.

[9] Hames and Leonard, *Modernizing the Monarchy*, op. cit.

the new monarch. It is worth remembering the words of a former Archbishop of Canterbury, Cosmo Gordon Lang. On Sunday 13 December 1936, the Archbishop broadcast to the nation. The Prime Minister at the time, Stanley Baldwin, described what he said as 'the voice of Christian England'. The Archbishop said that it was strange and sad that the King 'should have sought his happiness in a manner inconsistent with the Christian principles of marriage and within a social circle whose standards and ways of life are alien to all the best instincts and traditions of his people'.[10]

The Supreme Governor of the Church of England obviously needs to embrace the orthodox Christian faith; and for a Supreme Governor who is unmarried, it means either a life of sexual abstinence (a life which many fine single people lead – with loneliness, yes, but also with new fulfilments) or marriage to a woman without a husband still living. An heir to the throne not willing to meet those conditions *must forfeit the Crown and stand down*, as, indeed, King Edward VIII did. That was tragic but necessary. The monarch can and should help Britain to be true to the Christian tradition. That is especially important as we enter the twenty-first century with such a need to repair the moral and spiritual fabric of the nation.

## SEX, LIES AND VIDEOTAPE

If there were ongoing problems with the monarchy in the UK as the new millennium approached, there most certainly were problems with the Presidency in the US. As the most powerful man in the world, the President of the United States inevitably acts as a world focus. In the case of the President in office at the end of the twentieth century, sadly it was a focus for dishonesty and immorality.

The serious issue behind the videotape of President Clinton's testimony to the Grand Jury from the White House on 17 August 1998 was highlighted in the press, on the radio and on television as 'sex'. Hence the reporting of the sordid details of his relationship with Monica Lewinsky. Just as important, however, if not more important, were the lies or alleged lies contained in the testimony.

[10] Marcus Loane, *Men to Remember*, Canberra, Acorn, 1987, p. 41.

Indeed, the vast quantity of salacious material published was an attempt by Kenneth Starr to prove that President Clinton had been lying.

The modern world in the last part of the twentieth century was awash with lies. President Clinton's actions were a symptom of this moral disease. Lying was now apparently accepted and, in some situations, acceptable. Not surprisingly, there was a growing loss of confidence in public leaders in government, the law, business, medicine and, sometimes, the Church.

In America the change was well documented, beginning with 1960. That was the year the American people were genuinely astonished. They discovered that President Eisenhower had lied when he was asked about the U-2 spy plane which had been shot down over Russia. By the mid-1970s, after lies from President Johnson over US involvement in Vietnam and from President Nixon over Watergate, 69 per cent of the American people, according to a national poll, agreed that 'over the last ten years, this country's leaders have consistently lied to the people'.[11]

The erosion of contemporary morality in terms of lying has a long history. Undoubtedly the 1960s moral revolution had a great effect. More recently, however, there has been an escalation in lying. In the 1980s there was a veneer of morality during the Thatcher–Reagan years, but some younger politicians brought on over that period were involved in a new 1990s epidemic of deceit and decadence. There is now no longer the honourable, immediate resignation from office after exposure and then immersion in some piece of quiet charitable work. Instead there can well be an absence of shame, the enjoyment of fortune and some form of media celebrity status for the liar or deceiver.

In the late 1990s lying began to look like a way of life in the wake of the Clinton saga. Or it may be that we have now learnt to be more suspicious.

At the end of September 1998 there came the good news of the release of two British hostages from Chechnya, Camilla Carr and Jon James. The Foreign Office denied that a ransom had been

---

[11] *Cambridge Survey Research*, 1975, 1976, in Sissela Bok, *Lying*, New York, Vintage Books, 1989, p. xviii.

paid. However, *The Times* reported on 22 September that 'a meeting at the Foreign Office between a Russian millionaire businessman and a senior British official with experience of intelligence and counter-terrorism appears to have played a crucial part in the release of the two Britons ... no one in Whitehall doubted that the meeting between Mr Berezovsky [the Russian] and Mr Budd [the Briton] helped to finalize the deal that led to their freedom.'

How in the public world of today can you know what to believe? It may not have been a technical 'ransom', in the same way that President Clinton argued he had not had a technical 'sexual relationship' with Miss Lewinsky. On 17 January 1998, in his deposition in the Paula Jones civil law suit, he said, 'I have never had sexual relations with Monica Lewinsky. I've never had an affair with her.' But after tape recordings from Linda Tripp, statements by Monica Lewinsky and then his own confessions, we know that he had. Is this the regular way words are now used by government officials? If so, it needs to be recognized that civil society (and what we call civilization) will be hard pressed to sustain itself if such a culture of suspicion and de facto lies is allowed to continue. This is not said simply to moralize. It is hard reality.

## THE BIBLE

What does the Bible have to say about lying and lies? The Ten Commandments do not have a direct prohibition against lying as such. But the ninth commandment forbids 'false testimony' – 'You shall not give false testimony against your neighbour' (Exodus 20:16).

The psalmists and wisdom writers were more direct. Psalm 34:13 says, 'Keep your tongue from evil and your lips from speaking lies.' Proverbs 12:22 says, 'The LORD detests lying lips, but he delights in men who are truthful.' And the prophets uttered God's condemnation of lying religious leaders: 'For they have done outrageous things in Israel; they have committed adultery with their neighbours' wives and in my name have spoken lies' (Jeremiah 29:23).

The New Testament is also direct and definite. First, it gives us Jesus' own teaching. He taught that the devil was behind all lying as

58

'a liar and the father of lies' (John 8:44). He taught that the truth was liberating – 'the truth will set you free' (John 8:32). He taught that the Holy Spirit was 'the Spirit of truth' (John 14:17). And he said to Pilate, 'For this reason I was born, and for this I came into the world, to testify to the truth. Everyone on the side of truth listens to me' (John 18:37).

The apostles were direct, too. Here is Paul instructing the Colossians: 'Do not lie to each other, since you have taken off your old self with its practices' (Colossians 3:9). Here he is instructing the Ephesians: 'Put off falsehood and speak truthfully' (Ephesians 4:25). Truth, however, must be spoken 'in love'.

The book of Revelation says these are matters of great consequence. It says that 'everyone who loves and practices falsehood' will ultimately be 'outside' the heavenly city, in a situation of unimaginable awfulness (Revelation 22:15). That is why the gospel of Christ – the gospel of repentance and forgiveness – is such good news. But there can be no hope if people do not recognize that there is a problem to repent of and falsehood that needs to be forgiven.

## OTHER WRITINGS

This clear teaching from the Bible is not always echoed in modern writing, even some modern Christian writing. Take the *Dictionary of Christian Ethics* from the SCM Press, which contains the following statement: 'It is clear that there may be circumstances in which it is right to tell a lie … The only way to have the sensitivity of spirit to know when a lie is called for in particular circumstances is to be habitually truthful.'[12]

Written in 1967, this is proposing a justifiable falsehood – something the New Testament never entertains. But this is now a common view and widely held. President Clinton may have held it. One medical doctor wrote as long ago as 1955 in *The New England Journal of Medicine*:

---

[12] Ronald Preston, 'Lying', in John Macquarrie (ed.), *A Dictionary of Christian Ethics*, London, SCM Press, 1971, p. 202.

*Above all, remember that it is meaningless to speak of telling the truth, the whole truth, and nothing but the truth to a patient. It is meaningless because it is impossible ... Since telling the truth is impossible, there can be no sharp distinction between what is true and what is false ... So far as possible, do not harm. You can do harm by the process that is quaintly called telling the truth. You can do harm by lying ... But try to do as little harm as possible.[13]*

Here the criterion of harm makes this a utilitarian ethic (if it works, it is acceptable, or 'the end justifies the means'). The lawyer Charles Curtis seems to be even stronger in his convictions: 'I don't see why we should not come out roundly and say that one of the functions of the lawyer is to lie for his client.'[14]

Hitler used a utilitarian ethic to justify lying to millions. He was not the first national leader to say that the good of the State justified lying, but he was probably the first to talk about the 'big lie'. In *Mein Kampf* he wrote, 'The great masses of the people ... will more easily fall victims to a big lie than to a small one.'[15] He proved the truth of that proposition in his own terrible way. But he was only following the lead of his compatriot, the philosopher Nietzsche, who had written some time before, 'A great man ... he rather lies than tells the truth.'

Surely the clock must be turned back to that earlier Christian ethic – the biblical ethic which the Church and the Christian world followed for centuries. That is why a president, as a symbol, is so important. His lying, in the words of Hannah Arendt, makes it hard for us 'to take our bearings in the real world'. This happens after brainwashing and it may also happen if presidential and ministerial lying is simply shrugged off as a minor peccadillo. Hannah Arendt writes,

*It has frequently been noted that the surest result of brainwashing in the long run is a peculiar kind of cynicism, the absolute refusal to believe in the truth of anything, no matter how well it may be established. In other words, the result of a consistent and total substitution*

[13] Bok, *Lying,* op. cit., p. 227.
[14] Ibid., p. 146.
[15] Ibid., p. 134.

*of lies for factual truth is not that the lie will now be accepted as truth,*
*and truth be defamed as lie, but that the sense by which we take our*
*bearings in the real world – and the category of truth versus falsehood*
*is among the mental means to this end – is being destroyed.*[16]

More and more, we are all now drifting into 'a peculiar kind of cynicism'. That is the measure of the problem, and it is extremely unhealthy. If, on the other hand, senior figures in public life caught up in scandals were to resign, that would help to rehabilitate truthtelling as an essential public and social cement. Of course, a President can be forgiven by God and his wife. There were reports that Bill Clinton was seeking that forgiveness. King David, in the Old Testament, was in a similar situation after his affair with Bathsheba (2 Samuel 11 and 12). He genuinely repented and was forgiven (Psalm 51). But he still suffered. Being King, he could not resign. He had to stay and experience the consequences of his sin in the form of Absalom's rebellion and worse. Our politicians, however, and even our monarchs, are not Old Testament kings. They *can* resign. Sometimes it is right that they should do so.

## CLASSICAL CHRISTIAN DOCTRINE

The classical Christian doctrine on lying which we need to recover was articulated by Augustine and it was strict:

*But every liar says the opposite of what he thinks in his heart, with*
*purpose to deceive. Now it is evident that speech was given to man,*
*not that men might therewith deceive one another, but that one man*
*might make known his thoughts to another. To use speech, then, for*
*the purpose of deception, and not for its appointed end, is a sin. Nor*
*are we to suppose that there is any lie that is not a sin, because it is*
*sometimes possible, by telling a lie, to do service to another.*[17]

[16] Hannah Arendt, 'Truth and Politics', in Peter Laslett and W.G. Runciman (eds), *Philosophy and Society*, New York, Barnes and Noble, 1967, p. 128.

[17] Augustine, *Enchiridion*, XXII, in Marcus Dods (ed.), *The Works of Aurelius Augustine*, vol. ix, Edinburgh, T & T Clark, 1873, p. 92.

A white lie is still a lie. There is no 'holy' lying. Augustine was supported in this by John Wesley:

> *If any, in fact, do this – either teach men to do evil that good may come or do so themselves, their damnation is just. This is particularly applicable to those who tell lies in order to do good thereby. It follows, that officious lies, as well as all others, are an abomination to the God of Truth. Therefore there is no absurdity, however strange it may sound, in that saying of the ancient Father, 'I would not tell a wilful lie to save the souls of the whole world'.*[18]

Opponents of such a view ask: 'What about the case, cited by the philosopher Kant, of a would-be murderer who inquires whether "our friend who is pursued by him had taken refuge in our house" and mere silence or evasion will not work?' Samuel Johnson, for example, said, 'The General Rule is that truth should never be violated; there must, however, be some exceptions. If, for instance, a murderer should ask you which way a man has gone.' Cardinal Newman, however, took issue with Johnson, saying it was not as simple as that:

> *As to Johnson's case of a murderer asking which way a man has gone, I should have anticipated that, had such a difficulty happened to him, his first act would have been to knock the man down, and to call out for the police; and next, if he was worsted in the conflict, he would not have given the ruffian the information he asked at whatever risk to himself. I think he would have let himself be killed first.*[19]

Kant himself supported Augustine and Wesley. He argued that there was a duty of truthfulness in all situations. He said that a lie always harms mankind generally. And it harms the liar himself by destroying his human dignity and making him subhuman: 'By a lie a man throws away and, as it were, annihilates his dignity as a man.'[20]

---

[18] John Wesley, *Sermons*, quoted in Bok, *Lying*, op. cit., p. 32.

[19] John Henry Newman, *Apologia Pro Vita Sua*, London, Fontana Books, 1959, p. 365.

[20] Immanuel Kant, *Doctrine of Virtue*, quoted in Bok, *Lying*, op. cit., p. 32.

## THE TRAGIC SITUATION

Augustine, of course, knew of the problem cases. He knew cases in the Old Testament where deception seemed to achieve good results. He denied, however, that there was such a thing as justifiable falsehood. True, he argued that some lies are worse than others. He had, in fact, an eightfold distinction worked out, with the worst being lies in teaching about God and the least being lies that do no harm but seem to help someone:

> *It cannot be denied that they have attained a very high standard of goodness who never lie except to save a man from injury; but in the case of men who have reached this standard, it is not the deceit, but their good intention that is justly praised, and sometimes even rewarded. It is quite enough that the deception should be pardoned, without its being made an object of laudation.*[21]

What that analysis points to is this. If a good person does lie in an impossible situation, it is not to be seen as a 'right action'. Rather, the whole situation is to be seen as a tragedy. That is because all lies are evil. The individual is being caught up in a totality of evil. A good person, according to Augustine, is, and should feel, guilty if they lie to save the life of another. But God will forgive the lie, if there is repentance. Augustine thought as he did because he had a clear belief that this life is not all there is. Heaven and hell await. He knew that death kills the body, but lying kills the soul. He argued, therefore, that to lie to save the life of another is a foolish bargain: 'Therefore, does he not speak most perversely who says that one person ought to die spiritually so that another may live corporally?'[22]

Augustine also believed in the sovereignty of God. To lie in the hope of helping another presupposes that your information is correct, that you have a level of omnipotence, and that there is no other way out.

---

[21] Augustine, *Enchiridion*, XXII, op. cit., p. 193.
[22] Augustine, *On Lying*, quoted in Bok, *Lying*, op. cit., p. 44.

The debate about lying was not simply an academic exercise for Augustine and his generation. Many of the early Christians were given the opportunity to lie to save their *own* lives. The question the authorities asked them was: 'Do you believe in Jesus Christ?' If they admitted it, they were martyred. If they did not, they were freed. Should they tell or act a lie? Some did. Many did not. They refused to give in to Caesar and the enemies of Jesus. Through their commitment to the truth, the Christian world has enjoyed a culture of truth for centuries. In time this has allowed much to develop and evolve in the West in terms of scientific achievement and democratic institutions. These can only work on a basis of truthfulness. Without doubt, this classical Christian tradition of never lying has played an important part in Western civilization.

Today we could be seeing that civilization unravel. And the centre of gravity for the Christian moral tradition could well change, with enormous long-term consequences. It changed in the early days of the Church when it moved from Jerusalem to Antioch. It then moved from Antioch to Rome. After that it moved from Rome to Northern Europe and the US (and Australia). Why could it not now move to a new location? The 1998 worldwide Lambeth Conference of Anglican bishops meeting at Canterbury, which upheld biblical orthodoxy against liberal Western deviations, confirmed this possibility: the guardianship of Christian doctrine and the Christian moral tradition in the Protestant episcopal churches could now relocate to Africa, South East Asia and parts of South America. If this was seen as marginalizing the Church of England, it would undoubtedly have implications for English Church–State relations and consequently our whole British 'moral ecology'.

## OBJECTIVE TRUTH

The classical Christian tradition is not just about truth-telling at all times, however. It underlines objective truth and the importance of loyalty to such truth in a way the twentieth century began to forget. Modern views on lying focus on the discrepancy between the lie uttered and the thought in the mind. But the classical Christian tradition is just as concerned with the discrepancy between the statement uttered and reality or fact – what is objectively true. Today leniency is employed if something false is said in ignorance, but not if it is intentional. Denying God and affirming immoral behaviour are held to be acceptable, even by many who say they are false statements, because of ignorance. Previously it was said that ignorance was culpable *because it caused others to suffer*. The common view today is that we are entitled to be ignorant of the truth but not to pervert it.

The Bible, however, does not allow us to think that ignorance is so easily excused. Nor do Roman law or our own legal system simply pass over the guilt of ignorance. While attaching to them lesser degrees of blame, the Old Testament certainly refers to sins of ignorance, and in the parable of the two servants in Luke 12:47–8 Jesus says, 'That servant who knows his master's will and does not get ready or does not do what his master wants will be beaten with many blows. But the one who does not know and does things deserving punishment will be beaten with few blows.'

The classical Christian tradition also linked truth-telling with justice. In the eighteenth century Bishop Butler linked falsehood with injustice and unprovoked violence as a cardinal vice. He said that 'veracity as well as justice is to be our rule of life'. Today justice and 'social justice' have high moral status, but truthfulness (and sexual morality, which is linked to truthfulness through fidelity) has become dispensable – witness Prince Charles and Bill Clinton.

# CHAPTER FIVE

# EUROPE

## THE EVANGELICAL ALLIANCE AND EUROPE

Having studied 'classics' (Greek and Roman languages and civilization) at school and university, Europe has an inevitable attraction for me. Among my earliest memories are those of my grandfather speaking French. He was fluent and thought the rest of his family should be so as well. Going back a generation or two, there were Germans on my mother's side. Part of our family is Belgian. I am not, therefore, by nature or nurture a Eurosceptic or 'anti-Europe'. However, serious questions – without conclusions – have been forced on me over time. Other questions were raised in the early 1990s.

For many years, during the period of its expansion in the 1980s, I was a council member of the Evangelical Alliance. From being a small group, it expanded under the leadership of Clive Calver. During that period it probably became more charismatic than mainline evangelical, and politically more left than right. Nonetheless, it developed into a main force in British Christianity. It seemed reasonable, therefore, for the Alliance to have an interest politically in Europe. Already there were European networks for Evangelicalism. The Alliance decided, as a small step, to arrange for a modest delegation to visit Brussels. I was a member of this group in June 1992.

Personally I found it very instructive, hosted as we were by Sir Fred Catherwood, an MEP and Vice-President of the European Parliament as well as President of the Evangelical Alliance. We also met with some senior European officials. Sir Fred is distinctly pro-European in political terms – not unnaturally, being an MEP. His little paperback called *Pro-Europe?* sets out his thinking.[1]

I was surprised by the enthusiastic pro-Europeanism of most of my fellow Evangelicals. I had assumed that everyone would have questions about the power of bureaucracies, the loss of sovereignty and the value system of the European Union. But no! It seemed that they had few worries, or at least they did not voice them. This made *me* ask questions all the more.

Does the new Europe mean that the British monarch will hardly matter any more within a world of globalization and supranationalism? If so, why have concerns about Prince Charles? Are we seeing the primacy of the nation-state receding in Europe and the rest of the world? Or is such supranationalism and the attempt to 'harmonize' states actually fuelling incipient tribalisms which are rooted not in political arrangements but exclusively in blood or ethnicity? Some of these tribalisms, as we know, have terrifying consequences.

As we enter the twenty-first century, these are unresolved issues of great significance.

## EXTREMES

Let me begin our discussion on Europe with the extremes. Here are two very different quotations which express opposite and extreme views on our subject:

> *The basic elements in European conflict are race and religion. The confederacy of powers, which are centred around the Babylonish Roman Catholic religious system, are also partly Esau-orientated in race descent – Prussia in particular. This explains the continuing strategy to replace the world leadership of the Birthright nations of Celto-Saxondom who, being of Jacob-Ephraim descent, have the birthright commission from the Almighty to lead the nations in peace.*
>
> *Our national governments, and most Protestants today, have little or no understanding of this underlying struggle for supremacy in*

[1] Fred Catherwood, *Pro-Europe?*, Leicester, Inter-Varsity Press, 1991.

*Europe that has been going on during the 20th century ... The creation of the European Union is a final throw.*

So writes 'Watchman' in the January/February 1998 edition of *Wake Up!* – the magazine of an apparently extreme fringe 'British Israelite' group.

Contrast that with the more sober remarks of Winston Churchill – but in one sense also extreme, if quietly so – in a celebrated speech made on 19 September 1946 at the University of Zurich, soon after the end of the Second World War.

*I wish to speak to you to-day about the tragedy of Europe. This noble continent comprising on the whole the fairest and the most cultivated regions of the earth, enjoying a temperate and equable climate, is the home of all the great parent races of the western world. It is the fountain of Christian faith and Christian ethics. It is the origin of most of the culture, arts, philosophy and science both of ancient and modern times. If Europe were once united in the sharing of its common inheritance, there would be no limit to the happiness, to the prosperity and glory which its three or four hundred million people would enjoy. Yet it is from Europe that have sprung that series of frightful nationalistic quarrels, originated by the Teutonic nations, which we have seen even in this twentieth century and in our own lifetime, wreck the peace and mar the prospects of all mankind.*

*And what is the plight to which Europe has been reduced? Some of the smaller States have indeed made a good recovery, but over wide areas a vast quivering mass of tormented, hungry, care-worn and bewildered human beings gape at the ruins of their cities and homes, and scan the dark horizons for the approach of some new peril, tyranny or terror. Among the victors there is a babble of jarring voices; among the vanquished the sullen silence of despair. That is all that Europeans, grouped in so many ancient States and nations, that is all that the Germanic Powers have got by tearing each other to pieces and spreading havoc far and wide. Indeed, but for the fact that the great Republic across the Atlantic Ocean has at length realized that the ruin or enslavement of Europe would involve their own fate as well, and has stretched out hands of succour and guidance, the Dark Ages would have returned in all their cruelty and squalor. They may still return.*

*Yet all the while there is a remedy which, if it were generally and spontaneously adopted, would as if by a miracle transform the whole scene, and would in a few years make all Europe, or the greater part of it, as free and as happy as Switzerland is to-day. What is this sovereign remedy? It is to re-create the European family, or as much of it as we can, and provide it with a structure under which it can dwell in peace, in safety and in freedom. We must build a kind of United States of Europe.*[2]

Two very different voices! But both very extreme. Both give a hard time to the Teutonic nations (who presumably equate with the 'Esau-orientated' Prussians). One is advocating a hard-line nationalism; the other a hard-line internationalism.

How do we begin to cut through the Gordian knot that is Europe? We will start not on a theological but on a more mundane level, with a simple question: What makes for a successful organization – *any* organization – whether a church, a club, a business or a nation?

Four things, surely, are always necessary:

1  An agreed agenda
2  Competent leadership
3  Enabling structures
4  Meeting needs, whether of your members or your markets

It will be helpful, therefore, to analyse Europe and the European project under those four headings. If you are not strong and healthy in all four areas, whatever organization you are in – from the local fellowship of a church, to the nation-state or to a union of states – there will be major problems.

[2] Winston Churchill, 'Churchill on Europe', in David de Giustino (ed.), *A Reader in European Integration*, London, Longmans, 1996, pp. 44–5.

## WHAT IS THE AGREED AGENDA?

First, then, what is the *agreed agenda* of Europe? This is the one thing above all others that is necessary. Without an agreed agenda, an agreed idea of what you are about, organizations soon fall apart. You can only live on PR and 'hype' for so long.

Sir Fred Catherwood is quite clear about the objective of the new Europe. 'The first objective of the Community,' he says, 'is to create peace in place of Europe's terrible tribal wars, the last two of which cost 50 million dead.'[3]

Undoubtedly this was the overriding concern of the early founders of post-war Europe and their institutions. Jean Monnet, the great architect of modern Europe, had this as his goal. But he also had another goal: quite publicly he expressed his motivation for establishing a new European order as being an admiration for the glories of the old Holy Roman Empire.

That is the second objective many have for the European Union. As a student at Oxford in the early 1960s, I can remember getting into discussion on Europe with my tutor. He was championing the proposals in 1962 for Britain's entry into the European Economic Community (EEC), as it was then called. These proposals came to an abrupt end in January 1963 when de Gaulle of France vetoed Britain's application. My tutor, a man of enormous intelligence but no particular Christian commitment, surprised me. He unashamedly said that his desire for a European Union was quite romantic. He liked, he said, the thought of reconstructing the old Holy Roman Empire.

The dream of a united Europe has a long history. It certainly goes back to the Romans themselves. At the peak of its power, Rome ruled Europe from the Pyrenees to the Rhine – but they never really conquered Germany, the area to the east of the Rhine and north of the Danube. Charlemagne had the good sense to learn the lesson. When he was crowned Holy Roman Emperor in AD 800, he tried to win the support of the Germanic princes. But the Holy Roman Empire did not last. Napoleon, Kaiser Wilhelm II and

---

[3] Fred Catherwood, 'Britain and Europe', in Martyn Eden (ed.), *Britain on the Brink*, Nottingham, Crossway, 1993, p. 17.

Hitler all had ideas of creating a united Europe, but by force. There was, interestingly, a Nazi memorandum written in June 1943 for the German Ministry of Foreign Affairs. This was a planning document that foresaw a 'European community', a 'closer community' of countries which voluntarily embraced 'European solidarity' and 'European obligations'.[4] The *dream* of a united Europe certainly has a long and wide history.

The third objective for a united Europe is economic benefit. This is nothing new either. Before the Second World War the Hungarian economist Elemer Hantos argued powerfully that the unfettering of European commerce would bring about a unified economic region. He believed that European unity required high levels of employment, low prices and an expanding market economy. Economic security would be the true foundation of political stability.[5]

So what is wrong with all of these objectives? Are these not good aspirations? Yes, in a way.

The real problem, in terms of Europe having an agreed agenda, is this: Jean Monnet, the father of the European Community, and master politician that he was, never really declared his hand. He believed that the Continent and its long-term unity did not need a single grand act of union. Rather it would come about by a slow and steady process – treaties, policies, commissions and regulations which would spawn and have a growing effect. In other words, 'Don't tell anyone you want to go big!' This is what he wrote in 1952 to Robert Schuman, the founder of the European Coal and Steel Community: 'Europe will not be made all at once, or according to a single plan. It will be built through concrete achievements which first create a de facto solidarity.'[6]

First of all, therefore, came the European Coal and Steel Community. That in time lead on to the European Economic Community. But without clear goals publicly expressed, conflicts of interest were inevitable. Monnet's hidden agenda for the development of a new and slowly developing European Empire was one

---

[4] de Giustino (ed.), *A Reader in European Integration,* op. cit., pp. 16–21.
[5] Ibid., pp. 9–10.
[6] *Time Golden Anniversary Issue – Europe 50,* Winter 1996, p. 48.

thing, but it did not always go hand in hand with the much lower and limited aim of financial gain and security. Potential conflict was evident in those early days of the European Coal and Steel Community. Harold Macmillan, the former British Prime Minister, declared, 'Our people will not hand over to any supranational authority the right to close our pits or our steel works.'[7] What is new? And, of course, there are problems with both visions – of a new, great empire and of economic gain.

A new Holy Roman Empire – and sadly now without the 'holy' dimension – would be very difficult to sustain. As we will see (in Chapter 13), common religious beliefs will take on more importance in the State in the twenty-first century – witness the appeal of Islam in many Arab countries already. So a secular Europe would have – and is having – a bad start. The complications of the modern world also mean there is huge difficulty in having one political unit steered from what is hoped to be a unifying centre.

That was part of the issue at the time of the Reformation. As is well known, the Reformation dealt with fundamental theological issues such as the fact of the grace of God, the primacy of faith in Christ alone, and the authority of the Bible. But also at issue was the independence of local Provinces. People in outlying parts were less and less willing to be told what to do by people hundreds of miles away in Rome. The distant rulers did not know local facts and so could not solve local problems. The opposition to the papacy was in part due to the fact that it provided an inefficient system. That system simply benefited the fat cats in Rome rather than the locals in the Provinces. Those realities are the same today.

What, then, of the vision of economic benefit? That too is under debate. On 1 January 1999 some nations gave up their power to mint and manage their own money. That is a key element in modern government. For them the process is now all controlled by a European Central Bank. The European Monetary Union is taking shape. If there were an 'agreed agenda' in existence, that would be fine. The problem is that the European Union is only half a free-trade area – for services and industrial goods. In agriculture it is a wasteful cartel, as some have called it, designed to protect farmers.

[7] de Giustino (ed.), *A Reader in European Integration*, op. cit., p. 34.

'One half of the EU budget ($45 billion) goes into farm support to sustain high prices. Another $33 billion bails out Spain, Portugal and Greece.'[8] Facilitating aggressive industry does not go well with propping up poor farmers. And French farmers are quite expressive on the subject: they are capable of storming city halls in order to have their needs met.

It is clear that there are many problems over an agreed agenda for Europe.


## COMPETENT LEADERSHIP

Secondly, what is the level of competent leadership in Europe? The EU has six main institutional bodies for leadership:

1 The European Parliament, which has few teeth but it did manage to dismiss the entire European Commission along with its President for incompetence and mismanagement in the early part of 1999.

2 The European Commission itself, which is the EU's executive – this is made up of 20 Commissioners, appointed by member governments for five years. It proposes Community laws, puts them into effect and manages EU policies.

3 The Council of Ministers, which decides all laws and so is effectively the legislature. It is made up of government ministers from the member states who lead on the subject under discussion (e.g. Agriculture, Transport, etc.).

4 The European Council, which is made up of the Heads of State and meets in summit twice a year to give overall political direction.

5 The European Court of Justice, which interprets and applies Community law.

6 The Court of Auditors, which oversees the Community budget.

You may say this seems reasonable. The trouble is that it all means a huge bureaucracy. Europe is so big. That means more work for

---

[8] *Time*, 19 January 1998.

everyone. If you are now a British minister you have more trips to Brussels than you had before. That means more work. There are only 24 hours in the day, so you delegate work. You cannot read all the papers. And when there is little agreement in an organization over the agenda and people have different value systems, you cannot assume compliance and easy problem-solving. An element of force, in the form of policed rules, becomes necessary. This gives power to the enforcers and power to the bureaucracy. That is dangerous. They are even tempted to create problems.

Ivan Illich has described the inherent problems for new professionals in modern bureaucracies like the EU. They are, he argues, tempted to generate disabling institutions. He tells how they 'need clients in order to survive ... and they create and define problems, diseases and deficiencies which they, and they only, have the skills to put right. They disable their clients in order to enable them, creating thereby a spurious dependency and problems which need never have been invented.'[9]

Let us assume, however, a benign bureaucracy and a well-intentioned leadership for Europe. We are faced then with a more fundamental question in terms of politics and government: 'What is the State for?' What ought a government to be doing anyway? It is a vital question. In Christian thinking there are those like John Calvin who hold that the State is there for four purposes:

1  To promote civil justice and outward morality.
2  To restrain sin (hearts may not be changed by the law and they may be totally depraved, but you do not have to live out what is evil).
3  To promote humanity (to let love guide and rule).
4  To help the Church.

Calvin wanted a cooperative relationship between Church and State. That is one view. Martin Luther, on the other hand, took a more pragmatic view. He believed that the State was to be more minimal and primarily there to curb the worst excesses of sinful

---

[9] Quoted in Charles Handy, *Understanding Voluntary Organizations*, London, Penguin Books, 1988, p. 7.

men and women.[10] The differences of opinion between Calvin and Luther reflect an important Christian debate about the origin and scope of government. Andrew Goddard summarizes the debate neatly:

> *Some (classically Augustine) have argued that government is insti-*
> *tuted by God but as a post-Fall institution. Its task is to respond to*
> *human sin by upholding the common good and executing limited*
> *judgment over the community on the basis of a higher law. Its task is,*
> *in the words of Romans 13, 'to bear the sword' and 'bring punish-*
> *ment on the wrongdoer'. Others (classically Thomas Aquinas) believe*
> *that although government now has this juridical role, it was also orig-*
> *inally part of God's good created order. In creation it was ordained to*
> *have a directive role within human society even without sin.*

Goddard goes on to argue that the decision you reach on the relative merits of those two positions 'will prove of significance in relation to the EU's institutions. The EU is almost wholly a directive, administrative system of government.'[11]

It is true – modern European states are by no means minimal. They are more and more all-embracing, and even sometimes quasi-totalitarian in the sense of invading the whole of life. Europe thus has a more Aquinan or Calvinistic approach to politics, while nations such as the US have a more Augustinian or Lutheran approach. When you have a Christian society and Christian values – as was more the case in Europe in the past – a directive government poses fewer problems. When there is little agreement as to basic beliefs, when pluralism, materialism, secularism and often anti-Christianity in terms of sexual morality abound, there will be problems. And we have problems.

[10] For basic texts see Harro Höpfl, *Luther and Calvin on Secular Authority*, Cambridge University Press, 1991.

[11] Andrew Goddard, *The European Union: a Christian Perspective*, Cambridge, Grove Books, 1998, pp. 18–19.

## STRUCTURES

We come now to the third necessity for a successful organization: structures. The question here is, 'Are the EU's structures enabling?' There are a number of important issues that call for comment.

One of the great platforms behind the institution of the new Europe was not only peace but, in Churchillian terms, the desire for democracy. Jacques Maritain was the Christian thinker and father figure behind the Universal Declaration of Human Rights. He paralleled Jean Monnet on the world scene after the Second World War. Maritain argued powerfully that the Bible and the doctrine of freedom in the Bible mean that democracy is congruous with the gospel and should be pursued. Most Christians today would agree – but it is necessary to be careful.

In the name of democracy and everyone having their say, massive inefficiencies can be perpetrated. It is so easy in the name of democracy to confuse 'consent' with 'consensus'. Charles Handy puts it like this:

> *Effective democracy relies on consent. He or she who governs does so with the trust and consent of those who are governed, who have the right and power to get rid of the governor when that trust and respect are exhausted. Those in charge take the decisions, which can be implemented only with the consent of those who carry them out ... It is difficult, but it works very well with the right person in charge.*
>
> *Consensus on the other hand requires that everyone takes every decision. It is a travesty of democracy, time-consuming, irritating and fraught with politics and factions. It is usually so frustrating that it is quickly allowed to degenerate into an autocracy or the dictatorship of a clique if only to allow something, anything, to happen. Democracy is a dangerous slogan on its own.*[12]

The whole conception of the EU is *not* to have strong leadership. Therefore you have to play the game of 'consensus' with all those attendant problems.

[12] Handy, *Understanding Voluntary Organizations*, op. cit., pp. 5–6.

'Subsidiarity' is a related issue. Europe talks a lot about 'subsidiarity'. Subsidiarity is actually part of the teaching of the Roman Catholic Church. It says that there is a moral principle for a higher-order body not to do things that a lower-order body can do perfectly well. It is supposed to be the very opposite of centralism. It is supposed to give people as much responsibility as they can cope with.

If you have a huge and complex organization, however, like an empire, the very need for the coordination of subsidiary activities means an excessive concentration of power in the coordinators. In any organization the people who control information flow have disproportionate power and influence.

Also subsidiarity only works when there is an understanding of genuine federalism. What is federalism? It is *not* the same as decentralism, as Charles Handy explains: 'In decentralized structures the centre is still in command but has delegated a range of tasks to the periphery. In federalist constitutions, the centre is the residuary body, doing things which the parts cannot or do not want to do – delegation the other way round.'[13] Centralized structures mandate subsidiarity from the top. Genuine federalism mandates subsidiarity from the bottom. The danger in Europe is the prospect of decentralism instead of genuine federalism.

Has the Bible anything to say directly about these structural issues?

## A BIBLICAL VIEW

The Christian is to seek to live at peace with all men and women. Peace and peace-generating structures must, of course, be welcomed as Jean Monnet wanted and Fred Catherwood wants today. But there is a danger in overexalting structures and peace-keeping. It leads to the belief that war can be prevented by politics and other measures are then neglected. This happened after the First World War. Utopianism is a very dangerous trait in human politics. Only when Christ returns will swords be beaten into ploughshares, as the Christian understands it. Before then, as Jesus said, there will be 'wars and rumours of wars' (Matthew 24:6); and

[13] Ibid., p. 115.

that is due, not to political arrangements or the lack of them, but to human sin. James 4:1–3 says,

> *What causes fights and quarrels among you? Don't they come from your desires that battle within you? You want something but don't get it. You kill and covet, but you cannot have what you want. You quarrel and fight. You do not have, because you do not ask God. When you ask, you do not receive, because you ask with wrong motives, that you may spend what you get on your pleasures.*

The great need for Europe, therefore, is not union but conversion – peace with God in the first place. But the really great danger is the inherent danger of empires. That is why there is some truth in the references by Christians to the book of Revelation in respect of the European issue. The biblical teaching on 'empires' begins with the Old Testament account of Babel. Babel is a symbol and cannot be ignored.

Genesis sees the division of the world into nations as subsequent to the Fall. Unlike marriage or man's dominion over the earth (Genesis 1–2), the nations are not part of the original Creation. It is only in Genesis 10, after the Flood, that we meet the nations. We read in Genesis 10:32, 'The nations spread out over the earth after the flood.'

In Genesis 11 comes the account of Babel. The nations tried to unite. But with sin in the world, that unity was accompanied by pride and God saw that such an *imperium*, or united power, as was planned at Babel had to be restrained and judged. In building the Tower at Babel the people were uniting in a common project without reference to God. '*Babel*' relates to '*Babylon*'. Babylon becomes synonymous with any evil empire and therefore all evil empires in the Old Testament and also in the book of Revelation (Revelation 17–19). It stands for all godless power. Therefore, if the cap fits, nations and empires have to wear it, whether they are the empires of pagan Rome, Hitler, Stalin or their successors. The fact that some Christians exaggerate the material in Revelation is no excuse to neglect the warnings.

It is not that Europe inevitably *has to be* an evil empire, however. The Bible shows that God can work providentially in and through the nations. This is clear in Israel's history and in the New Testament. But nations and empires *without* God will be evil. And currently Europe appears to be ignoring God.

## MEETING NEEDS

Finally comes the question of meeting needs. What is best for the people of Europe – the real clients of the European project? Christians can easily live with most forms of government if there is relative peace and freedom.

Jesus lived under the first Roman Empire, the first extended Europe. The New Testament reveals an ambivalent attitude to the Roman Empire of the first century. Clearly Paul used the Roman Empire for evangelism – its roads and cities, its structures and peace helped the gospel go forward. But Rome was also demonic. Both minor and major persecutions took place, and there was much violence.

That, surely, is important for the question of how we should respond to Europe. Europe provides possibilities. It is also dangerous. Therefore we need to be 'as shrewd as snakes and as innocent as doves' (Matthew 10:16). We need to analyse the situation carefully and to make wise political judgements – which will be the least worse options in many cases – and then we need to evangelize. Ultimately Europe's needs will only be met by the gospel. Pentecost reversed Babel not by setting up new political structures but by the Holy Spirit convicting men and women of the truth about Jesus and his Resurrection and calling them to repentance through the preaching of the gospel. A European Mission is still more important than a European Union. Cultural and political achievements come from spiritual achievements.

'When St Paul sailed from Troy in obedience to a dream and came to Philippi in Macedonia,' writes Christopher Dawson, 'he did more to change the course of history and the future of European culture than the great battle which had decided the fate of the Roman Empire on the same spot more than ninety years before.' At the time it seemed so insignificant. But in reality Paul was 'turning the world upside down'. We only know of three of his converts: a businesswoman from Asia Minor, a slave girl who was a professional fortune-teller, and his jailer. 'These were the first European Christians – the forerunners of uncounted millions who have regarded the Christian faith as the standard of their European way of life.'[14]

Following its spiritual decline in the twentieth century, the only long-term hope for Europe in the twenty-first century is to be re-evangelized. A renewed spiritual unity will lead to economic and social unity. Without such spiritual renewal, European unity will at best be weak and at worst be repressive or totalitarian. A weak unity does not justify losing individual sovereignty; repressive unity is to be resisted at all costs.

[14] Christopher Dawson, *The Historic Reality of Christian Culture*, London, Routledge and Kegan Paul, 1960, p. 15.

# CHAPTER SIX

# THE RELIGION OF SECULAR HUMANISM

## UCS

After a state primary education up to the age of 11 in Stanmore, north London, I went for my secondary education to UCS (University College School) in Hampstead. UCS was originally part of University College, London. It was founded by, among others, James Mill, the father of John Stuart Mill, in the tradition of Jeremy Bentham, the early utilitarian. They wanted an educational establishment for freethinkers and nonconformists. As a pupil from 1950 to 1958 I found the school 'liberal' in the best sense of the word. There was freedom to be anything, including Christian.

The 1950s were, in some ways, years as decadent as any – not in outward expression, but in inward belief. A certain cynicism and rebelliousness then pervaded the Western world. When Anthony Eden decided to take back the Suez Canal in 1956, my contemporaries doing National Service were not far from mutiny. The main symptoms of discontent were at a more popular level, however. The Greek philosopher Plato once said, 'Change the music and you change the morals.' This prediction was true in respect of the 1950s. The change came with rock'n'roll, skiffle, Elvis and Cliff. It all seems relatively innocent now. But it did not at the time.

At such a time adolescent boys at school in north London were following every fashion; they asked all sorts of radical questions; and they read all sorts of books and periodicals – at least we did. Very few of these publications supported traditional Christian propositions and values. Instead they mostly provided reasons for believing what you liked and doing what you wanted.

For two years during this formative period we had a form master just down from Oxford where he had read English at Magdalen College. His tutor there had been C.S. Lewis. Lewis had not achieved his current popularity and worldwide reputation at that stage. We 'entry form' boys were all introduced to his writings in our religious instruction lessons, but they had little effect on me. For most of the time at school I was not sure what I believed.

I faced all the reasons for not believing the Christian faith from a fairly young age. Yet I also realized that believing was not to be equated with a lack of thought or a lack of intelligence. It was self-evident that people much cleverer than I, and who had a better grasp of weighing evidence, were believers. By itself this proved nothing, but it did dispel prejudice.

Another significant factor in my religious development was that our headmaster, C.S. Walton, took his own life by hanging himself during the Christmas holidays one year. I was in the sixth form (the most senior part of the school) by then. Inevitably it was a great shock. Walton was an amazing man – single, knowing every boy, dynamic, unconventional and radical. His death raised huge questions for me. UCS had stood, in my mind, for the brave new world emerging in the 1950s. After that death, however, my schoolboy logic was nudged in the following direction: if this was where the value system of UCS ended up – if this secular, humanistic, left-of-centre, artistic, anti-Establishment school ended up with a corpse swinging from the banisters – was it worth it? Doubts were being sown in my mind.

## 'UNIV', OXFORD

After University College School, London, I went up in 1958 to 'Univ' (University College), Oxford (there was no connection between the two). This college, I was later to learn, was where Richard Clayton had been a student. Clayton was the great Evangelical leader in Newcastle in the nineteenth century, in whose memory Jesmond Parish Church had been founded. Univ was also Bill Clinton's college!

By now I was a believer (of sorts), but in reality very ill-informed in terms of the Christian intellectual tradition. I did possess a good basic Bible knowledge, however, having been brought up in a Christian family. My other mental furniture included an elementary grounding in Classical literature and ideas; an elementary grounding in English, other European and Russian literature; an elementary grounding in the rationalist tradition – the tradition of the European Enlightenment; and the fruits of a first-hand acquaintance with a number of outstanding Christian people who were friends of our family. I can remember listening to stimulating lunchtime conversations with people like the Old Testament scholar H.L. Ellison, the New Testament scholar Donald Guthrie, and that unconventional missionary to China, Gladys Aylward.

I went to Oxford not just to study 'the great minds' of the Classical authors we had to read for Classical Mods in the late 1950s, but 'to learn about life' (to quote our late headmaster and his approach to the study of the Greek and Roman Classics). On my first day I received a letter from the University Chaplain, the vicar of St Mary the Virgin, saying in effect, 'Don't go to the OICCU (the Oxford Inter-Collegiate Christian Union) – they are fundamentalists!' Such a prohibition, of course, provided every incentive to explore what this group did. So I turned up at the Northgate Hall the next Saturday evening. An Anglican clergyman, the Rev. John Stott, gave a Bible reading on Hebrews. Spiritually I was not up to learning a great deal from the evening, but I saw nothing to which I should take exception.

In this new environment it was impossible to escape the claims of the Christian faith. Very many students were *committed* Christians. This was so different from school. At Oxford hundreds of people were going to church – churches of all sorts, Evangelical, Anglo-Catholic and Roman Catholic. At the two Evangelical churches I attended, St Aldate's and then St Ebbe's, often there was standing room only. I had never been to a church that was full before.

I eventually threw in my lot with the OICCU. I judged that, of the various Christian options at Oxford in the late 1950s and early 1960s, this was the best. This was where you would find more Christians faithful to the Bible and the apostolic faith, and where you would find more real spiritual life than elsewhere. And most members seemed to be Anglicans. It was not a focus for weird cultists, as its critics seemed to imply. In fact a resurgence of Anglican Evangelicalism had just begun. Young bloods were emerging who came to speak to us regularly – not only John Stott, but also J.I. Packer, Michael Green, Dick Lucas (of St Helen's, Bishopsgate) and the late David Watson.

Dick Lucas took the Oxford University Mission in 1961. This was the first he had ever taken and the first I had ever attended. It had a profound effect on me. There was a series of consecutive addresses giving a basic and simple, but overall, theology. I found them persuasive. The mission committee of the Christian Union had also asked college representatives to give to enquirers as follow-up literature a small book called *Henceforth* by Hugh Evan-Hopkins.[1] It was a simple book. As I was one of the college representatives, I thought I had better read it before giving it away.

Apart from the Bible, some C.S. Lewis and a biography of William Temple, this was the first Christian book I had ever read seriously. Such perversity is amazing. I had read a great amount of secular literature, but my reading of Christian literature, including the Christian classics that have been so formative of European culture, was almost zero. There was, however, a very full bibliography at the back of this edition of *Henceforth*. Having enjoyed that book, I started to work my way through those listed in the bibliography. So began my theological education.

The result of all this was that just as the 1960s were opening up and the revolution in Western society was beginning, undergirded by new anti-theologies and new immoralities, and just as people were thinking they were being avant-garde in rejecting the old certainties of the Christian faith and morality, I was going in the opposite direction. I already had the good fortune of being inoculated against this fashionable 1960s version of secular humanism – for which I am eternally grateful to UCS. For me this influenced my thinking about the wider society.

[1] H.A. Evan-Hopkins, *Henceforth*, London, Inter-Varsity Fellowship, 1959. 'A plea for serious reading' and the bibliography were not included in later editions.

## CREEPING TOTALITARIANISM

Secular humanism has been very significant in modern political development. In Western political thinking there have been three fundamental questions about government. First there is the question: 'Who is to rule and by what authority?' Generally the answer has been given in terms of a monarchy, an aristocracy or a democracy (in some shape or another).

The second question is about the areas or spheres of government. The central question here in the West has focused on what areas belong to the Church and what areas belong to the secular authority. It was Jesus who first said, 'Give to Caesar what is Caesar's and to God what is God's' (Mark 12:17). Inevitably after that command the relationship between the Church and the secular authority would become a major issue. As we have seen, there have been different points of view even within the Church. While Calvin would not allow the secular authority to 'rule' in the Church, he nevertheless thought it should support the Church all it could. Luther, on the other hand, felt that the secular authority should go 'no further than the body, goods and outward earthly matters'.[2]

There is also a third and often ignored question. This is to do with the scope and expectations of secular authority. Since the rise of secular humanism the secular authority in the State has not only tried to take over the role of the Church, it has also tried to achieve on earth what the Church believed could only be achieved in heaven – varieties of human perfection. In consequence, what has evolved over the last 200 years has been a 'creeping totalitarianism', even in the so-called liberal societies of the West. This is indeed a sinister development.

With the discovery of electricity and the invention of the telegraph, the telephone and radio communication, governments acquired enormous power. Such power, in the context of secular humanism, has led governments to become utopian. There is a revival of the old heresy of Pelagianism – the belief that human beings can perfect themselves through their own efforts. But what is distinctive in modern Pelagianism is that 'government' is seen as

[2] Martin Luther, 'On Secular Authority', in Höpfl, *Luther and Calvin on Secular Authority*, op. cit., p. 23.

the chief means to achieve this goal of human betterment. Governments, therefore, continually have to seek more power for what has been described as 'the hope of salvation through politics'. This development is in sharp contrast to government where 'the aim is not to tell people how to live, but to maintain arrangements within which people can safely pursue the remarkable multiplicity of imaginable possibilities that human beings, left to their own devices, will bring forth'.[3]

Secular humanism is, therefore, a subtle and dangerous pressure towards totalitarianism in modern public life – on both the left and the right, and in liberal societies. The most notorious and evil totalitarianisms of the twentieth century sprang from secular humanistic ideologies – on the left Marxist socialism under Stalin and Mao Tse-tung, and on the right Fascist socialism under Mussolini and Hitler.

There are also dangers in Britain and America, however. In 1931 a British report of a committee presided over by Hugh Pattison Macmillan on banking and finance spoke about the growing preoccupation of government with 'the management of the life of the people' and claimed this was 'a change of outlook of the government of this country in recent times'. J.M. Keynes (of Bloomsbury) was the principal writer of the report.[4] Even if Keynes could manage economic life (which many now doubt), his track record on his own moral life (see page 45) suggests that he would not be good at managing the moral life of other people.

Where, however, did this secular humanism come from? It clearly did not start from scratch in the 1960s, although at the time it seemed like it.

## 10 NOVEMBER 1793

To find the source, we can go back to the morning of 10 November 1793, more than 200 years ago. That was when 'an extraordinary religious event' took place in Paris, in the Cathedral of Notre Dame

[3] Timothy Fuller, 'Editor's Introduction', in Michael Oakeshott, *The Politics of Faith and the Politics of Scepticism*, New Haven, Yale University Press, 1996, p. xix.
[4] Quoted in Oakeshott, ibid., p. 65.

– a 'Festival of Liberty and Reason'. As crowds of officials and onlookers entered the cathedral, a bizarre sight confronted them. Franklin Baumer tells us:

> *The insignia of Christianity [were] covered up and their place taken by the symbols of a strange new religion. Rising up in the nave was an improvised mountain, at the top of which perched a small Greek temple dedicated 'To Philosophy' and adorned on both sides by the busts of philosophers, probably Voltaire, Rousseau, Franklin, and Montesquieu.*[5]

Halfway down the side of the mountain was an altar of Reason, before which a torch of Truth was burning. Then came the high point of the ritual: out of the temple appeared a beautiful woman, an actress of the Paris Opera, dressed in red, white and blue, who personified Liberty. The assembled congregation then offered worship to 'Liberty'. Hands were stretched out to her as they sang a hymn written by Marie Joseph Chénier:

> *Come, holy Liberty, inhabit this temple,*
> *Become the goddess of the French people.*

It was soon decreed by the Constitutional Convention that Notre Dame should now be known as the 'Temple of Reason'.

This 'religion' did not last long, but it marked one of the beginnings of the secular humanism that has been seducing Western society ever since. And it was religious in form.

Of course, there is another sort of 'humanism' – the distinguishing mark of much of Renaissance Europe and the Reformation. The Renaissance was a time when there was a new interest in human nature. But the God of the Bible, the God and Father of our Lord Jesus Christ, was not excluded. Such a humanism is concerned with human nature in all its fullness – the nonrational and spiritual as well as the rational and material; it is concerned with learning in all its aspects – history, the fine arts, philosophy and theology as well as science.

[5] Franklin L. Baumer, *Religion and the Rise of Scepticism*, New York, Harbinger, 1959, p. 35.

Humanism of this sort, when Christian, is a noble thing, and there have been outstanding Christian humanists. C.S. Lewis himself was a twentieth-century Christian humanist. Christian humanism comes from the doctrine of Creation and the fact that mankind is made in God's image and so must be respected and valued.

Secular humanism as it affects the West and the world today is very different. Its roots go back to eighteenth-century France and the so-called 'Enlightenment' rather than the Renaissance and the Reformation.

In the eighteenth century there was an aggressive assault against the Christian faith. This was the background to the event in Notre Dame described above. One of the key figures was Voltaire: 'For the better part of half a century he was the most powerful influence in European thought,' as one commentator has said.[6] He identified Christianity as an 'infamous thing' to be crushed (*'écrasez l'infâme'* was 'Voltaire's battle cry ... repeated ... with the monotony of an unvarying refrain'[7]). He wanted to replace it with a religion of reason, virtue and liberty. A new cult was being proposed, 'drawn from the bosom of nature'. This would from now on be 'a natural religion'. Indeed, this was an anti-Christian revolution. Parallel to the revolution in politics, there was a revolution in religion. New 'religions' were proposed, but they did not all follow the same pattern.

## THE ENLIGHTENMENT

First, there were the deists – that is to say, people who believed in a supreme being (they were not atheists), but did not believe in the God of the Bible. Theirs was a sort of 'Freemasonry' religion. If you do not believe in Christ as Saviour, it seems reasonable only to have to affirm a creed like the Republican Creed of 1793: 'I believe in a supreme being, who has created men free and equal, who has made them to love and not hate one another, who wishes to be honoured by virtues and not by fanaticism.'[8]

[6] G.R. Cragg, *The Church and the Age of Reason*, London, Penguin Books, 1960, p. 399.
[7] Ibid., p. 240.
[8] Baumer, *Religion and the Rise of Scepticism*, op. cit., p. 38.

In addition to the deists there were the nationalists. These generated a 'religion of the Republic'. In other words, they deified the fatherland (and left a sinister legacy, as we saw only too well in the twentieth century).

Finally, there were those who favoured a 'religion of humanity', a phrase invented by Tom Paine, the British radical dissident. For him it meant a faith in mankind and our ability to establish a new world. And it promised a new dawn of happiness, social justice and peace.

Any such cults faded with Napoleon's later Concordat with the Pope, reached in 1801, when Roman Catholicism was restored as the state religion of France. But this religious ferment at the end of the eighteenth century meant that things would never be the same again in France, the rest of Europe or America. In fact, the results of this unique attack on the Christian faith from the philosophers of the Enlightenment are still with us.

At the heart of Enlightenment religion were two propositions. The *first* proposition was that if God exists at all, he is distant and certainly does not interfere in this world in any way. That is the classic deist position. It denies miracles. It denies any real incarnation – i.e. denies that Jesus Christ was divine and one with his Father, as expressed in the Bible and the creeds of the Church. It denies any revelation from God – we, therefore, have to find out everything ourselves. In his eighteenth-century book *The Age of Reason*, Tom Paine embodies this rejection of revealed religion: 'I do not believe in the creed professed by the Jewish church, by the Roman church, by the Greek church, by the Turkish church, by the Protestant church, nor by any church that I know. My own mind is my own church.'[9]

If the first proposition of Enlightenment religion is deism and the distance of God, the *second* proposition is the inherent goodness in, or perfectibility of, men and women and the denial of sin. This has the consequence of denying morality and universalizing religion. If, in principle, everyone is inherently good, it makes it difficult to say that any action is inherently bad, or any idea inherently false. This leads to a weakening of moral

[9] Thomas Paine, *The Age of Reason*, Secanus, N.J., Carol, 1997, p. 50.

judgement and an acceptance of all views, values and religions as being 'positive'.

In these two propositions, then, was the beginning of a huge conflict between the Christian faith and embryonic secular humanism. It focused not on theology but anthropology – on the understanding of mankind and human nature. The Bible, however, says clearly that human nature is fallen. This is how people are born. There is a universal moral disease of epidemic proportions, known as 'sin'. Sin is real. Until that is dealt with, there is no hope for mankind. That is why the Cross of Christ is so central to the Christian message – on the Cross Jesus bore our guilt and forgave our sins.

## CONDORCET AND VOLTAIRE

Condorcet (along with Denis Diderot) was the editor of the *Encyclopédie*. This magnum opus – an 'Encyclopedia of the Arts, Sciences and Crafts' – was the great means of communication for the new humanist faith. Condorcet was a leading exponent of the 'indefinite perfectibility of the human race'. It was with that assumption that he wrote his *Progress of the Human Mind* – a work that has been called the 'last will and testament of the Enlightenment'. 'No bounds have been fixed to the improvement of the human race...' he wrote. 'The perfectibility of man is absolutely indefinite ... Everything tells us that we are approaching one of the grand revolutions of the human race.'[10]

Condorcet knew, of course, that at present the world was not where it should be. He knew there were still crimes and injustice in abundance. So how did he adjust to contemporary evils? He tells us in his famous last words:

> *It is in the contemplation of this picture [of posterity] ... that [the philosopher] finds his true recompense for virtue. The contemplation of this picture is an asylum in which the memory of his persecutors does not follow him, an asylum in which, living in imagination with*

[10] Quoted in Baumer, *Religion and the Rise of Scepticism*, op. cit., p. 74.

*mankind re-established in its rights and in its true nature, he can forget mankind corrupted and tormented by greed, fear, envy. It is in this asylum that he truly lives with his fellows, in a* heaven *which his reason has created, and which his love of humanity embellishes with the purest joy.*[11]

Something sad and strange is going on. The deistic humanists are substituting the expectations of an earthly golden age (a myth, if ever there was one) for the hope of heaven – a depressing eschatology indeed. Condorcet's colleague Diderot was quite explicit: 'Posterity is for the philosopher what the other world is for the religious.'[12]

Voltaire was more robust. It is bizarre in the light of the realistic picture Condorcet paints of 'mankind corrupted and tormented by greed, fear, envy', but nothing was more anathema to the deists – and indeed to the Enlightenment as a whole – than the doctrine of original sin. It was an obsession with Voltaire. He attacked Blaise Pascal for his talk about sin time after time, calling him the 'sublime misanthrope'. Voltaire's *Philosophical Dictionary* makes his position clear: 'We are told loudly that human nature is essentially perverse ... nothing is more ill considered.'[13] He also attacked Augustine, as many still do, for expounding the doctrine of original sin.

The concept of original sin is presented so clearly in the Bible, but that would not have convinced Voltaire. He wanted to say to each individual, 'You are all born good; consider how awful it would be to corrupt the purity of your being ... Remember your human dignity ... Man is not born wicked; he becomes wicked.'[14] At a stroke Voltaire rendered unnecessary – or so he thought – both the atonement and Christ (and, of course, it allowed him his mistress, the Marquise de Châtelet).

Not only was morality denied or eroded by this approach, however: religion was universalized. 'Multifaithism' soon developed. The 'one catholic Church' was no longer considered holy and apostolic. Instead it had to embrace the wise of the whole

[11] Ibid., p. 75.
[12] Ibid.
[13] Voltaire, *Philosophical Dictionary*, London, Penguin Books, 1972, p. 298.
[14] Ibid., p. 299.

world, from Peking to Paris. As the Englightenment was dawning, the poet Alexander Pope referred to the emerging syncretism when he equated Yahweh (Jehovah), the Father God of the Bible, with Jupiter (Jove), the pagan Roman God:

*Father of all! in ev'ry age,*
*In ev'ry clime ador'd,*
*By saint, by savage, and by sage,*
*Jehovah, Jove, or Lord.*[15]

In the final analysis, Enlightenment humanistic deism failed. It never really became a substitute for orthodox Christian faith. It was a mixture of the good and the bad, and its philosophy was a matter of wishes, offering false long-term hopes that could only lead to disillusionment. It was, of course, anti-Christian, though its deism gave it credibility with the undiscerning.

That said, it did pioneer and help stimulate some much needed social change, such as came later through penal reform. The Enlightenment philosopher Cesare Beccaria, who had visited the prisons of Milan, wrote his *Essay on Crimes and Punishments* in 1764. It was a case, as the Bible might put it, of the children of this age being wiser than the children of light – those trying to keep the Christian faith. It was, however, only when the humanitarian ideals were married to evangelical religion that significant results were achieved. Some in the humanist tradition did want to abolish slavery, for example, but it was the evangelical William Wilberforce who delivered the goods. Humanistic deism failed in Britain because of the evangelical revival in the second half of the eighteenth century and the first half of the nineteenth century, of which Wilberforce was a part.

Humanistic deism held neither the masses, nor the intellectuals for long, many of whom moved from deism to an extreme scepticism or even atheism. But deism never died completely. Like a garden weed, deism is always popping its head up somewhere, just when you think it is gone for good. In the modern Church it is

[15] Alexander Pope (1688–1744), *Universal Prayer.*

present in the form of theological liberalism and the views of people like the former Bishop of Durham, David Jenkins.

## THE NINETEENTH CENTURY

Moving on to 1882, we find Friedrich Nietzsche, whom we have already come across, writing the parable of the madman. In the parable, the madman rushes into the market place and cries out, 'I am looking for God ... Where has God gone? ... I shall tell you. *We have killed him* – you and I ... God is dead ... That which was holiest and mightiest of all that the world has yet possessed has bled to death under our knives – who will wipe this blood off us?'[16]

Nietzsche was mentally unstable himself (probably due to a sexually transmitted disease), but he was drawing attention to an important fact: those opposed to the Christian gospel had moved into the next stage and a new mood was discernible. They had graduated to the stage of aggressive doubt and aggressive disbelief.

William Gladstone, the British Prime Minister, put the *annus horribilis* of this change of mood as 1872. In that year he said:

> *It is not only the Christian Church, or only the Holy Scripture, or only Christianity, which is attacked. The disposition is boldly proclaimed to deal with root and branch, and to snap utterly the ties which, under the still venerable name of Religion, unite man with the unseen world, and lighten the struggles and the woes of life by the hope of a better land.*[17]

Nor was it just church people who saw the problem. The writer Matthew Arnold, too, saw that there was a revolution in thinking about religion. Everywhere, he said, there was a 'spread of scepticism'. That was certainly true of the educated classes.

This was the period of the growing debate between religion and science. It was at this time that Thomas Huxley invented the word 'agnostic'. Auguste Comte, the French philosopher who succeeded

[16] R.J. Hollingdale (tr.), *A Nietzsche Reader*, London, Penguin Books, 1977, pp. 202–3.
[17] Baumer, *Religion and the Rise of Scepticism*, op. cit., p. 131.

Condorcet (he was born four years after Condorcet died), had already invented the words 'sociology' and 'positivism'. Positivism was a theory of social evolution. Comte argued that society went through three stages of development: first the theological or fictitious stage, then the metaphysical or abstract stage, and finally the scientific or positive stage. Comte was trying to get society to move from the metaphysical stage to the scientific. When he tried to develop a quasi-church and a religion of humanity to promote his views, Thomas Huxley called it 'Catholicism minus Christianity'.

With all these ideas in the air, it is not surprising that in 1851 a freethinker called George Holyoake wanted less alienating terms than 'infidel' or 'atheist' to be used for those who opposed the traditional Christian faith. This is a common ploy. Unpleasant concepts can be anaesthetized by changing their names – you call foeticide 'abortion'; you call buggery 'gay sex'; and you call fornicators 'the sexually active'. The term that Holyoake discovered was 'secularist', and in 1851 he helped to found a 'National Secular Society'.

Then came Herbert Spencer (1820–1903). Spencer is particularly significant as the great champion of philosophical evolutionism. In the tradition of Comte, this is a view that sees society continually improving itself, learning from its mistakes. Spencer extended Comte's ideas, taking them on where Comte left off. In 1867 he wrote in his *Principles of Sociology* that social life has a natural tendency to develop from simple to complex forms, and steadily to get better. He had actually begun to develop his views *before* Darwin's *Origin of Species* was published in 1859. Darwin was part of a wider philosophical climate. Spencer claimed that Darwin confirmed his views. 'Progress,' he said, 'is not an accident, but a necessity. Surely must evil and immorality disappear; surely must man become perfect.'[18]

Spencer was not totally atheistic in his social Darwinism, however. He believed in 'an ultimate existence':

*Very likely there will ever remain a need to give shape to that indefinite sense of an ultimate existence, which forms the basis of our*

[18] Quoted in Alec R. Vidler, *Essays in Liberality*, London, SCM Press, 1957, p. 12.

*intelligence. We shall always be under the necessity of contemplating
it as some mode of being; that is – of representing it to ourselves in
some form of thought, however vague. And we shall not err in doing
this so long as we treat every notion we thus frame as merely a symbol,
utterly without resemblance to that for which it stands.*[19]

Humanism *is* a religion. That must be insisted upon. The word
'secular' is clever – it seduces people into thinking that secularism,
which in practice means non-Christian humanism, is not a religion
or religious in any way. Many educators and media gurus hold that
it is more neutral to be a humanist than a Christian. They need to
be resisted: we are, in fact, talking about another religion.

## THE LAST PHASE

The last phase of humanism occurred in the 1930s. The year 1933
saw the rise of Hitler. It also saw the publication of the famous
*Humanist Manifesto.*[20]

This *Manifesto* explicitly identified humanism as religious. What
it deplored was 'the identification of the word *religion* with
doctrines and methods which have lost their significance and
which are powerless to solve the problem of human living in the
Twentieth Century'.

Among the major theses of its 'religious humanism' were the
following:

- 'Religious humanists regard the universe as self-existing and not
  created.'
- 'Humanism asserts that the nature of the universe depicted
  by modern science makes unacceptable any supernatural or
  cosmic guarantees of human values.'
- 'Religious humanism considers *the complete realization of human
  personality* [italics mine] to be the end of man's life and seeks its
  development and fulfilment in the here and now.'

[19] Baumer, *Religion and the Rise of Scepticism*, op. cit., p. 280.
[20] *Humanist Manifestoes I and II*, Buffalo, N.Y., Prometheus Books, 1973.

- 'In place of the old attitudes involved in worship and prayer the humanist finds his religious emotions expressed in a heightened sense of personal life and in a co-operative effort to promote social well-being.'
- 'Man is at last becoming aware that he alone is responsible for the realization of the world of his dreams, that he has within himself the power for its achievement.'

Notice that last point particularly, made just six years before the Second World War broke out. Notice, also, that the authors here are not denying the existence of God. By their silence they appear to leave the possibility open, but the presumption is that trust in God can have no practical effect. Whether or not God is thought to exist, mankind must live, they imply, as though he did *not* exist.

Another major thesis of the manifesto was that moral values could have no 'supernatural or cosmic guarantees'. That is to say, there can be no morality based on the Bible. The only morality to be recognized is what comes from human experience. There are no absolutes.

The phrase 'the complete realization of the human personality' seemed innocent enough at the time, but this would later prove to be of huge significance. It lay at the root of the far-reaching moral and cultural revolution that took place in the 1960s.

This *Humanist Manifesto* was, in fact, generally ignored at the time and the authors are now largely forgotten. But its influence was spread nonetheless through the giant of the group and the principal author of the document, John Dewey (1859–1952), the philosopher and educational theorist. The manifesto certainly reflected his views, and through this document he was able to disseminate them in strategic places – colleges of education, for example. His views have shaped modern education in the West to a profound degree, steering it away from its Christian roots and off in a secular humanist direction. This has had disastrous consequences, as many would argue, and it has undoubtedly led to our current de-moralization.

## CONCLUSION

Forty years later there was a second manifesto – *Humanist Manifesto II*. There was nothing substantially new, except that it was more aggressively opposed to traditional religion. Also, while the 1933 edition had been silent on the subject of sex, the 1973 document decided to come clean. Among other things, it said this: 'In the area of sexuality, we believe that intolerant attitudes, often cultivated by orthodox religions and puritanical cultures, unduly repress sexual conduct.' It goes on to say, 'Short of harming others or compelling them to do likewise, individuals should be permitted to express their sexual proclivities and pursue their life-styles as they desire.'[21]

The influence of these two manifestoes is out of all proportion either to the size of the groups responsible for them or to the numbers distributed. Their significance is that they have influenced the values of the 'new class' of those working in the educational empire, the media and the therapeutic services. As James Hitchcock says,

> *Many people imbibe their message without realizing that it is the creed of a particular movement. They have cleverly preempted the vocabulary of freedom: 'All we want is the right to believe our own creed, as we concede to you the right to believe yours. Let us do away with all forms of intolerance.' Yet in practice ... humanists are intolerant of religious belief.*[22]

Christians must oppose such secular humanism precisely because of its intolerance and manipulation. Its history may be complex, but its roots need to be known so that appropriate strategies to combat its current influence can be developed.

As we have seen, this influence is not just on issues of private belief. Undoubtedly *secular* humanism is related to various forms of totalitarianism – and that includes the more subtle form emerging in so-called liberal societies.

[21] Ibid.
[22] James Hitchcock, *What is Secular Humanism?*, Ann Arbor, Servant Books, 1982, p. 15.

The follower of Christ, however, can never be anything other than a *Christian* humanist. God has made humankind. This is a good world, but fallen. That is why we need to recover a sense of sin. But this is not dehumanizing. It is, rather, the only way to a true recovery of how God intended mankind to be. Such an understanding is the way to *true* humanism. The true humanist preaches the Cross of Christ *and* is interested at the same time in God's wonderful world. The doctrine of Creation and the fact that mankind is made in God's image means that every believer must respect, be interested in, and – as far as they are able – study all that goes to make up the life of men and women, both as individuals and together in human societies.

The Christian humanist must also cultivate a 'liberal mind' – but that does not mean at the expense of being firmly 'conservative' in respect of God's truth when necessary. As Alex Vidler puts it, 'A liberal-minded man is free from narrow prejudice, generous in his judgment of others, open-minded, especially to the reception of new ideas or proposals for reform. Liberal is the opposite not of conservative, but of fanatical or bigoted or intransigent.'[23]

Christians should be truly conservative *and* truly liberal. They can also be confident. Since the Enlightenment, Christianity has withstood 200 years of the fiercest intellectual criticism. Emil Brunner pointed out that the case is not the same for secular humanism:

> *Two hundred years ago, scoffing Voltaire, probably the most famous man of his time, prophesied that all would soon be over with the Bible. The house in which this boast was made is today one of the offices of a great Bible society. Voltaire's name is almost forgotten; the Bible has had, in the meantime, an incredible career of triumph throughout the world.*[24]

[23] Vidler, *Essays in Liberality*, op. cit., p. 21.
[24] Emil Brunner, *Our Faith*, London, SCM Press, 1949, p. 17.

# CHAPTER SEVEN

# FUNDAMENTALISM, EVOLUTION AND CREATION

### PHILOSOPHY

Being at Oxford and attempting to study philosophy in the early 1960s was a remarkable experience. Oxford was then the centre of the academic philosophical world. It was almost mediaeval in the way it attracted people from many countries.

Ludwig Wittgenstein, the Cambridge genius, was dead by then (he died in 1951), but his pupils lived on. He had taught them to look at language in a new and precise way. They continued the project, a number of them based in Oxford. Thus the 'linguistic movement' was spawned from Wittgenstein's seminars in Cambridge during the 1930s and 1940s.

Many of his pupils were bewitched, so it was said, by the eccentricities of the master. One pupil not bewitched, however, was George Paul, tutor at University College, Oxford (and incidentally brother-in-law of Michael Ramsey, the then Archbishop of Canterbury). Before George Paul was tragically drowned in a sailing accident one Easter, I remember him boasting, 'You will never be the same again after doing philosophy here with us.' He was so right.

Oxford linguistic philosophy did clear our heads, even if our heads were not as adequate as some of our tutors might have wanted. Wittgenstein said that other philosophers had put the fly into the bottle; his job was to let it out. Others had confused; now was the time to clarify.

Of his contemporaries, Wittgenstein no doubt had in mind men like Bertrand Russell, with whom he had formerly collaborated, and A.J. Ayer, an atheist and humanist, a signatory to the *Humanist Manifesto II*, and famous for his 1936 book called *Language, Truth and Logic*, which popularized 'logical positivism'.[1] It was against this form of positivism that many were reacting and it was being exposed as a misleading fraud.

Ayer was saying, for example, that all religious language was 'meaningless'. This was highly disturbing for Christians as it suggested that you could not meaningfully carry on a conversation about the faith. This provocative claim was made because of the principle of 'verification', which said in effect two things: first, that a statement is true where it is 'necessarily' or 'analytically' true (as in, 'If he is a bachelor, he is unmarried,' which is necessarily or analytically true by definition or from the meaning of the words); and second, that a statement is true where it can be 'empirically verified', i.e., proved by sense experience or observable experiment. Everything else is 'meaningless'. Following this principle, therefore, the statement 'God is love' is meaningless. In the words of Ayer, 'All utterances about the nature of God are nonsensical.'[2]

How was such an argument countered? It was countered by a more careful analysis of the words used. This revealed that logical positivists like Ayer were using a linguistic sleight of hand when they used the term 'meaning'.

## LINGUISTIC ANALYSIS

Take, for example, the words 'The King of France is wise' (a sentence actually discussed at the time). For a logical positivist this should be 'meaningless'. You cannot test this by inspecting the King of France's wisdom or lack of it. There is no King of France. But the words are plainly not 'meaningless'. Baby noises may be 'meaningless', but not sentences of this kind.

---

[1] A.J. Ayer, *Language, Truth and Logic*, London, Gollancz, 1958.
[2] Ibid., p. 115.

The way out of the impasse was pointed out by P.F. Strawson (now Sir Peter Strawson), our other philosophy tutor at Univ.[3] He argued that you must distinguish between the sentences themselves and the 'use' of sentences to make statements. You then see that meaning relates to the sentences as such; truth relates to the *use* of sentences in making statements.

It would be perfectly legitimate, for example, for an immigrant child in Britain today, whose vocabulary was weak, to ask for the meaning of the sentence, 'The King of France is wise.' It would be illegitimate, however, to ask, 'Is it true?' But that question, 'Is it true?', would have been legitimate if asked at the time of the French monarchy.

The point is obvious. We can give the *meaning* of a sentence even when there is no question of it actually being used in the present and when, therefore, there is no question of it being 'empirically verified'. Giving the meaning is rather like giving general directions for its use at *some time or other*. The *truth or falsity* of such a sentence, however, can only be a live issue when it is actually being used in a live setting.

'Meaning' is different from 'truth'. That is why we have both words. Meaning depends on whether a sentence *could* ever be used. This is altogether different from whether a sentence is true or false.

With regard to religious statements, the sensible person realizes that if there is a God, the words 'God is love' can be used of him. They are not meaningless. But unless we believe in a God 'who is there', we will not use sentences of this type to pass on information about him.

This may look rather banal. For many, however, this sort of exercise was liberating. It was particularly liberating when this discipline of precision was applied to more 'metaphysical' questions. The linguistic school of philosophy had a bad press for not dealing with serious issues, and its apparent pedantic analysis of words exasperated many. This was unfair. Sheer nonsense is talked too often about serious matters, not least when it comes to theology, politics and morality. This needs to be corrected. However, wider issues, including scientific issues, were gradually addressed by some of

[3] P.F. Strawson, *Logico-Linguistic Papers*, London, Methuen, 1971, pp. 12–13.

these philosophers. Stephen Toulmin, a 'linguistic' philosopher of science, challenged our thinking with his long 1957 essay 'Contemporary Scientific Mythology'.[4]

From my schooldays I had absorbed uncritically the view that on the subject of Creation, science tells you 'how' while the Bible tells you 'why'. I had no great worries at that stage. It seemed perfectly possible, and theologically necessary, for God to have been able to generate human beings by any means he chose – and that must include evolution. However, I was also aware that the doctrine of evolution, as commonly taught, had been instrumental in many people losing their faith. With that background, and a liberality of mind that I thought was Christian, I read Toulmin with interest.

He had already suggested in his book *The Philosophy of Science* (originally published in 1953) that with some scientists you should not, in the words of Einstein, 'listen to their words, [but] fix your attention on their deeds'.[5] He had some physicists especially in mind. He was saying that results are what matter; do not believe the theories they give you as being a true or *ultimate* explanation. Toulmin developed the view that it is helpful to see some scientific theories as models with built-in inferring techniques which help you to make deductions, rather than as 'descriptions' of reality. He argued this in respect of the Principle of the Rectilinear Propagation of Light. In that theory, at the very least, the statement that 'light *travels* in straight lines' is odd. It shows that words are not being used with their normal meanings.[6] In the same way, when physicists earlier in the century said that 'desks are not really solid; they are a mass of moving atoms', they were changing the meaning of words. I can remember to this day Mrs Austin, the widow of the great philosopher, J.L. Austin, pressing her desk in one of our tutorials and saying, 'But this is what we *mean* by "solid". It doesn't matter what James Jeans [a famous physicist and astronomer] says is going on inside it.'

We must therefore be careful with some scientific theories and explanations. They can be helpful. But they are not always the

[4] Stephen Toulmin, 'Contemporary Scientific Mythology', in Stephen Toulmin, Ronald W. Hepburn and Alasdair MacIntyre, *Metaphysical Beliefs*, London, SCM Press, 1970.

[5] Stephen Toulmin, *The Philosophy of Science*, London, Arrow, 1962, p. 16.

[6] Ibid., p. 22ff.

straightforward descriptions of reality they seem to be at first. Ordinary words and concepts can have their meanings subtly changed. This disorientates the unwary.

The most significant point for me in 'Contemporary Scientific Mythology' was the observation that 'as the subject matter of physics provides the imagery of despair, so that of biology provides the imagery of hope.'[7] What is that all about? Simply this: the Second Law of Thermodynamics obliges us to think of the universe as running down, but the popular understanding of evolution is that the universe is getting better and better. It is therefore difficult to see how *both* of these pictures, *if they are real predictions*, can be true at the same time.

Toulmin's suggestion is that such theories are one half science and one half 'metaphysics'. Metaphysics are background beliefs or assumptions about ultimate things. So Toulmin's view is that 'the Running-Down Universe [and] Evolution with a capital E ... are two examples which ... are not so much scientific discoveries as scientific myths.'[8] This is not, in itself, to argue that the scientific theories on which these views are based must be immediately rejected as 'scientific' theories. They may be the best we can do to make sense of the data at the moment. They may be good theories. But we have to ask questions about *precisely* what they are saying. Are they descriptions or are they models?

It is to questions about how theories relate to Creation (the beginning of things) that we must now turn. And we do so realizing that these questions are now having, once again, a serious political relevance.

## EDUCATIONAL ISSUES

In the United States the debate over evolution and Creation is being treated by some as a defining issue in education. It is therefore significant, whatever our views on the subject, that in August 1999 the Kansas school board, according to *The Times* newspaper,

[7] Toulmin, 'Contemporary Scientific Mythology', op. cit., p. 63.
[8] Ibid., pp. 4–5.

'voted to delete evolution from the state school curriculum, delighting religious conservatives, enraging secular scientists and achieving what the mighty American religious establishment tried and ultimately failed to do in 1925'.[9]

But what needs defining? The answer is the role of the school, as modern societies become progressively more secular; as governments become more totalitarian and monopolize education; and as Christian parents object to the assumptions, views and values often being taught to their children. One set of views to which many Christian parents object converge around evolution as it is often taught. Christian parents who object over this or other issues are certainly not all mindless obscurantists. Many of them, indeed, are better educated than the teachers who are teaching their children.

The situation is serious because state schools are no longer the educational institutions they once were. In the nineteenth century, when modern schooling developed in the West, education was basically seen as an introduction to literature and science (at a range of levels). But now, with the breakdown of the family and with little church or chapel attendance, the school is attempting to give moral, spiritual, social and political training as well. That, however, means children are being indoctrinated more heavily in the belief systems which the secular authority endorses. While in Britain there is supposed to be a Christian input, often in practice these belief systems in the schools are anything but Christian. And if in some science subjects there is 'one half science and one half background beliefs', it is not surprising that Christian parents object from time to time.

Christian parents, not unnaturally, see these educational issues as important. Christopher Dawson put it like this:

> In politics Christianity can accommodate itself to any system of government and can survive under the most severe forms of despotism and autocracy. And in the same way, it is not bound to any economic system and has in the past existed and expanded in a world of slavery as well as in a world of freedom, under feudalism and capitalism and state socialism. But if it loses the right to teach it can no longer exist.

[9] *The Times,* 14 August 1999.

*The situation was entirely different in the past when most people were not educated and when church and chapel provided the only channel of popular instruction. But today, when the whole population of every civilized country is subjected to an intensive process of schooling during the most impressionable years of their lives, it is the school and not the church that forms men's minds, and if the school finds no place for religion, there will be no room left for religion elsewhere. It is no accident that the introduction of universal compulsory state education has coincided in time and place with the secularization of modern culture.*[10]

The evolution and Creation debate highlights a serious issue in respect of the relationship between Christians and the secular authority. The subject cannot be ignored.

## COSMOLOGY

The last decade of the twentieth century saw a renewed interest in Creation, evolution and 'creation science'. Typical was the interest in the 1992 findings of the US Cosmic Background Explorer satellite (COBE). *Time* magazine claimed on 4 May of that year, 'By peering back into the beginning of time, a satellite finds the largest and oldest structures ever observed – evidence of how the universe took shape 15 billion years ago.'

In what sense is that true, if it is true? How does it relate to the traditional Christian understanding about Creation? And how does it fit in with Genesis 1:1, where we read, 'In the beginning God created the heavens and the earth'? Here is one response to that last question:

*Natural scientists and philosophers have attempted to explain nature or the world; but not one of their theories or suggestions has remained firm or unshaken; each has been overthrown by its successor ... Those for whom the concept of 'God' is meaningless are unwilling to admit that a rational being was in control at the inception of the Universe ...*

[10] Dawson, *The Historic Reality of Christian Culture*, op. cit., pp. 87–8.

*Take the 'materialists' – those who say matter is all there is, matter is ultimate, or put more technically, atoms, molecules etc. (invisible entities) coalescing make up the visible world. It is because they don't know how to say, 'In the beginning God created the heaven and the earth' (Gen 1.1). An atheistic philosophy of the world has misled them; and it appears then that nothing governs or rules the universe, but all is given up to mere chance.*

*To guard us from such an error the writer of the creation narrative in Genesis, with his very first words, flashes into our minds the name of God. 'In the beginning God created.' What a glorious order. He first establishes a beginning. Then he adds 'created' to show that what was made was a very small part of the power of the creator.*

This is not someone arguing against Darwin in the nineteenth century. This is from the pen of someone writing in the fourth century, Basil of Cappadocia.[11]

We are in great danger of thinking that issues of science and religion belong exclusively to modern times. We tend to feel that the problems of Genesis have only come with the advent of Newtonian physics and Darwinian biology – and perhaps the 'Big Bang' theory. That is self-evidently not so.

The elemental Christian view of 'origins' is expressed neatly and profoundly in Hebrews 11:3: 'By faith we understand that the universe was formed at God's command, so that what is seen was not made out of what was visible.' This is known as *creatio ex nihilo* – creation out of nothing – as opposed to the idea that there was an ever-existent 'material' universe out of which God formed the world. There was, Hebrews teaches, no eternal dualism of God *and* matter. God was responsible for creating the material universe. There was, therefore, a 'beginning', and history is to be thought of as linear and not cyclical.

Whether something in reality corresponds to a 'Big Bang' depends on the facts, as yet unknown. But the Big Bang cannot be the biblical 'beginning'. The Big Bang as it is presented today occurs within the framework of our categories of space and time. The biblical creation account, however, *includes* the creation of

[11] Basil of Cappadocia, *Hexaemeron*, Homily 1.2.

space and time. However we take the language of Genesis, the first act of Creation was of time – of day and night through the creation of light and darkness: 'And there was evening, and there was morning – the first day' (Genesis 1:5).

## THE CHRISTIAN TRADITION

It is worth keeping in mind some words of Augustine on Genesis.

> *In these questions two things are to be observed. First, that scriptural truth be unshakenly maintained. Secondly, that since the Divine Scripture may be expounded in many ways, it is not right to attach oneself so strictly to any one interpretation as still to maintain it after sure reason has proved that what we suppose to be contained in scripture is false.*[12]

We should also heed Thomas Aquinas and his second of 'two ways of reasoning'. He was discussing the cosmological theories current in the thirteenth century. 'In astronomy,' he wrote, 'the explanation by eccentrics and epicycles is propounded because, when this position has been adopted, the sensible appearances of the heavenly motions can be accounted for. Nevertheless this explanation is not a conclusive proof, because the appearances might perhaps be accounted for by adopting a different position.'[13]

In the thirteenth century this was a wise thing to say. Three centuries later, Copernicus would reject the old Ptolemaic system of astronomy with the new claim that the earth goes round the sun. In the light of contemporary knowledge, the old Ptolemaic hypothesis was useful. It helped many sailors navigate at night. In time, however, a neater hypothesis – that of Copernicus – became the preferred theory. 'The appearances of the heavenly motions'

---

[12] Augustine saw three ways of viewing Genesis: first, literally (or materially); secondly, metaphorically (or spiritually); or thirdly, a mixture of the two. Augustine says, 'I prefer the third [view]', *De Gen. ad litt.* VIII, 1, quoted in Henri Blocher, *In the Beginning – the Opening Chapters of Genesis*, Leicester, Inter-Varsity Press, 1984, p. 36.

[13] Thomas Aquinas, *Summa Theologicae* I, xxxii, 1 *ad* 2, quoted in E.L. Mascall, *Christian Theology and Natural Science*, London, Longmans, Green and Co., 1957, p. 54.

certainly were better 'accounted for' by this hypothesis, as Galileo confirmed with his telescope.

We may not be able to conceive it at present, but why should there not be another 'Copernican revolution' totally altering the way we model the physical universe? Our present knowledge would then seem primitive. At present the *model* we use is accurate enough for space craft to navigate by – indeed, it is very accurate. But when we are asked to believe a suggestion as to what happened 15 billion years ago, caution is appropriate. Unlike models of our solar system, such a suggestion cannot be verified by direct space investigation.

We are being asked by some to believe that the universe burst into being as a submicroscopic, unimaginably dense knot of pure energy flying outwards in all directions, spewing radiation. We must avoid the temptation to say that this description is logically like the descriptions in Julius Caesar's *Gallic War* or Luke's *Acts of the Apostles* – literal history. Surely it is more reasonable to say that, as a model, the 'Big Bang' can account for a range of discoveries, can lead to new thinking, and can fit in with other theories in physics. But whether there ever *was* a Big Bang in the same way as in factual history there once was an eruption of Mount Vesuvius is a very different matter. And of course – a vital issue – when you try to think about or imagine an event like the 'creation of all things', it is logically unique. There is no way you can discuss it in terms of ordinary induction and analogy, which is the normal way of developing scientific theories. There is no analogy in this case.

Is it, in fact, possible to say anything useful or explain anything about something that is totally unique, such as the 'creation of all things'? Yes, it is. It was Professor H.L.A. Hart, an Oxford lawyer from this period of linguistic analysis (and also teaching at Univ), who argued in his inaugural lecture that explanations of unique items are perfectly possible. He used the example of a 'trick' in a game of cards. How do you explain that? You explain it not by saying that it is 'analogous' to a 'goal' in a game of football. That helps no one. You explain it by explaining the whole game. Then it becomes obvious what a trick is.[14] So the Christian argues that if you

---

[14] H.L.A. Hart, *Definition and Theory in Jurisprudence*, Oxford, Clarendon Press, 1953, p. 14.

explain the whole account of Creation, redemption and the last things as the Bible gives them in broad outline, they can be *sufficiently* understood. As Paul says in 1 Corinthians 13:12, 'Now we see but a poor reflection as in a mirror; then [at the end of time, with Christ's return] we shall see face to face. Now I know in part; then I shall know fully, even as I am fully known.'

## MONTEFIORE, JOHNSON AND 'SCREWTAPE'

For the last 100 years Cosmology has not been the real problem, however. The problem has been more with the origin of mankind and human evolution. Then, in the last decade of the twentieth century, cracks appeared in the edifice of evolutionary theory as it is popularly understood.

In 1995 Hugh Montefiore, the former Bishop of Birmingham, wrote the following letter as a book review in the *Church Times*. It was in the style of one of C.S. Lewis's *Screwtape Letters* and was entitled 'A theory unnaturally selected'.[15] It shows up some of the cracks.

*Dear Wormwood,*

*I am writing because I want more precautions taken to safeguard our position on the scientific front. The general belief in the West that Darwinism explains the evolution of species has been our greatest triumph, and has given enormous satisfaction to our Father Below.*

*The assumption that mankind has emerged from a purposeless process of evolution resulting from the accumulation of small random mutations which were to the advantage of individual members of a species, and made them fitter to survive, has robbed millions of faith in the existence of the Enemy, or reduced him to the status of a 'blind watchmaker'.*

*But I scent danger ahead. You have done very well to prevent reviews of small and easy-to-read books like* Darwin on Trial *(Monarch, 1994). The eminence of its author Philip E. Johnson, a Berkeley law professor, and his disclosure of the threadbare nature of our arguments, could have done us great damage.*

---

[15] *Church Times*, 21 April 1995.

*Fortunately, we have been so successful that anyone who tries to debunk neo-Darwinism is generally regarded by society as a crank. You must keep on preventing those scientists who are adherents of the Enemy from criticising evolution through natural selection. You must try to spread abroad the idea that the only alternative to Darwinism is the belief that the world was created by the Enemy in six days. Don't try to persuade people that Darwinism is true – we know it isn't – but that there is no alternative explanation that is credible today.*

*A few practical hints. If anyone objects that there is no concrete evidence that any new species has actually evolved by micromutations, divert attention from the facts by saying it is logically possible. Suggest that major changes might in principle come about through small mutations in an embryo, but never try to explain how, for example, a reptile producing eggs could turn into a mammal producing live young.*

*When it comes to fossils, beware of the palaeontologists, because they tend to be against us. No transitional intermediates have ever been found in the vertebrate sequence or elsewhere; so hammer on about animals with similarities to two classes, and never mention the differences, or why there were sudden extinctions or why some species persist for millions of years. So you should hide the fact that the fossil problem is getting worse, not better. Pretend that we simply need to find more fossils. Assert that similarities in molecular structure between species prove a common ancestry – although, of course, they don't.*

*What really scares me is the thought that some well-known biologist may say that anyone looking objectively at the evidence would regard Darwinism as highly improbable. But it's unlikely: too many vested interests are at stake.*

*Your affectionate uncle, SCREWTAPE*

## EVOLUTION

The old certainties with regard to evolution are being challenged today. As Philip E. Johnson himself says,

*Every history of the twentieth century lists three thinkers as pre-eminent in influence: Darwin, Marx and Freud. All three were*

*regarded as 'scientific' (and hence far more reliable than anything 'religious') in their heyday. Yet Marx and Freud have fallen, and even their dwindling bands of followers no longer claim that their insights were based on any methodology remotely comparable to that of experimental science. I am convinced that Darwin is the next on the block. His fall will be by far the mightiest of the three.[16]*

Such a fall for Darwin would certainly be highly significant, because popular Darwinism has been used to dethrone God. As the philosopher of science Del Ratzsch puts it, 'Evolution, along with the new cosmologies and backed by the undentable prestige of science, became part of a gratifyingly sophisticated excuse for unbelief – a ticket out of an oppressive universe with a God who set boundaries and made demands, into one where we set the rules and the cosmos itself was the only limit.'[17] Darwinism, indeed, became a new secular religion. The serious consequences have been seen especially in our schools. An official American 'Position Statement' for biology teachers from 1995 excludes any mention of divine design or control: 'The diversity of life on earth is the outcome of evolution – an unsupervised, impersonal, unpredictable and natural process of temporal descent with genetic modification that is affected by natural selection, chance, historical contingencies and changing environments.'[18]

How, then, is this confidence being challenged? There are three areas that come together in the debate on evolution: the scientific, the philosophical and the theological. From all these perspectives serious questions are now being asked.

In the scientific area it is now being seen that Darwin's *Origin of Species* had a level of plausibility in 1859 more because of the developing culture of unbelief (see Chapter 6) than because of its scientific merit. There was nothing new in the idea of evolution as such. Jean Baptiste Lamarck, a French zoologist, had published *Zoological Philosophy* in 1809. This spoke of life in its simplest form emerging

---

[16] Philip E. Johnson, *Defeating Darwinism*, Downers Grove, Inter-Varsity Press, 1997, p. 113.

[17] Del Ratzsch, *The Battle of the Beginnings*, Downers Grove, Inter-Varsity Press, 1996, p. 7.

[18] Johnson, *Defeating Darwinism*, op. cit., p. 15.

from non-life by small steps and in increasing complexity. But Darwin's theory caught on where Lamarck's had not because of the theory of natural selection, which was given the status of natural law and seemed to be something of a hidden power. It told *how* it all happened, or so it seemed. T.H. Huxley, who described himself as 'Darwin's bulldog', said the hypothesis of natural selection in the *Origin of Species* at last offered a 'cautious reasoner' an alternative to the 'creation hypothesis'.

## Questions

People were wanting to escape from any idea of 'creation'. Natural selection enabled them to do that. Confirmation that there were clearly anti-religious motives in wanting to find such a hypothesis now comes from Richard Dawkins, the contemporary Oxford zoologist. He writes, 'Darwin made it possible to be an intellectually fulfilled atheist.'[19] Dawkins has promoted this evolutionary atheism with great zeal, but his attitude is only one side of the story. A senior palaeontologist at the British Natural History Museum, along with many others, reflects the more sceptical approach. Not so long ago, at a lecture for experts in his field, he asked his audience the following question:

> *Can you tell me anything you know about evolution, any one thing ... that is true? I tried that question on the geology staff at the Field Museum of Natural History and the only answer I got was silence. I tried it on the members of the Evolutionary Morphology seminar in the University of Chicago, a very prestigious body of evolutionists, and all I got there was silence for a long time and eventually one person said 'I do know one thing – it ought not to be taught in high school.'*[20]

The palaeontologist went on to suggest that both evolution and creationism are forms of pseudo-knowledge. His subsequent remarks do not allow us to be sure what he really thinks, but he certainly indicates that not all is straightforward.

[19] Quoted in Philip E. Johnson, *Darwin on Trial*, Crowborough, Monarch, 1994, p. 9.

[20] Ibid., p. 10.

One problem is that 'evolution' can mean any number of things, from the obvious truth that bacteria evolve resistance to certain antibiotics or the obvious truth that as a matter of fact so often 'the fittest survive', to the questionable metaphysical proposition that mankind 'evolved' entirely through purposeless, mechanical forces.

First, therefore, we must always ask, 'Are we talking about "micro-evolution" within species? Or are we talking about the "macro-evolution" of the cosmos?' The former clearly takes place. But what is the evidence for the latter?

More and more people are expressing doubts. Simple natural selection and the survival of the fittest, driving an ideology of evolution, no longer has the plausibility it once possessed. The zoologist Pierre Grassé, speaking of Julian Huxley (T.H's grandson) and other evolutionary biologists, now says that their 'evolution' was

> *simply the observation of demographic facts, local fluctuations of genotypes, geographical distributions. Often the species concerned have remained practically unchanged for hundreds of centuries! Fluctuation as a result of circumstances, with prior modification of the genome, does not imply evolution, and we have tangible proof of this in many panchronic species [i.e. living fossils that remain unchanged for millions of years].*[21]

As significant as the questions about human evolution are the new findings in geology. Following the relatively recent eruption of Mount St Helens in the US on 18 May 1980, the work of Steve Austin is reintroducing catastrophe theory. The volcano's eruption and the succeeding years have provided a real-time laboratory for testing theories of geological formation. What has been discovered is mind-stretching. The research has discovered that canyons and rock layers, far from taking millions of years to develop, can form in a few years if natural volcanic forces are great enough.[22] It also has major implications for coal theory.

This is all in sharp contrast to the earlier ground-breaking geological theories of men like James Hutton (1726–97),

[21] Ibid., p. 27.
[22] See the video lecture, Steve Austin, *Mount St Helens: Explosive Evidence for Catastrophe in Earth's History*, Creation Science Foundation, Queensland, Australia.

suggesting a general 'uniformitarianism' and an absence of catastrophes (such as the Flood). This uniformitarianism led to the view in the nineteenth century that the earth's history consisted of successive, unimaginably long geological epochs. This was a necessary condition for Darwin's theories to be plausible.

Questions are now also being raised about radiocarbon dating. One hypothesis concerns the decay of the earth's magnetic field, positing an exponential rate of decay, thus giving a stronger magnetic field in the past. This would have shielded the earth from cosmic radiation and produced lower amounts of carbon 14. Whether this is convincing or not, little by little the unquestioned assumptions of ideological Darwinism are at least being put up for discussion.

## PHILOSOPHY AND THE BIBLE

The challenge is not only in matters of science. The philosophy of science, as we have seen, is raising questions about the logical nature of scientific hypotheses. Are they to be considered 'descriptions' of reality, or are a number of them more like 'models' which have built into them inferring techniques that help us solve problems? The model may be *based* on reality, but it is not to be taken as *a picture* of reality.

There is now also a challenge to the critics of the Bible and their general stereotype of the biblical 'fundamentalist'. It is at last recognized that the so-called 'fundamentalists' of the early part of the twentieth century were far from being the type of bigots popularly portrayed in films such as *Inherit the Wind*. The men, for example, who wrote the series of essays called *The Fundamentals* between 1910 and 1915, and from which the word 'fundamentalist' is derived, were for the most part distinguished scholars. B.B. Warfield, the fundamentalist of fundamentalists and one of the essayists, was a Professor at Princeton in the US and an intellectual giant. For the record, he believed that evolution could be a method God used in Creation. He was actually a 'theistic evolutionist'.

Another essayist and great fundamentalist, James Orr, a Professor of Theology at Glasgow, was concerned that evolution theory was denying the doctrine of original sin and the Fall. His views have been summarized by Kirsten Beckett as follows: 'If evolution is guided – and not necessarily slow, but proceeding with sudden mutations which introduce new factors – then the problem is changed. It may not be possible to *prove* that original man was sinless, but there is now room for such an origin.'[23]

So how did the fundamentalists treat the Bible? In Volume I of *The Fundamentals* James Orr wrote,

> *What I see in these narratives of Genesis is that, so true is the standpoint of the author, so divine the illumination with which he is endowed, so unerring his insight into the order of nature, there is little in his description that even yet, with our advanced knowledge, we need to change. You say there is the 'six days' and the question whether those days are meant to be measured by the twenty-four hours of the sun's revolution around the earth – I speak of these things popularly. It is difficult to see how they should be so measured when the sun that is to measure them is not introduced until the fourth day. Do not think that this larger reading of the days is a new speculation. You find Augustine in early times declaring that it is hard or altogether impossible to say of what fashion these days are, and Thomas Aquinas, in the middle ages, leaves the matter an open question. To my mind these narratives in Genesis stand out as a marvel, not for its discordance with science, but for its agreement with it.*[24]

Therefore he believes the following:

> *It is clear that the narratives of Creation, the Fall, the Flood, are not myths, but narratives enshrining the knowledge or memory of real transactions. The creation of the world was certainly not a myth, but a fact, and the representation of the stages of creation dealt likewise with facts. The language used was not that of modern science, but, under divine guidance, the sacred writer gives a broad, general picture which conveys a true idea of the order of the divine working in*

[23] Kirsten Beckett, 'Darwin and the Fundamentalists', *Kategoria*, no. 2, winter, 1996, p. 51.

[24] James Orr, 'The Early Narratives of Genesis', in R.A. Torrey, A.C. Dixon et al., *The Fundamentals Volume 1*, Grand Rapids, Baker Books, 1993, p. 237.

*creation. Man's fall was likewise a tremendous fact, with universal consequences in sin and death to the race. Man's origin can only be explained through an exercise of direct creative activity, whatever subordinate factors evolution may have contributed.*

He concludes,

*In these narratives in Genesis and the facts which they embody is really laid the foundation of all else in the Bible. The unity of revelation binds them up with the Christian gospel.*[25]

So speaks one of the great voices of Fundamentalism. This approach is not obscurantist. It did not treat the texts in a wooden fashion, ignoring their literary form. And it realized that 'the language was not that of modern science'.

## OTHER VOICES

As James Orr said, Christians down the centuries have realized that the language of Genesis must be respected. The records of Genesis 1–3 are clearly not like the records of the Acts of the Apostles. Writing in the sixteenth century, Calvin said in his commentary on Genesis, 'Moses wrote in the popular style, which, without instruction, all ordinary persons endowed with common sense are able to understand.'[26]

More recently, in 1950, Pope Pius XII spoke of the early chapters of Genesis in *Humani Generis*:

*Although it is not right to judge them by modern standards of historical composition, such as would be applied to the great classical authors, or to the learned of our own day, they do nevertheless come under the heading of* history ... *These chapters have a naïve, symbolical way of talking, well suited to the understanding of a primitive people. But they do disclose to us certain important truths.*

[25] Ibid., p. 240.
[26] Ibid., p. 237.

Chapters 1–3 of Genesis still raise certain questions. But after nearly 150 years of detailed argument and analysis, many thoughtful people at the beginning of the twenty-first century are coming to the conclusion that Darwin does not provide the answers. Is it not wrong, therefore, to give the ideology of evolution a privileged place in our education today? As a 'myth' or 'model' it may have value if it secures results. But it should not then be taught, with all the secular prejudices we are now so used to, as reflecting 'what *really* happened' in history. T.H. Huxley invented the word 'agnostic' with regard to belief in God. Surely agnosticism with regard to the theory of evolution is what is now called for in our schools. This is not an unreasonable demand for Christians to make in respect of twenty-first-century state education.

# CHAPTER EIGHT

# RELATIVISM, EDUCATION AND MULTIFAITH RELIGION

## THE SUDAN

On leaving Oxford in 1964 I was made to confront the issue of other religions. For a short period I worked with CMS (the Church Missionary Society, as it was then called) in the Sudan. Seconded to work for the American Mission (the missionary branch of the United Presbyterian Church, the largest of the Presbyterian groupings in America), I was teaching English and Scripture. I also had a responsibility for the English language Anglican service which CMS held for southern Sudanese in Omdurman on Sundays.

I had stayed on at Oxford to complete a degree in theology, at the very time when the new theology and morality of Bishop John Robinson and his friends were beginning to erode the Christian faith. His book *Honest to God* was published in my last year at Oxford. It was also a time of waning missionary zeal. What, after all, was there to tell non-Christians in other parts of the world if much that you read about Jesus in the Bible was a myth? There was nothing really new in this 'new' theology. It was old theological liberalism with a new face. In 1879 Cardinal Newman summarized its essence like this: 'Liberalism in religion is the doctrine that there is no positive truth in religion, but that one creed is as good as another ... It is inconsistent with any recognition of any religion as *true*. It teaches that all are to be tolerated, for all are matters of opinion.'[1]

---

[1] Quoted in Vidler, *Essays in Liberality*, op. cit., p. 10.

When faced with an actual 'other religion', this approach becomes multifaithism. Multifaithism is a treating of all religions as ultimately the same – all interesting, all to be experienced and none to be privileged.

Most of the Africans that I met saw through the folly of all this. Mission bureaucrats in England and America, however, seemed less perceptive. Such a minimized gospel, therefore, was part of the prevailing mood back home when I went to Africa in the 1960s. The theological revisionism which went alongside this view was generating a culture of relativism. It was this that undergirded the new multifaithism. 'There is one thing a professor can be absolutely certain of,' writes the American academic Alan Bloom about his own students. 'Almost every student entering the university believes, or says he believes, that truth is relative ... Relativism is necessary to openness; and this is the virtue, the only virtue, which all primary education for more than fifty years has dedicated itself to inculcating.' The threat for the relativist is therefore clear: 'The true believer is the real danger.'[2]

This is frightening, but it is the stuff of political correctness in the Western world and the Western Church. Bloom sees the social consequences of such relativism where there are no agreed beliefs. He asks, 'When there are no shared goals or vision of the public good, is the social contract any longer possible?'

With that intellectual climate developing in the West, I took off from London Heathrow airport in one of the original Comet jet aircraft in October 1964 to fly to Khartoum, the capital of the Sudan. Rioting and tear gas met me on my arrival, as the government of the day was being overthrown. A new period was beginning – a period of tyrannical rule from the Muslim north with dreadful persecution of the Christian and animist south. Tragically, this has continued on and off ever since.

RIOTS

Soon I was at work at the Omdurman Commercial High School, teaching Higher (i.e. A-level) Scripture and English literature.

[2] Alan Bloom, *The Closing of the American Mind*, New York, Simon and Schuster, 1987, pp. 25–6.

Imagine my surprise on finding that the national mission authorities in America had decreed that Christian mission schools should have Muslim clerics come in to teach the Muslim pupils about Islam. In the north of the Sudan most of the students were Muslim. But the Muslim students in our own school came there of their own free choice. I could not believe it. Was that what Christians in America and Britain were sacrificially giving money to missions for – to subsidize the indoctrination of Muslims by Muslims? I had gone there to teach the Christian faith (in a sensitive way, I trust) to Muslims, not to provide a free environment for the spread of Islam. The theory was that the more Muslim students knew of Islam, the better would be their dialogue with Christian students.

The reality was very different. There seemed to be a growing distance between Muslim and Christian students, and in our school a growing opposition from some Muslim students to the headmaster, a fine northern Sudanese who was a black Arab but Christian. Far from Christian–Muslim relations improving, the opposite was happening. It was not long before I looked out of the glassless window of my classroom during a lesson and saw hundreds of boys (16–18-year-olds) storming over our school's perimeter wall. Joined by a number of our own Muslim pupils, they proceeded to break up the school. The main object of attack was our northern Christian headmaster. Eventually I had to close my class, go out into the quadrangle and make for the headmaster's study. There was only one other 'white' teacher around. As 'Horatios at the Bridge', we blocked the way into the headmaster's study while these violent Sudanese adolescents fought to get to him. We thought that the rioters would be less likely to attack us, being expatriates. It was not a pleasant experience. Tanks soon arrived, but the northern soldiers only looked on. It was not until the classrooms had been vandalized, desks broken, lights ripped out and general mayhem had been wreaked that the troops entered the campus and threw tear gas to disperse the crowds. I could hardly avoid the conclusion that the multifaith approach to mission was not a great success.

At the time this particular school was one of the very few places in the entire Sudan – an area the size of Europe – where southerners could receive a school education. All the schools in the south (as well as the hospitals) had been closed. In Omdurman we were able to provide some help for the fortunate few. But not now: the school had to shut. Unilaterally and privately, I decided to give some of the southern students tuition in my home. That was all I could do.

The closure of the school was not the end of our troubles. The Presbyterian American Mission Centre in the middle of Khartoum was also totally destroyed one Sunday evening soon afterwards. The large centre had contained a radio station, missionary residences and educational and sports facilities. This time literally thousands of northern Sudanese were involved in a siege, attacking some southerners who had come to the mission centre for protection. People were killed that night in the city.

Killing generally was increasing in the Sudan. One of our teachers, an able southerner, went to a wedding in Malakal one week and he reported that a large number of the male guests were shot by the (northern) army at the reception. Remarkably, he managed to escape.

Perhaps understandably, in the light of these experiences, I have some reservations about multifaithism and, indeed, about Islam. The Muslims I taught were delightful. A few of the teaching staff covering technical subjects were Muslim and they were great colleagues. We had a good time socially. I just thought they were quite wrong in what they believed. Their Muslim faith offered instruction, but not salvation. They saw ignorance as the problem, not sin or that deep moral corruption that exists in every human heart. And my conviction was growing all the time that, as a faith, Islam gave rise to a political culture that did not sustain the tolerance and freedom I believed to be vital. The doctrine of hell should lead to the belief that God will not force belief. Nor must we.

To argue this in the 1960s was hard, and it was getting harder all the time. In the late 1980s I was giving a lecture at Newcastle University. During the question time I said that I preferred the political arrangements of the West, where they had been influenced by the Bible, to the political arrangements of many repressive Muslim societies.[3] I said I would rather live in Newcastle, where

[3] See the arguments in David Holloway, *A Nation under God*, Eastbourne, Kingsway Publications, 1986.

there was freedom for Christian churches (and for mosques), than in Tehran at that time under the mullahs. This public expression of preference was greeted with horror by a number of students. One threatened to report me to the Race Relations Board. To argue for the rightness of Christianity (*not* of the West) and the wrongness of Islam (or of any other faith or philosophy) in our now stridently relativist culture is very difficult indeed. The odds are stacked against you – particularly so in the vital and influential field of education.

## EDUCATION AND THE NEW CLASS

There is an obvious interaction between schools and the institutions of higher education where teachers are taught what to teach. And there is a crisis in these higher institutions. The President of Johns Hopkins University in the United States summarized the problem like this: 'The failure to rally around a set of values means that universities are turning out potentially highly skilled barbarians.'[4]

To indicate how low we have sunk spiritually in higher education, we can take as examples two of the most famous universities in the world – Harvard in the US and Oxford in the UK. Harvard's original charter contains the following educational mandate: 'Everyone shall consider the main end of his life and studies to know Jesus Christ which is eternal life.'[5] The motto of Oxford – as can be seen from the Oxford University crest – is '*Dominus illuminatio mea*', the opening words of Psalm 27 – 'The Lord is my light.' That mandate and that motto, however, are miles away from the current educational philosophies of Harvard and Oxford.

How has this change come about? If there are flaws in secular humanistic philosophies, as we saw in Chapter 6, why do people accept them?

Ever since the evolution of the 'sociology of knowledge' in Germany in the 1920s – popularized to the English-speaking world by Karl Mannheim – we have known that the social environment

---

[4] In J. Stanley Oakes, Jr, 'The Last Hope for the University', in Roy Abraham Varghese (ed.), *The Intellectuals Speak out about God*, Chicago, Regnery Gateway, 1984, p. xxii.

[5] Ibid., p. xxii.

powerfully conditions beliefs. The sociology of knowledge is common sense. The principle is simply that when, for example, postmodern intellectuals say that we must be sensitive to this or that aberrant behaviour or new set of anti-Christian views, it is not just reason that dictates these new attitudes. There is a 'plausibility structure' in place which means people are *conditioned* to feel that such new morality or new beliefs are reasonable. This 'feeling' of reasonableness often has little to do with logic and much to do with social conditioning. Today this social conditioning is effected not least by education and the media – and what goes on in education and the media is being determined by the 'new class'.

The American sociologists Peter and Brigitte Berger (and others) have highlighted the importance of this 'new class' in the analysis of contemporary society. The new class hypothesis contradicts the common assumption that modern democracies are ruled and run by the 'middle class'. It argues, instead, that in all advanced capitalist societies the middle class has split. On the one hand there is the 'old' middle class – producing goods and services and made up of business people and the older professions. On the other hand there is a 'new' middle class – producing 'knowledge', through education and the media (especially the electronic media) as well as through the administration and delivery of social and therapeutic services.

Brigitte Berger says this new class 'controls many of the institutions central to the so-called post-industrial society ... the vast educational empire, the media ... and a seemingly boundless therapeutic apparatus, as well as increasing segments of both public and private administration.'[6] And the new class is seeking to extend its power and influence. It has vested interests in increasing centralism, as centralized funding – like the tax system or the BBC licence fee – often provides most of its support. Furthermore, it has acquired far greater influence than the old middle class, because as a 'knowledge class' it can direct and control communal information.

It also pervades the world of the Church, which then further affects the world of education in terms of religious education. As in

[6] Brigitte Berger, 'The "New Class" as Guarantor of "the Good Life"', in Richard John Neuhaus (ed.), *Guaranteeing the Good Life: Medicine and the Return of Eugenics*, Grand Rapids, Eerdmans, 1990, p. 1999.

the wider society, so in the Church: members of the new class are not in a majority, yet they have disproportionate influence. Many of the Church's leaders – both clergy and central bureaucrats – are part of the new class. This is ensured by today's higher education, which is coloured by new-class assumptions and attitudes.

The new class is in a linear succession from the European humanistic Enlightenment. Apart from the basic Enlightenment convictions that man is perfectible through education or evolution and that God, if he exists, is distant, the main emphases of new-class values cluster around the concept of human self-fulfilment. The new class also has a scant regard for history and the past. It follows Kant's view of 'enlightenment' as human beings and human society growing up from 'immaturity'. It is 'immature' to rely on 'the guidance of another' or the wisdom of the ages. Common sense calls much of this 'reinventing the wheel'. New class enthusiasts call it 'exploration'.

It is these people, 'new class' clerics and laypeople from the churches, who often find their way onto the Local Education Authority committees which determine the religious syllabuses in our schools. And it is these people who too often seem to staff the teacher training institutions in our universities and colleges. They are also present in the central Church committees which deal with education. As I explained above, these are people socially conditioned to respond in predictable ways to a whole range of issues. It is not surprising, therefore, to find a disproportionate amount of liberal theology and multifaithism in our schools.

New-class values *are* less sympathetic to the orthodox Christian faith than the values held by the rest of the population. One American study in 1985 contrasted 3,000 members of the public with nearly the same number of journalists. According to the results, while only 49 per cent of the public were in favour of abortion, 82 per cent of the journalists were. While as many as 74 per cent of the public wanted worship or prayer in state schools, only 25 per cent of the journalists did. These results cannot be explained away by saying, 'It's all a matter of education.' In a comparison between business executives and journalists, 76 per cent of the executives thought adultery was wrong, but only 47 per cent of the journalists did. Only 13 per cent of the executives said they had no religious faith, but 50 per cent of the journalists said they had none.[7] This is not the only study with these sorts of findings. They provide evidence of the anti-religious and immoral views of the gatekeepers of public knowledge and information as we enter the twenty-first century.

## IGNORANCE OF THE CHRISTIAN FAITH

As a result of the 'agreed syllabuses' for religious education adopted by a number of Local Education Authorities, our children are now often illiterate in terms of Christianity. While I was on the General Synod, I heard the then Home Secretary, Douglas Hurd, say that for many children it was as though the Old Testament had never been written. A MORI poll at Easter 1991 revealed appalling ignorance, especially among young people, of the basic elements of the Christian faith. Reporting on this poll, the press said, 'Many Church leaders and politicians laid the blame firmly at the feet of the country's education system.'[8]

The prevailing culture of relativism is also to blame. Openness to everything is fair, if you believe the humanistic assumption that in principle everything is good. Few of us actually believe that, however. We do not want to be 'open' to Muslims killing southern Sudanese, or Serbs killing Muslims in the Balkans, or a host of wicked actions being perpetrated around the world. We want to say that some things are wrong absolutely, and for good reasons. We also want to say that some things are true. Many want to say that Jesus Christ is the way, the truth and the life, and that this particular truth is as relevant for public life as it is for private life. We do not believe we should *force* our views on anyone. We do believe, however, that we should seek to persuade and educate people into the truth.

Are there grounds for such beliefs, however? Is it reasonable to talk about the uniqueness of Jesus Christ? Some will say that belief

[7] Thomas R. Dye, Harmon Zeigler and S. Robert Lichter, *American Politics in the Media Age*, Pacific Grove, Brooks/Cole, 1992, pp. 96, 101.

[8] *Sunday Express*, 31 March 1991.

in Christ's uniqueness is due to ignorance or arrogance. But ignorance is a two-way argument. Many orthodox Christians have considerable experience of other religions, more so than their opponents. And it must be stressed that truth has nothing to do with arrogance, pride or humility. Rather it has all to do with facts. The claim to Christ's uniqueness and finality – he has no successors – is a truth claim and, therefore, it is a matter of fact. All claims about Jesus cannot therefore be right or true. Peter Cotterell, an English missiologist, puts it like this:

> *Islam says Jesus wasn't crucified. We say he was. Only one of us can be right. Judaism says Jesus was not the Messiah. We say he was. Only one of us can be right. Hinduism says that God has often been incarnate. We say only once. And we can't both be right. Buddhism says that the world's miseries will end when we do what's right. We say, you can't do what's right: the world's miseries will end when we believe what is right.*
>
> *The fact is that the world's religions may agree about the peripheral matters but they disagree precisely about the most important matters of all. Any intelligent person could decide that all religions are wrong. Any intelligent person could decide that one is right and the rest wrong. But no intelligent person can seriously believe that all religions are essentially the same.*[9]

This is not Western triumphalism. To say that Christ is unique is not to say that other cultures are therefore automatically inferior while all is well with the West; nor is it even to say that Christian activities are unique. The uniqueness lies simply in *the person in whom Christians believe*. It is Christ who is unique, not the West or the followers who worship him.

We have to be alert on all fronts. A major problem will come in society and in our schools not from the main religions wanting to disagree, but from 'New Age' spirituality. This is the religion made for an age of 'openness' and of the relativism being taught at schools, in universities and by the media. It is basically the belief

[9] In *The London Bible College Review*, 1989; see Peter Cotterell, *Mission and Meaninglessness*, London, SPCK, 1990, pp. 209–27 for a fuller analysis of Islam.

that the 'spiritual' is good and all is 'one'. It is the assumption that God can be known directly in the human spirit. It is a mystical pantheism. If we are spiritual, we will find God in our inner selves, it says, so Jesus Christ is unnecessary. Before long we are into Earth Mother mysticism and the occult. But that is another story.

## THE CULTURAL LIMITATIONS OF KNOWLEDGE

Multifaithism is an ongoing threat. There is already some syncretistic, multifaith worship in schools – and sometimes also in churches.

Multifaithism is motored by three pressures. Paul Knitter refers to these in the preface to *The Myth of Christian Uniqueness* as: one, 'the historico-cultural limitations of all knowledge and religious beliefs'; two, 'religious experience [being] infinite'; and three, 'the confrontation with the sufferings of humanity and the need to put an end to such outrages'.[10]

These are big issues, and I will just touch on them here. Knitter is going back to the sociology of knowledge, and the concept that the social environment powerfully conditions beliefs. Most of this is common sense, as I said before. It is clear that, apart from a few areas of direct personal experience, human beings require the social support of people who think the same way in order to maintain their beliefs about reality. For example, an individual does not need someone else to prove that he has toothache. But he does need social support for a wide range of religious and moral beliefs. Peter Berger puts it like this: 'Physical pain imposes its own plausibility without any social mediations, while morality [or religion] requires particular social circumstances in order to become and remain plausible to the individual.'[11]

In modern societies, these social circumstances form a range of 'plausibility structures'. Take the armed forces or British public schools as examples. So long as people are in such institutions,

---

[10] John Hick and Paul F. Knitter (eds), *The Myth of Christian Uniqueness*, London, SCM Press, 1987, pp. ix–xi.

[11] Peter L. Berger, *The Heretical Imperative*, London, Collins, 1980, p. 18.

certain values will be plausible in an unquestioned way. Once they move out and 'migrate' to other social contexts, these values may be questioned. This is surely obvious.

We can also say that there is a direct relationship between the cohesion of institutions and common beliefs, values and world-views. When a school is strong and effective, its pupils will most likely have the same value system with regard to discipline, manners and the importance of hard work. Similarly, when institutions break up, there will be a break-up of plausibility structures and consequently a weakening of every belief and value that depends on social support. So a weak school will have pupils who are likely to be disorderly, disobedient and lazy.

In part this is the reason why multifaith worship is such a sensitive issue; and why multifaith worship in cathedrals and abbeys is *super*sensitive. It is, in itself, an act of institutional deconstruction. If it is right to do it, fine; but if it is wrong, it is a much more serious issue than mere theological sloppiness. It is destroying the social support of belief (biblical Christian belief as upheld by the Church down the ages) for many people.

We need not develop this further. All we need to note is the following: Knitter seems to be aware of the fact that people require social support for beliefs and that their own social environment is a factor in what they believe. In his jargon this is 'the cultural limitation of knowledge and religious beliefs'. But the suggestion that we *therefore* have to accept multifaithism is simply wrong. It is to confuse *how* we come to believe with *what* we believe. Truth questions *still* have to be faced.

The sociology of knowledge in no way removes questions of truth. It can show why modern people find it easier to believe in electricity than in demons, but the question of whether demons really exist still remains. The sociology of knowledge can show why modern Christians feel reluctant to say that Jesus Christ was God's unique and final revelation to mankind, but the question of whether he was or whether he was not also still remains.

## RELIGIOUS EXPERIENCE

Knitter goes on to talk about 'religious experience' as the second lead into multifaithism. Since Friedrich Schleiermacher, a German theologian at the beginning of the nineteenth century, there has been a belief in a reservoir of 'world spirituality'. All religions then tap into this one source and draw up nourishment for their own varieties of 'religious experience'. This, it is said, means that all religions are basically related and 'one'. Add to that the effect of the 'History of Religions School' at the beginning of the twentieth century, which not only mapped out but tried to synthesize the religions of the world, thus reinforcing a concern for experience. Add to that various pronouncements on interfaith matters by the WCC (the World Council of Churches) in the second half of the twentieth century. Then add the Roman Catholic post-Vatican II stress that God's grace is given not only to adherents of non-Christian religions but even to some atheists. And finally, add the Roman Catholic Karl Rahner's talk about 'anonymous Christians' – some people of other faiths whom, he said, ought to be regarded as 'Christians'. If you take all these things on board, do not then be surprised when you find you have both a growing belief in the value of *any* religious experience and also new 'plausibility structures'.

Now put yourself in the position of a member of the clergy who has inherited this legacy through theological college, conferences, periodicals and synods. You are asked to take a stand against the multifaith philosophy – say with respect to your local school. How would you respond? As a result of this theological tide, you would probably *feel* that it is reasonable to support interfaith ventures (even when your head tells you otherwise). This feeling, however, may well have nothing to do with theological logic – it is, in fact, socially conditioned.

With regard to religious experience, traditional Christian theology has always been cautious. As Jesus said in the Sermon on the Mount, 'Many will say to me on that day, "Lord, Lord, did we not prophesy in your name, and in your name drive out demons and perform many miracles?" Then I will tell them plainly, "I never knew you. Away from me, you evil-doers!"' (Matthew 7:22). Here were people with dramatic 'religious experience', but that did not justify them in the sight of Christ.

Interest in religious experience is, however, reinforced by the 'concentric circle' way of looking at other religions. This seeks to weigh the relative merit of the varieties of religious experience in the world. This approach may have spread originally from Roman Catholic teaching such as that contained in the Papal Encyclical *Ecclesiam Suam* of 1964. The model is of the Roman Catholic Church forming the centre circle; then a little further out are other Christian Churches; beyond them is a circle of other theists; beyond that a circle of various animistic and non-theistic religions; then on the far edge are the secularists with no religion at all.

Is it correct, though, to measure other religions by their nearness to or distance from Christianity? As Lesslie Newbigin said,

> *The other religions are not to be understood and measured by their proximity to or remoteness from Christianity. They are not beginnings which are completed in the gospel. They face in different directions, ask fundamentally different questions and look for other kinds of fulfilment than that which is given in the gospel. They turn, as Otto said, on different axes.*[12]

In the parable Jesus tells in Luke 18:9–14, was the Pharisee or the tax collector nearer to God? The Pharisee, no doubt, could claim a whole range of religious experiences. He was committed to 'fasting' – a tried-and-tested adjunct of religious experience. But it was the tax collector who went down to his house 'justified'. He had *no* 'religious experience'. He simply recognized his need and prayed: 'God have mercy on me, a sinner.'

## JUSTICE

Knitter also expresses a concern for justice and 'the sufferings of humanity', as his third element of multifaith motivation. His argument is that to assert the truth of the Christian faith against other

---

[12] Lesslie Newbigin, *The Finality of Christ*, London, SCM Press, 1968, p. 44.

religions and worldviews is essentially a denial of justice. Justice demands toleration.

As I said in Chapter 1, there is so much confusion over the meaning of 'toleration'. It has been argued that if you are truly tolerant of others, you will not critically evaluate their beliefs. But this is to equate tolerance with indifference. There is a commonly held but mistaken view that tolerating a religion is primarily a matter of not making a judgement about it. That is not the case. Tolerance involves the acceptance of something about which you have come to a negative opinion or negative judgement.

Let me quote a humanist, non-Christian writer on this very point – Professor Bernard Crick:

> *Reacting against the religious disputes of the seventeenth century, toleration both as a state policy and an educated attitude began to spread in Britain in the eighteenth century. But let us remember one essential thing about tolerance. It arises because people do differ on fundamental and important things, but wish to limit the practical effect of their differences. Tolerance is not complete acceptance, still less permissiveness; it is modified disapproval.*[13]

He is clearly right. Asserting the truth of the Christian faith (evangelism is one form of this) is not necessarily intolerant. It should not be classed as a denial of justice. Indeed, as Lesslie Newbigin also says, not to evangelize people of other faiths is unjust: 'It surely is a very peculiar form of racism which would affirm that the good news entrusted to us is strictly for white Anglo-Saxons!'

Moving on from the pressures which drive multifaithism, however, we must turn to more direct theological issues, as a great amount of 'good stout resolute nonsense' (to quote Lord Halifax) is talked about it.[14] The claim to the uniqueness and finality of Jesus Christ is a truth claim and, therefore, a question of fact. All claims, as we saw earlier, cannot be right. When it comes to the Christian faith we are talking about a 'gospel', or 'the good news' about what God has done in history. We are not talking about 'good ideas'. The

[13] Bernard Crick, 'A Humanist Perspective', in Haddon Willmer (ed.), *2020 Visions*, London, SPCK, 1992, p. 112.

[14] Ibid., p. 113.

question is, therefore, 'Did God do certain things or did he not?' Christians claim that the central action of God in history is in the incarnation, death and resurrection of Jesus (see Chapter 12). But God's action in revealing himself through the prophets and later through Jesus' apostles is also vital. Their teaching is what you have in the Bible. So what does the Bible teach about other faiths?

## THEOLOGICAL ISSUES

A fair reading of the Bible, I believe, would suggest five main reasons for rejecting current multifaith theology and philosophy, and these are outlined below.

*First,* what we read of the world's religions in the Bible is very often negative. When Paul was having an afternoon off in Athens and saw the evidence of other religions in the city, he did not think about the possibilities for interfaith worship: 'His spirit was provoked within him' (Acts 17:16), and he ended up trying to convert the Athenians.[15]

*Secondly,* God can choose whom he likes to receive his grace. Melchizedek and Jethro in the Old Testament come to mind as two unlikely characters outside the ancient covenant community. But there is no suggestion that their 'religions' could in any way be *viable alternatives* to the covenant revealed to Abraham and Moses.

Likewise, in the New Testament the Wise Men received divine guidance, but there is no suggestion that they were saved by their own religion. In fact, God brought them to worship the child Jesus.

Later on in the New Testament we read that the prayers of the Gentile Cornelius were heard by God. Peter therefore concluded that 'in every nation any one who fears [God] and does what is right is acceptable to him' (Acts 10:34). But Cornelius himself said, under divine prompting, that 'salvation' required more than those prayers: it required the preaching and message of Peter, i.e. the gospel (Acts 11:13).

Clearly, preparation for faith occurs outside the community of the people of God. The story of the Ethiopian eunuch (Acts

[15] 1 Corinthians 8–10 is essential reading for an understanding of Paul's theology on these matters.

8:26–39) is another example of this process, and there are countless people following a similar course today. But the fact is that in whatever way God meets with people in other religious (or secular) settings, the Bible gives us no grounds for saying there is full salvation *apart from* acknowledging Christ. Other religions (or secular philosophies) may play a part in helping to identify needs, but there is no salvation except in the name of Jesus Christ (Acts 4:12). This is not 'anonymous Christianity' at all!

*Thirdly,* confusion comes through failing to distinguish the Holy Spirit's dual work – in creation and universal history on the one hand, and in redemption and salvation history on the other. Ever since the Reformation there has been a tendency in the West to make redemption everything and to ignore creation. The result is that God's work is assumed to be always and only redemptive, even when what he is doing is creative. Of course, he is engaged in redemptive work for, in and with the person of Christ and through the preaching of the gospel; that is his great work. But we must never ignore his creative activity – his direct activity in sustaining our wonderful world, which people of all faiths and none can explore and develop; and his indirect activity through the creative and artistic skills he gives to people of all faiths and none.

With that background, the traditional categories of 'general' and 'special' revelation and 'common' and 'saving' grace are helpful. General revelation is what God reveals of himself by creation, in nature and through conscience. Special revelation is God's revelation in Christ and through the prophets and apostles (i.e. now through the Bible). Common grace includes all the blessings of this life – the sun shines on the righteous and the unrighteous, after all. Saving grace is salvation and redemption through Christ alone.

Much of the interfaith confusion, surely, comes because general revelation, understood in other religions, is seen to be special and common grace, experienced in other religions, is seen to be saving.

*Fourthly,* confusion can also come, and a position of uncritical openness can be adopted, because of the way religion is often identified with culture. We may rightly wish to affirm elements of another culture that is shaped by a non-Christian religion. At the same time we may be critical of some (or much) cultural baggage present in Western Christianity. That is not the same, however, as affirming the truth of that other system of belief and worship, or rejecting the truth of Christianity. For the Christian the bottom line has to be that nobody comes to the Father except through Christ (John 14:6).

*Fifthly*, we should not say that God's common grace is never experienced in other religious (or secular) contexts; nor that general revelation is never heeded in other religious (or secular) contexts. Nevertheless, we must accept the recorded words of Jesus, who said that his Father seeks '*true* worshippers' (John 4:23). Worship should not only be in spirit but also *in truth*. For the Christian believer this will rule out misleading 'interfaith' worship experiences, of the kind that are sometimes forced on children in our schools.

## POSTSCRIPT

It is a fact that much interfaith activity is initiated by theologically liberal Christians. Kim Knott admits this. She sees interfaith dialogue as 'the liberal corrective to heavy-handed missionary activity and religious exclusivism on the part of Western, particularly British, Christians'. But she also says,

> Anyone involved in dialogue will willingly concede that it is a minority interest that captures the hearts and minds of very few traditional, evangelical, mystically oriented or nominal members of different faith communities. In addition, not all, but many, are Christian, and it is almost always Christians who are responsible for founding groups and writing about the dialogical enterprise.[16]

Multifaithism and interfaith activity is thus the agenda of a minority of theological liberals which is imposed on others. It needs to be resisted.

You may ask, 'Should there then be no dialogue with adherents of other religions?' It depends on what you mean by 'dialogue'. In

---

[16] Kim Knott, 'Points of View', in Haddon (ed.), *2020 Visions*, op. cit., p. 94.

the early days of multifaithism E.J. Sharpe identified a fourfold ladder of dialogue. He spoke of discursive dialogue (where you share beliefs), human dialogue (where you get to know each other as persons), secular dialogue (where you engage in joint social or political action), and interior dialogue (where you sink your differences and take on each other's spirituality).[17] There has been a consistent push to descend down this 'ladder' towards the fourth rung. Many Christians can cope, and cope happily, with the first three rungs. They just deny that it is possible to descend to the fourth and still retain Christian integrity. It is not possible to believe and worship as others believe and worship, if Jesus Christ is the *only* way.

In a desire to assert the rights of people of other religions and cults in Western society, the issues covered in this chapter cannot be swept under the carpet. Truth claims will never go away. Christians claim that Jesus *is* 'the way and the truth and the life' (John 14:6). If that is true, it is not unreasonable – indeed, it is wise – for the Christian faith and not other faiths to be privileged or 'established' (tolerantly) in the State.

[17] Eric J. Sharpe, 'Goals of Inter-Religious Dialogue', in John H. Hick (ed.), *Truth and Dialogue in World Religions*, Philadelphia, Westminster, 1974, pp. 77–95.

# CHAPTER NINE

# WAR OVER
# THE FAMILY AND
# ABORTION

## BRITAIN AND THE US

In the debate within Newcastle City Council that followed the lesbian adoption scandal (see Chapter 2), a councillor who was a Liberal Democrat, a psychiatrist and a member of our congregation suggested that a family where the mother and father were committed to each other for life was in the best interests of the child. For saying that he was attacked, verbally, as having 'obscene' views.

Later I was called a number of times to discuss the family and related issues on the radio, in television debates and at other meetings. On one occasion I was with senior people involved in government, social work and the Church. In something I had been asked to write I had made what I thought was an innocent and irrefutable observation. I had said that marriage best secures a stable and enduring relationship for two parents, and then went on to say, 'Society still recognizes healthy heterosexual monogamous marriage as the ideal and proper environment for child care and nurture.'

As with the city councillor, the reaction to my comment was unbelievable. It seemed as though I too had uttered an obscenity. What I had known for a long time then went from my head to my heart: there is a 'war over the family'.

At about this time, however, I heard on the radio an interview with a social scientist who suggested there was significant research to demonstrate that what I had said was true. The common-sense view that permanent, married families did better than alternative arrangements for bringing up children on a whole number of indicators was being confirmed by hard evidence (not least in terms of crime levels). The 'love family', where the relationship generally depended on the emotional state of the parents and their individual skills, was too fragile. The 'married family' had in addition institutional, traditional and social support. Research had now proved this to be better.

At the end of the interview I discovered that the social scientist was a local Newcastle University academic, Norman Dennis. I immediately purchased copies of his books, *Families without Fatherhood* and *Rising Crime and the Dismembered Family*.[1] To my delight I found that some of the thinking and research on the family that I had already come across in the US was being taken on board in this country too. Visiting the US almost every year in the 1980s and 1990s, I was able to keep abreast of American thinking in the areas of Church, State and society. I had the good fortune to be directed to books and articles that were unknown at that stage in the UK. My visits initially took place during the Reagan years, when America experienced both an increase in permissiveness and also a countermovement, first in terms of the Moral Majority and then later from the Christian Coalition.

Believing that the kingdom of God can never be coterminous with any party political programme, I had suspicions about some Christians in the US when they seemed to suggest that being a Christian meant being right wing. At the same time I was equally suspicious about many Evangelicals and Anglicans in the UK during the same period who seemed to suggest that being a Christian meant attacking Mrs Thatcher and being left wing. Neither of these points of view seemed to me to be tenable. However, there was much to learn from both sides, and I learnt a great deal from the contacts, the literature and the research from the US.

It was obvious in the US that a Judaeo-Christian countercultural revolution was being staged – a recapturing of the ground lost since the 1960s. And much of the work was being done by sociologists,

[1] Op. cit. (see Chapter 2).

social scientists, medical doctors and people of other disciplines rather than theologians. Among the leading writers were people such as Richard Neuhaus, Michael Novak, Peter Berger and Gertrude Himmelfarb.

## UNDER ATTACK

The family has been under attack for a long time. David Cooper, an associate of the psychiatrist R.D. Laing, wrote in 1974, 'The bourgeois nuclear family ... is the principal mediating device that the capitalist ruling class uses to condition the individual, through primary socialization, to fit into some *role complex* that suits the system.'[2]

This, of course, is a Marxist analysis. In *The Communist Manifesto* Marx and Engels wrote about 'the bourgeois clap trap about the family and education, about the hallowed relation of parent and child'.[3] Then Engels, in his book *The Origin of the Family, Private Property and the State*, wrote,

> With the transformation of the means of production into collective property, the monogamous family ceases to be the economic unit of society. The private household changes to a social industry. The care and education of children becomes a public matter. Society cares equally well for all children, legal or illegal.[4]

The implication is clear – one day there will be no need for the traditional family. Not surprisingly, in the 1920s Soviet Russia tried to organize its social life according to Marxist theory and attempted to dissolve family ties. It was a disaster. Professor P.A. Sorokin, the Harvard sociologist, describes the Russian attitude of the 1920s as follows:

[2] David Cooper, *The Grammar of Living*, London, Penguin Books, 1974, p. 14.
[3] Karl Marx and Friedrich Engels, *The Communist Manifesto*, London, Penguin Books, 1967, p. 101.
[4] Quoted in O.R. Johnston, *Who Needs the Family?*, London, Hodder and Stoughton, 1979, pp. 27–8.

*The revolution leaders deliberately attempted to destroy marriage and the family. The legal distinction between marriage and casual sexual intercourse was abolished. Bigamy and polygamy were permissible under the new provisions. Abortion was facilitated in the State institutions. Pre-marital relationships were praised; extra-marital relationships were considered normal ... Within a few years millions of lives, especially of young girls, were wrecked. The hatred and conflicts ... rapidly mounted and so did psychoneuroses. Work in the nationalized factories slackened. The government was forced to reverse its policy.*[5]

All this needs to be kept in mind when it comes to contemporary discussions on the family. The family in the West has been a main carrier of values for centuries. If you want to eliminate those values, therefore, why not eliminate their carrier as well? The Russian dissident Igor Shafarevich, in his book *The Socialist Phenomenon*, explains that 'the Socialist project of homogenizing society demands that the family be vitiated or destroyed. This can be accomplished in good measure by profaning conjugal love and breaking monogamy's link between sex and loyalty. Hence, in their missionary phases Socialist movements often stress sexual "liberation".'[6]

In any discussion on the family, sexuality and marriage, however, it is vital to distinguish pastoral matters from questions about the right order for society. There will be many people today who have experienced the pain and the disorder of sin in their sexual lives, their marriages or their families. Probably for the majority there will be some near relative or close friend for whom this is the case, even if they have no direct experience themselves. There are, therefore, pastoral needs that have to be met. And the first pastoral duty for the Church is to point men and women to Jesus Christ who, through the Cross, offers forgiveness for *all* sin – sexual, marital and familial included.

Jesus knew that in dealing with sex, marriage and the family we have a 'creation ordinance'. In Mark 10:6–9 while talking about

[5] Quoted in David Watson, *In Search of God*, London, Falcon Books, 1974, p. 72.

[6] Quoted in Joseph Sobran, 'What is this Thing Called Sex?', *National Review*, 31 December 1980, pp. 1604–5.

marriage, he referred to 'the beginning of creation' – 'But at the beginning of creation God "made them male and female. For this reason a man will leave his father and mother and be united to his wife, and the two will become one flesh." So they are no longer two, but one. Therefore what God has joined together, let man not separate.'

That is to say, sex and marriage have to do with something in nature or the way God has made the world. Domestic arrangements may vary from culture to culture. Sometimes few, sometimes many of a kinship group live in proximity or relative proximity. But whatever the arrangements, there always needs to be a 'nucleus' of a father and mother and their children; and this relationship of the father and mother should be permanent. Being 'one flesh' through sexual intercourse is only to take place after there is a 'leaving of father and mother' and a 'uniting' of husband and wife. This rules out all premarital, extramarital and homosexual sex.

Of course, this nuclear family must never be idolized, in the sense of taking the place of God. Some close family ties, Jesus knew, had to be sacrificed for his kingdom. But it was a *sacrifice*. It was not giving up something that was marginal or unimportant. It was giving up ties that were deeply significant and precious. And because these ties are so important, Paul says in 1 Timothy 5:8 that 'if anyone does not provide for his relatives, and especially for his immediate family, he has denied the faith and is worse than an unbeliever.'

Today there is a particular attack on the nuclear family underway. There is no way the nuclear family can be sidelined, however. In his book *Social Structures*, George Murdock analysed 250 societies and found that the nuclear family was the universal and basic social grouping. Not all those societies followed a Christian sexual ethic. Of the 250, 65 societies allowed general promiscuity to the unmarried and 20 others gave qualified assent to premarital promiscuity.[7] The great majority, however, appear to have required sexual restraint. What seems non-negotiable is the nuclear family.

---

[7] Johnston, *Who Needs the Family?*, op. cit., p. 41.

## SEXUAL RESTRAINT AND THE ANGLICAN REPORT

Marriage and premarriage patterns have huge significance. Another anthropologist, J.D. Unwin, in his monumental work *Sex and Culture,* tells us that his researches led to two general conclusions. The first is that 'the cultural condition of any society in any geographical environment is conditioned by its past and present methods of regulating the relations between the sexes.' The second is that 'no society can display productive social energy unless a new generation inherits a social system under which sexual opportunity is reduced to a minimum.'[8]

The tradition of the Western Christian sexual ethic and family pattern received remarkable support from this research. 'The greatest energy,' said Unwin, 'has been displayed only by those societies which have reduced their sexual opportunity to a minimum by the adoption of absolute monogamy.'[9] As Professor V.A. Demant of Oxford puts it, 'Part of the mastery over nature in man's own life has been a mastery over the sexual impulse, to a degree in European Christendom not known elsewhere. But it has been known or practised to some degree throughout mankind's civilized history. All cultural development has meant a limitation of sexual drives.'[10]

None of this information appeared in the report on the family from the Board for Social Responsibility of the General Synod of the Church of England, published in 1995 and called *Something to Celebrate.*[11] Its subtitle was 'Valuing Families in Church and Society'. Its conclusion was that the Christian understanding of the traditional family is overrated. Families have now changed. The two-parent family with children has given way to a 'richly creative' diversity that includes one-parent families, cohabitation and even gay relationships. Cohabitation is now, according to the report, acceptable. 'Christians [are] both to hold fast to the centrality of

[8] J.D. Unwin, *Sex and Culture,* Oxford University Press, 1934, pp. 340, 414.
[9] Ibid., p. 431.
[10] V.A. Demant, *An Exposition of Christian Sex Ethics,* London, Hodder and Stoughton, 1963, p. 100.
[11] *Something to Celebrate – Valuing Families in Church and Society,* London, Church House Publishing, 1995.

marriage and at the same time to accept that cohabitation is, for many people, a step along the way towards that fuller and more complete commitment.'[12]

The report, as usual with such Church publications, contained much that was good and interesting. But as Colin Hart, the director of the Christian Institute, said, 'The report is like a cup of coffee. It is no good saying that most of your cup contains good coffee if it also contains three teaspoonfuls of strychnine when even one will kill you!' That report, however, was only part of a trend among Christians. A short essay at the time in a set of Bible-reading notes claimed that 'the traditional family is far from either following an Old Testament model for family life or echoing the values of the kingdom of God.'

Of course, there is much in traditional family life that is fallen, that is not perfect. But to think that, this side of heaven, the ideal of a communitarian 'kingdom of God' can allow us to marginalize the 'traditional family' is a dangerous folly. It was proposed at the time of the Reformation by radical reformers, and it has been proposed since by millennial cults. It ends up with people today like David Koresh and his followers, and in their case the incineration at the Texan Waco disaster of 1993.

As the twentieth century ended, however, it seemed that change was in the air in the UK. The Church of England's Board for Social Responsibility, responsible for that earlier report *Something to Celebrate*, responded more positively to the British Home Office's Green Paper on 'Supporting Families'. At least it made the assertion that 'any weakening of marriage ... has serious implications for the mutual belonging and care that is exercised in the community at large.'[13]

## STATISTICS

As we enter the twenty-first century, it is established that family breakdown means that the UK has the worst teenage pregnancy

[12] Ibid., p. 115.

[13] A consultation paper, 'Stronger Families for Everyone', London, Conservative Christian Fellowship, 1999, p. 9.

rate in the whole of Europe. And that is despite the fact that the distribution of contraceptives to 14- and 15-year-old girls has risen in the last quarter of a century by over 1,000 per cent. Eight thousand girls under the age of 16 have unplanned pregnancies every year and half of these pregnancies end with abortion. Forty thousand teenagers have abortions every year.[14] The Conservative Christian Fellowship has asked: 'Is it more than a coincidence that the nearly five million abortions since the passage of the 1967 Act have coincided with an increasing problem of child abuse and family breakdown?'[15]

Something has to be done to reduce teenage pregnancies. The context is the erosion of marriage, with the antecedent erosion of sexual morality and the consequential erosion of the traditional family. Over one-third of all births in England and Wales are now occurring outside marriage.[16] Since 1972 the number of one-parent families with dependent children has tripled.[17] There are now 1.5 million lone parents.[18] And for every two marriages in the UK there is one divorce.[19] Nearly one in five unmarried men and women are cohabiting – but such couples are 50 per cent more likely to have divorced after five years of marriage, and 60 per cent more likely after eight years of marriage than those who have not cohabited.[20]

It would seem self-evident that unacceptable strains and stresses are resulting from these developments. Inevitably they are leading to malfunctioning family units, and an ethic of sexual freedom is leading to unwanted pregnancies, despite careful contraceptive advice.

A number of significant 'players', however, would not agree with that conclusion. There still seems to be considerable prejudice *against* the traditional Christian values and family patterns. Many theologically liberal church people, social workers, lawyers, adminis-

[14] Ibid., p. 11.
[15] Ibid.
[16] The figure is 36.7 per cent, given in *Population Trends (92) Summer 1998*, London, ONS, p. 61.
[17] *Social Trends (26)*, London, HMSO, 1996, p. 49.
[18] *Social Trends (29)*, London, ONS, 1999, p. 42.
[19] *Social Trends (26)*, op. cit., p. 57.
[20] *Social Trends (24)*, London, HMSO, 1994, p. 38.

trators and other professionals involved in this debate seem unwilling to face the facts. It is interesting to note the subtitle of Norman Dennis's study *Rising Crime and the Dismembered Family*, mentioned earlier in the chapter. It reads, 'How Conformist Intellectuals Have Campaigned against Common Sense'.

The facts do have to be faced, and with some urgency. These new 'family patterns' *are* causing untold misery and suffering in our society. Many of the young girls who become lone parents come from deprived backgrounds and face a life full of problems. Young middle-class 'lone parents' have a better chance of financial and social support to alleviate their problems, but for the poor there may be no such support. It is time for anger – particularly when it is often irresponsible middle-class media gurus and wealthy magazine editors who generate a climate of sexual permissiveness to entrap the young. But after anger must come action. At least there should be support for groups campaigning for sexual restraint and the 'married' family, and readiness to speak out against intellectuals conforming to the immoral agenda.

The facts are undeniable. The marriage and medical research body One Plus One has shown that family stress and marital breakdown have measurable negative health effects on many victims. 'There is a strong relationship between marital breakdown and premature death ... There is an extremely strong association between marital breakdown and depression, psychiatric morbidity, alcoholism, suicide and parasuicide ... Divorced men are twice as likely to die from heart disease as married men. Cancer rates are significantly higher in the divorced population.'[21]

Other research has shown that it can no longer automatically be said that in a case of marital conflict a divorce would better serve the interests of the children. A report prepared at Exeter University has confirmed that a bad marriage is often better than a good divorce for the children.[22] Divorce can lead to worse psychological and physical problems. In fact, divorce has a greater impact on a

[21] J. Dominian, P. Mansfield, D. Dormor and F. McAllister, *Marital Breakdown and The Health of the Nation*, London, One Plus One, 1991, pp. 13, 23; see also, F. McAllister, *Marital Breakdown and the Health of the Nation, 2nd Edition*, London, One Plus One, 1995, *passim*.

[22] J. Tripp and M. Cockett, *The Exeter Family Study*, University of Exeter, 1994.

child than the death of a parent. Perhaps the fact that the absent parent is 'out there somewhere' but not 'here with me' represents a particularly complex sense of loss for a child. Half the children surveyed were 'worried, self-deprecating, underachieving and showed evidence of the after-effects of a considerable trauma'. 'We know,' said John Tripp, 'that conflict is damaging in the sense that it undermines children's well being and makes them feel less good about themselves when their parents fight, but our data suggests that that's really a very minor effect compared with the effects that we see when a parent leaves the house or leaves the home.'[23]

It has also been reported that children of broken families are four times as likely to suffer stomach ulcers or colitis by the age of 26. Nearly 30 per cent of young people whose parents divorced before they were 5 years old showed delinquent behaviour before they were 21, compared with only 14 per cent of young people from intact families. And these children showed a great concern about betrayal, abandonment and not being loved.[24]

These facts and the increasing incidence of family breakdown mean that for the Church pastoral needs are greater than ever. The gospel offers strength, help and hope in suffering. But first the facts have to be faced. It is truly irresponsible to think of the new morality and new lifestyles, as the report *Something to Celebrate* suggests, in terms of 'human flourishing'.

It is also irresponsible for that Church of England report to stigmatize supporters of the traditional family by implying that they are part of the 'New Right'. It says:

> *The New Right sees the family – mother, father and children, with a periphery of other members – as the key institution of civil society: 'The family is the matrix within which the citizen is well formed or misshapen. No institution is so important yet so easily overlooked.' The New Right emphasizes the family's role in socializing its members, especially through teaching and enforcing responsibility. Mutual responsibility helps to maintain the family, helps individuals to grow and contributes to social stability.[25]*

[23] Dr John Tripp speaking on *BBC Panorama*, 7 February 1994.
[24] *Daily Mail*, 18 November 1991.
[25] *Something to Celebrate*, op. cit., p. 56.

Those on the political right do not have a monopoly of *concern* for the family. On the contrary, both the right and the left are partly to *blame* for today's problems. In the UK the Labour government under Harold Wilson in the 1960s was the first to legislate for permissiveness. The Tories under Margaret Thatcher and John Major paid lip service to the traditional family while at the same time overseeing its disintegration. At the time of writing, Tony Blair's 'New Labour' alternative has also failed to turn the tide.

The concern for the traditional family is a result of the Reformation – Luther's attack on the view that celibacy was more important than marriage; Calvin's doctrine of 'callings', including the calling to be married; and the Puritan ideal of the family as the base unit of the Church. Richard Baxter famously said in 1656, 'The family is the seminary of the Church and State, and if children be not well principled there, all miscarrieth.'

## ABORTION – FACTS AND FIGURES

Part of the sexual culture which is destabilizing the family is undoubtedly the easy availability of abortion. The way abortion evolved in the twentieth century was perhaps one of the century's most evil developments. Like bombing Serbia or Kosovo from 30,000 feet in the Balkan conflict of 1999, abortion can seem so anaesthetized. From that distance you do not see the cluster bombs decimate villages, destroy families and maim or scar innocent people. It is the same with abortion – or foeticide, as it should more accurately be called. The foetus is so small, the process apparently so clinical.

For many in the West at the start of the new millennium, 'the family' does not include the unborn. That is sinister. At least, however, questions are now being asked. There is now a growing confidence about voicing opposition to abortion that was not present even a few years ago. Ronnie Campbell, the Northeast Labour MP for Blyth, defied Tony Blair and the New Labour machine which marginalizes 'pro-lifers'. He publicly reported how activists tried to deselect him because of his views. Fellow MPs said that his career was at risk because he supported the then Liberal

Democrat MP David Alton and his proposals to lower the legal time limit on abortions. But he had the courage to stand up for what he believed, against the tide.[26]

What has especially concerned many, however, certainly amongst the Christian public, are official government figures such as those highlighted by the Christian Institute.[27] The figures available show that for married couples only 8 per cent of pregnancies are aborted, while for unmarried couples the figure is 33 per cent. And abortion is not a matter of poverty. Indeed, the most prosperous areas have some of the highest abortion rates, while areas of high unemployment have lower rates.

Most serious of all, out of 156,539 abortions in 1994 only 147 were carried out because the mother's life was in danger; in only 1,796 cases was there a risk that the child would be born handicapped; and in only 2 per cent of cases was there a grave risk of permanent injury to the mental or physical health of the mother. That means that *97 per cent of all abortions are performed for 'social' reasons.*

The 1967 Abortion Act never said that abortion was moral. It simply said that certain abortions would not be the concern of the criminal law. Practically that legitimized abortion for millions. But how, do you decide the morality of an abortion? Many people play a game of 'ethical snap'. Someone cites a case of a woman or girl in desperate poverty who wants an abortion; someone then 'snaps' that with horrific photos of dead foetuses and dismembered foetal limbs.

The pro-choice movement accuses anti-abortionists of being sentimental in the operating theatre. The pro-life movement accuses abortionists of being sentimental in the counselling room. Others say it is all a matter of motives: if the decision is made with reasonably unselfish motives, that justifies an abortion. But the Bible suggests that while bad motives make good actions morally hypocritical, good motives do not make wrong actions acceptable. Peter, no doubt, had some good motives in opposing the way of the Cross for Jesus, but Jesus saw his activity as satanic (Mark 8:33).

[26] *Sunday Telegraph,* 5 January 1997. For the record of how MPs have voted on this and other moral issues, see the Christian Institute's web page: http://www.christian.org.uk

[27] Christian Institute, *News Digest,* vol. 4, no. 1, 1997, pp. 1–2.

## THE CHRISTIAN TRADITION AND THE BIBLE

We need to note some history. Abortion was common in ancient Greece – hence the Hippocratic Oath for doctors: 'I will not give a pessary to a woman to cause abortion.'[28] It was also common in the Roman Empire. By the time of Christ, abortion was well known and common in the ancient world.

The coming of Christ and the spread of the Christian faith brought a challenge to the practice of abortion. In the period immediately following that of the apostles – the period of the Church Fathers – one of the distinctives which marked the Church off from the pagan world was its opposition to abortion.[29] This was a fruit of the gospel – the extension of care to the humblest of human beings, including human foetal life. Early canon law, and subsequent pronouncements, have in general defended the foetus as 'human' or 'human on the way' and so as worthy of Christian love and protection.

More recently, however, an ethic of 'justifiable foeticide' has evolved. This, too, claims a Christian basis, namely that human life itself does not have an absolute value, only a very high one. There may therefore be occasions when life can be taken or protection withdrawn. But such a serious action has to be justified. As with the 'just war', the right to act cannot be presumed. It has to be argued for.

Most would agree that a serious threat to the actual life of the mother is a justifying reason. Some argue that some congenital deformity is a justifying reason (some would also say that this has to be such that no life outside the womb can be maintained). But these and other difficult cases are very rare. As we have seen, most abortions are for 'social' reasons. That is why the issue is a serious moral question that Christians cannot ignore. It involves the taking of innocent life.

But is it, in fact, *innocent* life? Is actual *human* life being destroyed

---

[28] Nigel de Cameron, *The New Medicine*, London, Hodder and Stoughton, 1991, p. 25.

[29] 'Athenagoras' Plea' (35), in Cyril C. Richardson (ed.), *Early Christian Fathers*, London, SCM Press, 1953, p. 378.

in abortion or in embryo research? And why should conception be so important? What does the Bible say?

Exodus 21:22 refers to an injury to a pregnant woman. If she miscarries, the claims of the foetus are assessed as less than her own. But violence to the foetus *is* an offence. Mostly, however, the Bible speaks at a more general level. Ecclesiastes 11:5 says, 'As you do not know ... how the body is formed in a mother's womb, so you cannot understand the work of God, the Maker of all things.' Perhaps the Revised Standard Version's translation is better: 'You do not know how the spirit comes to the bones in the womb of a woman with child...' This suggests that there should be a certain agnosticism, or at least humility, in our thinking about antenatal life. We are not facing a blob of tissue, but a divine mystery, something we cannot understand fully; and the womb contains not only a body but a 'spirit'.

The basic philosophical question is this: 'Whose is the history of that which is in the womb – the mother's or a separate person's?' The Psalmist had no doubt. It was *his* history. *He* was in the womb: 'For you created *my* inmost being; you knit *me* together in *my* mother's womb' (Psalm 139:13, my italics). Isaiah said much the same thing: '*Before I was born* the LORD called *me*; from my birth he has made mention of my name' (Isaiah 49:1, my italics).

Most importantly, this is also the Christian understanding from the New Testament stories of the birth of Jesus. The incarnation of the Son of God began not with his birth but with his *conception*. So we say in the Creed: '*He* was conceived...' In so far as Jesus Christ reveals true man (as well as true God), the inescapable conclusion is that life in the womb is human from conception.

## HUMAN LIFE

The fundamental Christian belief is in a God who gives, a God of 'grace'. He 'gave' his only Son for our sins (John 3:16). And human life is a 'gift'. When Job was bereaved he said, 'The LORD *gave* and the LORD has taken away' (Job 1:21). Human life is 'given'; it is not 'achieved'. That is important. We do not 'achieve' our humanity by reaching certain standards of performance or development.

Nonetheless, in the debate on abortion (and embryo and foetal experimentation) many assume today that the word 'human' (and so the offer of protection) is to be applied only where there are certain 'achievements'. These 'achievements' are understood in terms of physical performance or psychological and mental development. This, however, is a totalitarian road. And it can go on to exclude from the category of the 'human' also certain physical or racial 'underachievements'. So, for example, Peter Singer, the Princeton Professor of Bioethics, says that mentally retarded children can be dispensed with – he is proposing infanticide;[30] and Hitler dispensed with millions of Jews through the terrible Holocaust of the Second World War.

If humanity is a 'gift', the first 14 days surely cannot be discounted as a period of 'nonbeing', any more than other periods of a person's life. Behind human procreation is the divine creation. Procreation is creation on behalf of God (*pro* being Latin for 'on behalf of'). Protection is to be offered to human beings not because they 'reach a certain stage of development' but because of the fact that they are all created by God *in his image*. 'Whoever sheds the blood of man, by man shall his blood be shed; for in the image of God has God made man' (Genesis 9:6).

So what are we saying if we say the foetus is 'human'? We are saying that in virtue of its genotype or genetic code it is a distinct being who has been *pro*created. It may be that God's creative powers, entrusted to men and women, have been misused, but that is not a ground for destroying what has been created. And what is created is a human foetus. It is not a human infant, nor a human adolescent, nor a human adult, nor a senile human being. If a senile person is a degenerating member of humanity, a foetus is a developing member. The boundaries of humanity are death and conception.

The foetus is not simply 'potentially' human either. Yes, the foetus only potentially has the characteristics it will develop in later life. The newborn baby only potentially has the characteristics it will develop as a toddler or teenager. But a foetus is more accurately

[30] J. Bottom, 'Facing up to Infanticide', *First Things*, no. 60, February 1996, pp. 41–4; Andrew Sloane, 'Singer, Preference Utilitarianism and Infanticide', *Studies in Christian Ethics*, vol. 12, no. 2, 1999, pp. 47–73.

'a human with potential'. An ovum or sperm – i.e. prior to conception – is 'potentially human'.

We should also not moralize, like bomber pilots, according to size. An embryo may look, and actually be, tiny. A village looks microscopic from 30,000 feet. It may not *feel* so bad dropping bombs from that distance, but innocent people are killed nonetheless.

There are many other problems to consider, including the guilt felt by those who have had abortions. The Church, therefore, must not only teach what is right. Again, it must teach that the good news is about forgiveness at the Cross of Calvary, where Christ bore the sins of the world, including the sin of abortion and the sins of others that lead to abortion. Some reading this may be scarred by having had, or being involved in, an abortion. The gospel is that Christ loves the sinner and forgives, but he hates the sin and always says: 'Go and sin no more.' That is on the pastoral level.

There is also, however, a political level. We have to remember that the health of a nation is not just measured by the growth of its economy, the rate of its inflation, its budget deficit, or its prestige 'millennium' buildings. There are other more important measurements.

You can measure a nation's health by how many families are broken, how many children are suffering because of those breakdowns, the attitude to the sanctity of human life, and whether the vulnerable, the innocent and the unborn are being protected. On all those counts – especially the last one – Britain would seem to be sick. Since the 1967 Abortion Act in Britain we have lost over 5 million lives through abortion – one in every five pregnancies. But the real evil, in the words of David Alton, is that 'in the short space of 30 years, a serious crime has become a right; a public question of law and ethics has become a personal choice; and a practice once firmly repudiated by the medical profession has become a tragic, routine medical procedure – so routine that clinics offer a lunch-box service.'[31]

In the Church and the State there is a need to have a consciousness with regard to the facts, and then a conscience over this State-sponsored killing which is a daily occurrence.

[31] David Alton, *The Paramount Human Right: the Right to Life*, Family Research Council Insight Paper, 1997.

# CHAPTER TEN

# THE BIBLE AND HOMOSEXUALITY

## ROBERT RUNCIE

Early in 1996 I was interviewed in Jesmond by the journalist and commentator Anthony Howard for a BBC Radio 4 series of programmes on the Church of England. These were to be broadcast in the late spring or early summer of that year. A number of people were involved, giving their views on a wide range of issues. I did my interview, then forgot all about it.

Quite suddenly, on Thursday 16 May 1996, the main media carried the headline, 'Runcie admits to having knowingly ordained practising homosexuals and describes the Church's current position as "ludicrous".' That evening, it was announced, in the second of a series of three programmes entitled *The Purple, the Blue and the Red*, the former Archbishop of Canterbury Robert Runcie would be asked by Anthony Howard whether he had knowingly ordained practising homosexuals. He was to answer:

> *Yes! I feel that's an answer that would do justice to a Panorama-Princess-of-Wales-interview. But it wasn't quite as dramatic as that because I have not knowingly ordained anyone who told me they were a practising homosexual and were living in partnership with somebody as if it was a marriage. I have not ordained anybody – in fact I have halted an ordination – when I discovered that. On the other hand, there have been times in my ministry when I have acted in a 'don't want to know way and why should I enquire way'. And I never*

*liked the prospect of inquiring into what happened in a man's bedroom unless he's prepared to tell me.*

Those who could read through the 'fudge', and knew the way some bishops operate, saw what this reply seemed to be saying. If Robert Runcie had reason to suspect that someone was a noncelibate homosexual, but the grounds of that suspicion were only through a third party or circumstantial, he would not check; he would go ahead and ordain. If, however, he knew that someone was a non-celibate homosexual and that they would openly be sharing the clergy home with a homosexual lover because they told the Archbishop outright, he would not ordain.

The 'blind eye' of bishops was common knowledge by then. In 1995 *The Times* ran a feature on a vicar in County Durham 'whose "wife" is another man' – a well-known activist and writer on gay matters. When this clergyman was ordained, he said, 'nobody ever asked [about my homosexuality]. It didn't seem to be an issue, and I never had any guilt.' His partner claimed that they are accepted in their parish because people 'have learnt what the Gay Christian Movement keeps on trying to persuade people: that accepting [homosexual relationships] doesn't mean accepting that anything goes.'[1]

Two of our own ordinands from Jesmond Parish Church, studying at a local theological college, were quite horrified when one of their number was placed by the college for training in this county Durham parish. The student concerned, who had moral objections, was particularly distressed because the college had not issued any prior warning about the situation – namely that the placement was to be with a vicar who lived openly with his homo-sexual partner. This sort of problem did not appear in the rather anodyne write-up in the newspaper.

[1] *The Times*, 23 March 1995.

## BACKGROUND

Why make a fuss about this? Is that not just homophobia? No. A phobia is an *irrational* fear – and irrational fear is clearly undesirable and something to be resisted. There can also be a *rational* fear of something, though – and that is legitimate in this context because there is an aggressive campaign being waged which is destabilizing our sexual culture. Its significance is wider than homosexual issues, affecting heterosexual relationships also, and thus marriage and the family. The homosexual campaign, however, is the motor currently driving much of the whole process. The Church is a key focus for its efforts. The ordination of practising homosexuals is important to the campaign because it will serve to legitimize same-sex relationships in a special way.

Of course, there are pastoral concerns that must be dealt with; that is where there must be listening, care, counselling and help. But it is sheer naïveté to fail to see that the issues for public debate are political and *not* pastoral. They are about the way we order our common life together. The tragedy is that those wanting pastoral care find it harder to be helped when the moral ground rules are being undermined. Bob Davies, an ex-gay man, describes how he read religious books that were trying to justify same-sex practices:

> *If only I could really embrace this viewpoint (I thought), all of the conflict I feel inside would be resolved. But ... a stronger conviction refused to budge from my conscience: this book is wrong. These arguments are wrong. Homosexuality is wrong! ... So I had a clear choice to make: would I obey God's word, or seek to reinterpret it in order to fulfil my desires?*[2]

My own involvement in this issue began when I was a member of the General Synod's Board for Social Responsibility in the late 1970s. In the mid-1970s there was pressure for the Board to set up a working party to study 'the theological, social, pastoral and legal aspects of homosexuality'. This pressure came from a conference

[2] Bob Davies and Lori Rentzel, *Coming Out of Homosexuality*, London, Hodder and Stoughton, 1995, p. 21.

of theological college Principals because of homosexual problems among ordinands at their colleges. The result was a working party set up under the former Bishop of Gloucester, John Yates. It reported to the Board in 1979 and its report (a liberal one), together with the critical observations of the Board, were published as one document under the title *Homosexual Relationships.*[3]

It was at that time that I was necessarily drawn into the discussion and had to undertake a considerable amount of research. The fruits of that I published in a book called *The Church and Homosexuality*. In it were two other papers by Michael Green and David Watson.[4] Following its publication, I was immediately drawn even further into the public debate.

There was a major debate in the General Synod in 1987 on Tony Higton's private member's motion, detailed below. By that time I had been elected onto the Standing Committee of the Synod and Tony Higton, a Synod member, asked for my support for his motion on homosexual relationships. I agreed because I felt the Synod had to make up its mind where it stood. The discussion and the dialogue had lasted long enough: by 1987 it had been going on for eight years.

In preparation for the debate, I helped with the publication of the report entitled *Sexuality and the Church*, which, in addition to one paper by Tony Higton, has two by Gordon Wenham on 'Heterosexuality in the Bible', one by David Wright, Dean of New College Edinburgh, on 'Homosexuality in the Early Church', one by me on 'The Recent Debate on Homosexual Relationships in the Church of England', and a final paper on 'The Causes of Homosexuality' by two psychologists from St Mary's Hospital in London. I still think this is one of the best introductions to a difficult subject.[5]

---

[3] *Homosexual Relationships – A Contribution to Discussion*, London, CIO Publishing, 1979.

[4] M. Green, D. Holloway and D. Watson, *The Church and Homosexuality*, London, Hodder and Stoughton, 1980.

[5] Tony Higton (ed.), *Sexuality and the Church*, Hawkwell, ABWON, 1987.

## THE 1987 DEBATE

The result of the debate in November 1987 was that the General Synod passed by a 98 per cent majority (403 for, 8 against, 13 abstentions) the motion that:

> *This Synod affirms that the biblical and traditional teaching on chastity and fidelity in personal relationships is a response to, and expression of, God's love for each one of us, and in particular affirms:*
>
> *1. that sexual intercourse is an act of total commitment which belongs properly within a permanent marriage relationship;*
>
> *2. that fornication and adultery are sins against this ideal, and are to be met by a call to repentance and the exercise of compassion;*
>
> *3. that homosexual genital acts also fall short of this ideal and are likewise to be met by a call to repentance and the exercise of compassion;*
>
> *4. that all Christians are called to be exemplary in all spheres of morality, including sexual morality, and that holiness of life is particularly required for Christian leaders.*

On the day, clause 3 of the motion at first simply read, 'that homosexual genital acts also fall short of this ideal'. Unlike cases of fornication and adultery, they were not specifically said to call for 'repentance', being sinful; they were only said to 'fall short of this ideal'. It was Peter Forster, a former staff member of St John's College, Durham (Bishop of Chester at the time of writing), who at my request proposed and carried the vital amendment which added the words 'and are likewise to be met by a call to *repentance* and the exercise of compassion'.

That motion is now the official mind of the Church of England – in so far as the Church of England has one. Homosexual genital acts are sinful. The House of Bishops, however, issued their own report soon afterwards, entitled *Issues in Human Sexuality*, published in 1991.[6] This appeared to contravene the decision of the Synod by ignoring that amendment in clause 3. In effect, the Bishops' report only affirmed that homosexual behaviour falls short of the ideal. It did not call for repentance. There was,

---

[6] *Issues in Human Sexuality*, London, Church House Publishing, 1991.

naturally, an outcry. The conclusions of this new document in respect of homosexual relationships in the view of the Bishop of Newcastle, Martin Wharton, were summed up as follows: '*Faithful, lifelong, committed and permanent relationships are permitted* – certainly amongst the lay-members of the church, but that cannot be the position for the priests.'[7]

Martin Wharton endorsed that position. Jesmond Parish Church and others had to take issue with him over this, not with any pleasure, but for the sake of the Christian gospel, and out of faithfulness to the Bible and historic Anglicanism. The vote of the bishops at the Lambeth Conference on Thursday 6 August 1998 proved that such a response is representative of the worldwide Anglican church. Those out of step with it are the liberal bishops and clergy. In what was a defining vote, the bishops passed the motion that the conference:

- commends to the Church the sub-section report on human sexuality;
- in view of the teaching of the Scripture, upholds faithfulness in marriage between a man and a woman in life-long union, and believes that abstinence is right for those who are not called for marriage;
- recognizes that there are among us persons who experience themselves as having a homosexual orientation. Many of these are members of the Church and are seeking the pastoral care, moral direction of the Church, and God's transforming power for the living of their lives and the ordering of relationships. We commit ourselves to listen to the experiences of homosexual people. We wish to assure them that they are loved by God and that all baptized, believing and faithful persons, regardless of sexual orientation, are full members of the body of Christ;
- while rejecting homosexual practice as incompatible with the Scripture, calls on all our people to administer pastorally and sensitively to all, irrespective of sexual orientation and to condemn an irrational fear of homosexuals, violence within marriage and any trivialization and commercialization of sex;

[7] BBC 1, *Look North*, 17 June 1997.

- cannot advise the legitimizing or blessing of same sex unions or ordaining of those involved in same sex unions;
- requests Primates and the ACC to establish a means of monitoring the work done on the subject of human sexuality in the Communion and to share statements and resources among us;
- notes the significance of the Kuala Lumpur statement and the concerns expressed in resolutions IV.26, V.1, V.10, V.23 and V.35 on the authority of Scripture in matters of marriage and sexuality and asks the Primates and the ACC to include them in their monitoring process.

This could not be clearer. The Bible's teaching is that there is to be heterosexual, lifelong, monogamous marriage or abstinence. Christians must care for people with a homosexual orientation and their experiences must be listened to. They are all loved by God. If they are baptized, believing and faithful (i.e. living according to the faith, and in this case that means marriage or abstinence), they can be assured they are full members of the body of Christ. No such assurance can be given to the unmarried who are not sexually abstinent.

Were the bishops at Canterbury right in their understanding of 'the teaching of the Scripture', however? What is 'the teaching of the Scripture' the bishops refer to?

### ASSUMPTIONS

Two fundamental passages from the Bible need to be kept in mind. The *first* of these is found in Matthew 11:23–4:

> And you, Capernaum, will you be lifted up to the skies? No, you will go down to the depths. If the miracles that were performed in you had been performed in Sodom, it would have remained to this day. But I tell you that it will be more bearable for Sodom on the day of judgment than for you.

We had a visit from *OutRage!*, an aggressive homosexual 'action' group, at Jesmond Parish Church in September 1991 because of the stand I (and my wife) had taken over lesbian adoption. We were the first church in the UK to have a service disrupted by this group when a service of Holy Communion was halted. The above passage from Matthew 11 was in the official lectionary of the Church of England for the following day, 16 September. It struck me powerfully. I believe that *OutRage!* is part of the modern-day equivalent of Sodom. And Sodom is evil. It stands in the Bible for violence and sexual sin. Sodom stands under the judgement of God, and we should be shocked by the life of Sodom.

According to Jesus, however, the sins of Sodom are by no means the worst in the book. Capernaum is worse than Sodom. Worse than homosexual orgies is what is going on in respectable Capernaum, says Jesus. And what is going on there? Complacency and indifference to himself, the Son of God and Saviour from guilt and sin – the sins of Sodom and Capernaum included. In his commentary on Matthew, A.E. Plummer says, 'Self-satisfied complacency, whether in the form of Pharisaic self-righteousness or in that of popular indifference, is condemned by Christ more severely than grosser sins.'[8] It is these things which, at the end of the day, lead to moral slippage, and give rise to the more overt sins of Sodom. In one sense the root is more serious than the fruit.

The *second* passage that must be kept in mind is John 8:3–11:

*The teachers of the law and the Pharisees brought in a woman caught in adultery. They made her stand before the group and said to Jesus, 'Teacher, this woman was caught in the act of adultery. In the Law Moses commanded us to stone such women. Now what do you say?' They were using this question as a trap, in order to have a basis for accusing him.*

*But Jesus bent down and started to write on the ground with his finger. When they kept on questioning him, he straightened up and said to them, 'If anyone of you is without sin, let him be the first to throw a stone at her.' Again he stooped down and wrote on the ground.*

*At this, those who heard began to go away one at a time, the older ones first, until only Jesus was left, with the woman still standing*

[8] Alfred Plummer, *An Exegetical Commentary on the Gospel according to St Matthew*, London, Elliot Stock, 1909, p. 165.

*there. Jesus straightened up and asked her, 'Woman, where are they? Has no-one condemned you?'*

*'No-one, sir,' she said.*

*'Then neither do I condemn you,' Jesus declared. 'Go now and leave your life of sin.'*

This passage surely teaches three things about dealing with sexual sin. Jesus has no time for those who are wrongly judgemental. It must always be a case of 'there but for the grace of God go I'. Jesus also showed care for the person who had sinned, and so must we. Finally, Jesus did not condone the sin. He clearly called what was done 'sin' and he called for repentance. So also must we.

## THE SECULAR WORLD

The context of this debate on homosexuality is not just the Church – it is also very much the world. In the 1970s the gay liberation movement came to the fore. In an article entitled 'Homosexuality: the Contemporary and Christian Contexts' Tom Driver argues that the gay liberation movement raised homosexuality to the level of political consciousness: 'As a result we can no longer deal with it as if it were merely a psychological problem or a question of private morality; rather it is now a question of public policy.'[9]

This is in line with Kate Millett's view in her book entitled *Sexual Politics*. She argues that 'the enormous social change involved in a sexual revolution is basically a matter of altered consciousness, the exposure and elimination of social and psychological realities underlining political and cultural structures. We are speaking, then, of a cultural revolution.'[10]

Surely she is right. That is why this is a serious issue and why the public is concerned with the debate in the Church. So much is at stake. Whether those involved fully realize it or not, there is an attack on traditional sexual ethical patterns underway, and these in

[9] In John J. McNeill, *The Church and the Homosexual*, Darton, Longman and Todd, 1977, p. 4.

[10] Kate Millett, *Sexual Politics*, London, Virago, 1977, p. 362.

turn affect the stability of the family. That is not to say that every actively homosexual person is wanting such an attack to take place. Some certainly do not want that, I am sure. But there is an underlying cultural drift. And in some lesbian and gay Christian circles the attack is overt. Bill Johnson, a practising homosexual clergyman, has said, 'As long as the Church is able to perpetuate the belief that marriage and the family are the highest form of human relationship it will be able to perpetuate itself as a heterosexual family-orientated institution ... heterosexual relationships and marriage as traditionally experienced are basically unhealthy.'[11]

This is moving towards a Gay Liberation Front position. In the 1979 Gay Liberation Front manifesto we were told bluntly, '*We must aim at the abolition of the family*,' and it went on to claim that the buttress of the family was Christianity: 'Christianity, whose archaic and irrational teachings support the family and marriage as the only permitted condition for sex.'[12]

The Lesbian and Gay Christian Movement (LGCM) moved towards this position with the publication of *Towards a Theology of Gay Liberation*. Its editor was Malcolm Macourt, who more recently has claimed, 'There are still strong moral laws about relationships.'[13] But what counts for him as 'moral' laws? In this book Malcolm Macourt first argues against the view that homosexuals are born and not made – against the view that there is a '*true homosexual* (that marvellous creation of 1950's reformers created to assist in the removal of the more gory anti-gay legal and social restrictions)'.[14] Then he argues for a *free and random* model of behaviour.

The 'ideal', he claims, is where you have a free choice between a number of options in a society,

> *in which young people, as they grow up, will become aware of a wide variety of life patterns: monogamy – multiple partnerships; partnerships for life – partnerships for a period of mutual growth; same-sex*

[11] Quoted in Richard Lovelace, *Homosexuality and the Church*, Lamp, London, 1978, p. 46.

[12] Quoted in Green, Holloway and Watson, *The Church and Homosexuality*, op. cit., p. 107.

[13] *The Times*, 23 March 1995

[14] Malcolm Macourt (ed.), *Towards a Theology of Gay Liberation*, London, SCM Press, 1977, p. 26.

*partners – opposite sex partners – both; chastity; living in community*
*– living in small family units; and so on. A world, furthermore,*
*where each young person becomes aware that each of these life patterns*
*is held in equal esteem in society. So that each will feel free to choose the*
*pattern or partners with whom they wish to share their lives – to choose*
*the person or persons with whom it* makes most sense *to them to*
*live.*[15]

This is the vision of the gay liberationists. The Christian gay liberationist will choose a pattern which 'makes most sense', in a way that allows him to love God and to love his neighbour. So argues Malcolm Macourt.

Others now talk more about 'commitment', but this seems to be a relative term. As we have seen, it is claimed that, the 'Gay Christian Movement keeps on trying to persuade people that accepting [homosexual relationships] doesn't mean accepting that anything goes.'[16] The reality, however, is otherwise. At the time of the 1987 General Synod debate the LGCM was promoting material that advocates promiscuous and degenerate homosexual sex.

In the October 1986 edition of the *LGCM Journal* there was a report that 15 copies of a sex guide for homosexuals seized from the LGCM by Customs and Excise had been won back by a European Court ruling. Richard Kirker, the LGCM secretary, was happily displaying copies of the book. What was in the book? Answer: a gay liberation agenda. Tony Higton summarizes the book as follows:

*The baths are recommended as a place to achieve more sex per hour*
*than anywhere else. The book favours having sexual orgies with*
*a crowd and advocates being playful in casual sex relationships.*
*The word 'promiscuity' is dismissed as irrelevant. An unattached*
*homosexual can have as much sexual experience as he wants. In*
*fact the book recommends having sex in threesomes (same sex or*
*mixed). Married homosexuals may have to deceive their wives about*
*their homosexual activities, but it is best for the couple to agree to a*

[15] Ibid., p. 25.
[16] *The Times*, 23 March 1995.

*promiscuous life style. Sex in public toilets is accepted. If someone is looking for a homosexual prostitute (an illegal practice) the book recommends consulting a prostitution service rather than simply picking someone up. However, the book gives advice on the art of 'cruising', which means going out on the streets or elsewhere looking for a stranger as a sex partner. Apparently many homosexuals use all their free time in 'cruising' and find it good fun and really rewarding. The book even accepts sadomasochism (or S and M), which involves the use of violence and cruelty in dominating a partner ... Not even the practice of ingesting human waste in the context of sexual activity is ruled out.*[17]

All this was in the book being promoted by the LGCM – a group that was given a celebratory service for 20 years of existence in Southwark Cathedral in the autumn of 1996.

## ANALYSIS

Whether or not the Church of England has recognized the real problem, social scientists certainly have. As Bronislaw Malinowski shows in his *Sex and Repression in Savage Society*, even an elementary culture demands some limits on sexual adventure.[18] Also more people are seeing that the homosexual issue is related to the whole psychosexual revolution. The statistics are now showing that the problem itself is a small issue. The percentages of people with homosexual problems are known to be nothing like the claim of one in 10. A survey published in the *British Medical Journal* found that only one in 480 were exclusively homosexual, while only 1.7 per cent had any homosexual intercourse – figures which are 'lower than is widely thought'. Most people claiming to be homosexual were actually bisexual.[19] The public is paying attention now because there is a growing awareness that the phenomenon of

---

[17] Higton (ed.), *Sexuality and the Church*, op. cit., pp. 9–10.

[18] See Demant, *An Exposition of Christian Sex Ethics*, op. cit., p. 100.

[19] D. Forman and C. Chilvers, 'Sexual Behaviour of Young and Middle Aged Men in England and Wales', *BMJ*, 29 April 1989, 298, pp. 1137–42.

homosexuality is linked to other problems. As we have seen, according to the British *Sexual Attitudes and Lifestyles* survey, 70 per cent of all men in Britain think that homosexual relationships are wrong.

The phenomenon is complex. Some homosexuals want help with their condition. Others simply want to be left alone. But then there are those who aggressively want to affirm their homosexuality and change the whole culture in which they live – and in the forefront of this campaign are a number of homosexuals within the Church. The danger with forcing this debate on the public in both the Church and the world is to overfocus on homosexuality. In reality the attempted homosexual revolution is just part of an attempted and wider sexual revolution. Christians, therefore, also ought to focus on and oppose any opinions, attitudes and practices which debase heterosexual sex as well as those which promote homosexual sex. The debate and the campaign are being motored especially by the homosexual community, however; so inevitably the discussion falls disproportionately on homosexual sex.

A fundamental axiom which became accepted by too many in the late twentieth century was that *sexual desire must be acted on.* Homosexuals in particular have accepted this axiom. It must be challenged, however, by the Christian. Why? Because Jesus Christ, the most normal and fulfilled of all human beings, did not act on his sexual desires. Unchallenged, this axiom leads to a dehumanizing consequence, namely that *a person becomes defined by their desires alone.* It also leads to a trivializing of sex such that sex becomes recreational and, like a sport, becomes subject to 'preferences' – you choose your game.

There is a growing awareness of links between this axiom and increasingly noticeable social problems. A liberation from constraint gives rise, in the end, to the appalling illegitimacy statistics we now face in the UK – to one in three babies born outside marriage and to a growing number of lone-parent families. Such results, including the long-term financial consequences, are making the West review its sexual ethics.

It is clearer than ever that no society can hold together without sexual constraint and without following certain sexual norms. But sexual constraints that give rise to heterosexual monogamous marriage – where there are father-committed families – are developed only with difficulty, and they are maintained only with difficulty. Society, therefore, cannot be indifferent to attacks on those constraints. That is why social norms for sexual behaviour have to be taught. And that is why it is often said that public anxiety about homosexuality is pre-eminently a concern for the young.

'But isn't all this just social pressure to conform to middle-class prejudices?' someone may still be thinking. No – it is a fair reading of the biblical evidence. The Bible is clear: sex is for heterosexual monogamous marriage alone.

## JESUS AND THE OLD TESTAMENT

Genesis, the first book in the Bible, presupposes that to be human is to share humanity with the opposite sex. This is part of God's original Creation – the creation of the man and the woman. The Genesis narrative is opposed to the Greek myth of an original hominid which was cut in two subsequent to creation. That myth produces a metaphysic which says that what is fundamental is 'being human': sexual differences are simply a matter of 'plumbing'. The Bible, on the contrary, says that what is fundamental is 'being a human male or a human female'. The two are equal but fundamentally different. And true sexual fulfilment relates to the complementarity of the male and the female – equal but different. That is the clear message of Genesis 1–2.

Then come the incidents in Genesis 19, the Sodom narrative. At one stage it was argued – not least by Sherwin Bailey in his *Homosexuality and the Western Christian Tradition* – that this is not about homosexual behaviour but only about inhospitality.[20] That is now rejected by serious scholars. The verb 'to know' in the account undoubtedly means 'to have sex'.[21]

In Leviticus there are prohibitions on homosexual genital acts (18:22 and 20:13). It is argued by some that other things are also

---

[20] D. Sherwin Bailey, *Homosexuality and the Western Christian Tradition*, London, Longmans, 1955, pp. 1–28.

[21] Green, Holloway and Watson, *The Church and Homosexuality*, op. cit., p. 22.

prohibited in Leviticus. That is true. But the Church of England's Article VII says, 'Although the law given from God by Moses, as touching Ceremonies and Rites, do not bind Christian men, nor the Civil precepts thereof ought of necessity to be received in any commonwealth; yet notwithstanding, no Christian man whatsoever is free from the obedience of the Commandments which are called Moral.' Article VII implies that Christians have long found problems with the application of the Old Testament. That is why we must go to the New Testament to find the guidelines to help us understand the Old. We can then go back to the Old Testament and interpret it in the light of Christ.

So what does the New Testament have to say? It is often said that Jesus had nothing to say about homosexuality, but the Bible does not record Jesus speaking about incest, rape, child abuse or bestiality either. John 21:25 says that many things Jesus taught were not recorded. He probably had no occasion to mention homosexuality, in fact, as the Jews of his day were strictly opposed to such practices. Judaism was unique among the religions of the ancient Near East in prohibiting homosexual sex.[22] By forcing the 'sexual genie', as someone has put it, 'into the marital bottle', it had a profound effect on the heightening of male–female marital love and of eroticizing marriage. In some cultures wives were mere child-producers: sexual pleasure was obtained from other men. The Jewish prohibition against homosexual relations was part of the process which helped to elevate the status of women.

Jesus did generally uphold the Old Testament laws on sexual behaviour (Matthew 5:27–30; Mark 7:21–3). He only spoke of sexuality in the context of lifelong heterosexual marriage (Matthew 19:4–9). He certainly stressed the need for love, but nowhere did he teach that a motive of love can justify anything. He never taught his disciples that because of 'love' they could ignore the Old Testament moral law: 'Do not think that I have come to abolish the Law or the Prophets; I have not come to abolish them but to fulfil them' (Matthew 5:17).

The New Testament also distinguished between the Levitical commands. There are a range of Levitical details that the New

[22] Alan Praeger, 'Why Judaism Rejected Homosexuality', *Mission and Ministry*, vol. 10, no. 3, Summer 1995, pp. 13–18.

Testament sees as provisional. Only from seeing what is actually taught in the New Testament is it possible to learn which commands are merely cultural or matters of hygiene for certain climates and so non-binding, and which are fundamental matters of basic morality and so permanently binding. For example, in the Old Testament a 'eunuch' was not fully accepted into the worshipping people of God, but in the New Testament the Ethiopian eunuch most certainly was (Acts 8:27–39). By contrast the New Testament makes it clear that practising homosexuals (and adulterers and fornicators, for that matter) are still not welcome until they repent.

It may not be quite true after all that Jesus had nothing to say on homosexuality. In Matthew 19:12 he said, 'For some are eunuchs because they were born that way; others were made that way by men; and others have renounced marriage because of the kingdom of heaven.' Here Jesus is teaching that some Christian people do not experience heterosexual marriage because of choice ('because of the kingdom of heaven'), others because of the fallenness of the world – either the fallenness of men (castration) or the fallenness of nature (birth). In the second century AD Clement of Alexandria certainly took that to refer to 'some men, [who] from their birth, have a natural sense of repulsion from a woman'.[23]

## PAUL AND THE GOOD NEWS

It used to be said that in New Testament times there was no understanding of a natural homosexual condition, therefore we cannot take the New Testament too seriously now that we know better. That is simply false. As early as the fourth century BC Aristotle distinguished between congenital and conditioned homosexuality. In the *Nicomachean Ethics* he says that homosexual practice is 'sometimes the result of congenital tendencies, sometimes of habit'.[24]

---

[23] *Miscellanies* 3:1.1, in J.E.L. Oulton and H. Chadwick (eds), *Alexandrian Christianity*, London, SCM Press, 1954, p. 40.

[24] J.A.K. Thomson (tr.), *The Ethics of Aristotle*, London, Penguin Books, 1955, pp. 205–6.

We cannot therefore ignore Paul's words in Romans 1 and his teaching on homosexuality. Some say that he is referring to 'perversion' and *not* 'inversion' (a settled condition). Had people in the first century known about a 'settled condition', they say, Paul would never had said what he said. But they *did* know. So Paul has to be taken at face value when he says in Romans 1:24, speaking of the judgement of God on sin, 'Because of this, God gave them over to shameful lusts. Even their women exchanged natural relations for unnatural ones. In the same way the men also abandoned natural relations with women and were inflamed with lust for one another. Men committed indecent acts with other men, and received in themselves the due penalty for their perversion.' Referring to these and other sins, Paul concludes in verse 32, 'Although they know God's righteous decree that those who do such things deserve death, they not only continue to do these very things but also approve of those who practise them.'

Of course, that is not the last word from Paul. The last word is his message of forgiveness at the Cross where Christ died for our sins. In the Church there will be sinners of all sorts, including those forgiven for sexual sin. There certainly were at Corinth. In 1 Corinthians 6, in a section on immorality, Paul says,

> *Do you not know that the wicked will not inherit the kingdom of God? Do not be deceived: Neither the sexually immoral nor idolaters nor adulterers nor male prostitutes nor homosexual offenders nor thieves nor the greedy nor drunkards nor slanderers nor swindlers will inherit the kingdom of God. And that is what some of you were. But you were washed, you were sanctified, you were justified in the name of the Lord Jesus Christ and by the Spirit of our God (vv. 9–11).*

It is sheer nonsense to say that people cannot change. There is much evidence to prove that they can. True, many are not changed. There are people who have experienced the forgiveness of Christ and the power of the Spirit who continue to struggle with homosexual temptations. But if we cease to define people by their sexual attractions, they are *not* 'homosexuals' – they are simply Christians having to deal with inappropriate sexual feelings. And that is something most Christians have to deal with from time to time. The key is not to be 'enticed'; and your strategy must be based on James 1:14–15: 'Each one is tempted when, by his own evil desire, he is dragged away and enticed. Then, after desire has conceived, it gives birth to sin; and sin, when it is full-grown, gives birth to death.'

That is why it is important to say 'No' in the early stages. That is why it is pernicious for bishops and other clergy to suggest that homosexual activity (or any sexual intercourse outside marriage) is permitted. It makes it hard for a person who is trying to say 'No'. And the 'gay agenda' is pernicious in reinforcing a 'gay identity'. People are *not* 'homosexuals' – a class on their own. We must insist that they are *just people* like everyone else.

Referring to homosexual orientation, David Mills puts it so well: 'An *orientation* is simply a recurring temptation whether your genes or your brain tissue or your toilet training or the devil or bad companions present it to you.'[25] The devil works at our weakest points, and for some that is sexual temptation; for others it is alcohol, or an uncontrollable temper, or money. Did the rich young ruler have an *orientation* to prefer wealth? It is better to say he was tempted to greed.

We all have different dominant temptations. No one, therefore, can be 'holier than thou'. But the Bible says we must learn to 'put to death whatever belongs to our earthly nature: sexual immorality, impurity, lust, evil desires and greed, which is idolatry. Because of these the wrath of God is coming' (Colossians 3.5). Then we are to 'clothe ourselves with compassion, kindness, humility, gentleness and patience' (Colossians 3.12).


## POLITICS AND THE STATE

Where does this leave us in terms of the State at the beginning of the twenty-first century? Certainly as the twentieth century closed it seemed that the British Government wanted to homosexualize the public culture.

On 20 May 1999 the National Westminster Bank sponsored a dinner for Stonewall, the gay campaigning group, at London's

---

[25] David Mills, 'Don't Throw Stones', *Mission and Ministry*, op. cit., p. 45.

plush Savoy Hotel. Among the 500 who attended were five Government ministers, including Jack Cunningham, the then 'Cabinet Enforcer'. He was reported as saying that lowering the age of consent for homosexual sex was a 'high priority' for the Government – in spite of the fact that male homosexual intercourse is inherently unhealthy and so costly to the public purse. He also promised that Section 28 of the Local Government Act 1988 would be repealed. 'To loud cheering, he said, "Section 28 was wrong in 1987. It is wrong in 1999. And it will go."'[26] Section 28 prevents a local authority 'promoting homosexuality' and 'promoting the teaching in any maintained school of the acceptability of homosexuality as a pretended family relationship'. Once this Section is removed, nondiscriminatory policies will make it very difficult to teach that marriage is the normal basis for family life. To privilege marriage as the preferred relationship can then be seen as 'indirect' discrimination against homosexuality.

In the words of the American judge Robert Bork, we are 'slouching towards Gomorrah'.[27] Following the normalization of homosexual sex, there are also moves afoot to normalize paedophilia, especially in the US.[28] But warning shots have also been fired in the UK. Peter Tatchell, the British gay campaigner, wrote in a letter to the *Guardian* on 26 June 1997, 'it is time society acknowledged the truth that not all sex involving children is unwanted, abusive and harmful'. Not surprisingly, his organization OutRage! 'is calling for the age of consent to be reduced to 14 for everyone, both gay and straight'.[29]

In relation to child sexual abuse it is, of course, a fact that girls who are heterosexually abused outnumber boys who are homosexually abused. That is not surprising, because 95 per cent of child sex offenders are men and the vast majority of men are heterosexual. But a 1998 Home Office study tells us that 'approximately 20–33 per cent of child abuse is homosexual in nature and about 10

---

[26] Stonewall press release, 21 May 1999, 'Section 28 WILL go'.

[27] Robert H. Bork, *Slouching Towards Gomorrah*, Regan Books, New York, 1996.

[28] See the extensive Family Research Council's study by Frank V. York and Robert H. Knight, *Homosexual Activists Work to Normalize Sex with Boys*, 1999, http://www.frc.org

[29] OutRage! press release, 14 February 1996, 'Valentine's Day: OutRage! Urges Age of Consent of 14'.

per cent mixed'.[30] That is a staggering percentage of the whole. If we take generally agreed figures, 0.3 per cent of men are exclusively homosexual and only 3.5 per cent of men have ever had a same-sex partner, and for half of those it was a one-off episode never to be repeated.[31] As the Christian Institute comments, 'It would be completely wrong to say that all homosexuals are child molesters, but it is true to say that homosexual abuse is over-represented in the crime statistics.'[32] These Home Office figures certainly fit in with other studies. Frank York and Robert Knight report that 'a study of Canadian paedophiles has shown that 30 per cent of those studied admitted to having engaged in homosexual acts as adults'.[33]

Surely there needs to be a public repudiation of our decadent culture. At the grass roots at least, the Church is often speaking out and taking action. Christian people in schools, on local councils and as doctors are refusing to be intimidated by the various gay activists whose influence they see growing not only in government, but in broadcasting, in the judiciary, in education, in the social services and, sadly, in the Church's leadership. Hence the need for reform in the Church.

Most Christian people do not see these as issues of 'human rights'. There is no human right to engage in anal intercourse or an act of gross indecency. As the gay activists rightly remind us, Article 1 of the 1948 Universal Declaration of Human Rights says, 'All human beings are born free and equal in dignity.' However, they do not go on to remind us that Article 29 says, 'In the exercise of his rights and freedoms, everyone shall be subject ... to ... the just requirements of morality, public order and the general welfare in a democratic society.'

It is self-evident that the Church needs to respond not only pastorally but also politically to this issue of homosexual relationships.

[30] Don Grubin, *Sex Offending against Children: Understanding the Risk*, Home Office, Police Research Series, Paper 99, 1998, p. 12.

[31] Johnson, Wadsworth, Wellings and Field, *Sexual Attitudes and Lifestyles*, op. cit., pp. 187, 191, 463.

[32] *The Age of Consent – The Case against Change*, The Christian Institute, Newcastle upon Tyne, 1999, p. 8.

[33] York and Knight, *Homosexual Activists Work to Normalize Sex with Boys*, op. cit., p. 8.

# CHAPTER ELEVEN

# STEMMING THE
# TIDE OF DIVORCE

## DOMESTIC EXPERIENCE

Quite unexpectedly and while I was still at Oxford, my mother died suddenly in 1961, aged 48. She left behind two infirm, elderly parents, whom she had been nursing, in our family home in north London. Her cousin, to whom we were hugely indebted, came to stay to look after my grandparents (her uncle and aunt).

She was a remarkable woman, my mother's cousin, a singer and pianist of distinction, who had married unhappily and then been divorced earlier in the century when divorce was not common. However, she refused to remarry when others advised it. Her Christian faith was probably less sure then than it became later, but she knew the drift of the Bible. She also knew the discipline of the Church of England. She believed remarriage after divorce was contrary to God's will and therefore wrong.

The consequences for her were a life of loneliness, undoubtedly. She had to bring up three children on her own. The glamour of the entertainment business and the concert hall were no more. In their place was a life in what many would call a backwater, but it was a life of usefulness where she could use her skills to meet needs. Her local Anglican church required someone to play the harmonium in the Sunday school. She agreed to help. This involvement meant that, somehow, she found herself with the local church party going to Billy Graham's famous Harringay Crusade in 1954. Her church was not an Evangelical one, and Billy

Graham was not really her style, but she was clearly helped in her own spiritual life by that crusade.

It was this woman who first made me think seriously – in the early 1960s – about the issues of marriage, divorce and remarriage. On the one hand, I had the excellent discipline of enforced Bible study as I was reading theology at Oxford. I had to come to terms with the New Testament texts on marriage and divorce. On the other hand, I was able to observe this relative at close quarters and learn about her strict views on divorce and remarriage and see the consequences in her life. I was challenged. I was forced to ask: what was more important – to have aimed at enjoyment and wealth through remarriage; or to have forgone some obvious advantages, but then to have lived a life where her children were reasonably brought up, where she herself undoubtedly grew in her faith in God and where she was free to be useful to others?

By contrast I also had before me the experience of someone else at the same time – a young husband, a keen Evangelical Christian involved in Christian work. But his wife fancied another man and slept with him. The sinned-against husband was counselled by a well-known church leader, who told him that Christians could divorce for adultery and then remarry. So he did just that. His Christian work, however, took a nose-dive in consequence, and took decades to recover.

Those and similar life experiences were part of the context for my reading of the biblical texts on marriage, divorce and remarriage.

## SOCIAL CONSIDERATIONS

The moral revolution of the 1960s was also part of the context for my reading of those texts. A strict ethic with regard to marriage seemed to many by then to be unnecessary and old fashioned. But, 30 or 40 years later, the result of this revolution has been an astronomical increase in marriage breakdown and divorce. Along with abortion, one of the main social evils as we enter the twenty-first century in the West, and certainly in the UK, is divorce. It is now impossible to read Jesus' teaching on divorce and remarriage without thinking about what is happening all around us.

In England and Wales there were only two or three divorces per year for centuries. It was only in 1914 that the number reached 1,000, then it reached 10,000 in 1942. In the words of Norman Dennis of Newcastle, 'that meant that the vast majority of British adults found some way to live *permanently* with another adult of the opposite sex under the same roof'.[1] Things changed dramatically in the 1960s. From having one of the lowest rates of divorce, England (together with Wales) has become the divorce capital of Europe. Divorce rates have now passed the 150,000 per year mark. England and Wales are simply symbols and symptoms of the West at large.

The common assumption now is that marriage is an institution for adults, aimed at achieving adult happiness. If it is not making both partners happy, why not divorce? It has been forgotten that marriage is about stable families, strong communities and healthy societies. And children do suffer. It is not 'better to come from a broken home than to live in one', as used to be argued.

Speaking of divorce and the permissive culture (and what has followed it), Professor A.H. Halsey of Oxford, a former Reith Lecturer, summarizes the current findings (some of which we looked at earlier) like this:

> *No one can deny that divorce, separation, birth outside marriage and one-parent families as well as cohabitation and extra-marital sexual intercourse have increased rapidly. Many applaud these freedoms. But what should be universally acknowledged is that the children of parents who do not follow the traditional norm (i.e. taking on personal active and long-term responsibility for the social upbringing of the children they generate) are thereby disadvantaged in many major aspects of their chances of living a successful life. On the evidence available such children tend to die earlier, to have more illness, to do less well at school, to exist at a lower level of nutrition, comfort and conviviality, to suffer more unemployment, to be more prone to deviance and crime, and finally to repeat the cycle of unstable parenting from which they themselves have suffered.[2]*

[1] Norman Dennis, *Who's Celebrating What?*, Newcastle, The Christian Institute, 1995, p. 4.

[2] A.H. Halsey, in the Foreword to Dennis and Erdos, *Families without Fatherhood*, op. cit., p. xii.

STEMMING THE TIDE OF DIVORCE

Halsey is aware that we are dealing with *averages*. He is not main-taining that traditionally reared children are all healthy, intelligent and well behaved; nor that children from broken and parentally deprived homes will all turn out to be unhealthy, unintelligent and criminal. But *on average* what he claims will be true: 'It must be insisted that no contrary evidence is available to contradict the average differences postulated by the stated thesis.'[3]

The divorce culture needs to end. Social science leaves us with no doubt. It is a disaster for young and old alike.

## THE CHURCH OF ENGLAND AND THE BIBLE

What do the Bible and the Church of England teach about divorce and remarriage? It is crucial to know, because there is so much confusion over the matter.

The Bible contains an unequivocal statement in the Old Testament book of Malachi: '"I hate divorce," says the LORD God of Israel' (2:16). The Church of England is also unequivocal. Its view is clear. In 1955 the then Archbishop of Canterbury, Geoffrey Fisher, summed up the Anglican position on divorce and remar-riage as far as Church discipline was concerned – and this is still the position as we enter the new millennium, whatever some bishops may say. He said,

> The attitude of the Church of England, shortly put, is
>
> (a) No marriage in church of any divorced person with a partner still living, since the solemnizing of a marriage is a formal and offi-cial act of the Church, and the Church must not give its official recog-nition to a marriage which (for whatever cause) falls below our Lord's definition of what marriage is;
>
> (b) But the relation of such people to the Church or their admission to Communion is another matter, one of pastoral care for the sinner, and properly a matter of pastoral discretion.[4]

[3] Ibid., p. xiii.
[4] *Marriage and the Church's Task*, London, CIO Publishing, 1978, p. 2.

How true, though, is this Anglican teaching to 'our Lord's definition of what marriage is'? To answer that will require a detailed look at the texts. At the risk of oversimplification, Jesus' teaching can be summarized as follows.

*First*, he taught that there *will* be divorce because of hardness of heart (Mark 10:5), but this is wrong, as is remarriage. He taught that 'what God has joined together, let man not separate' (Mark 10:9). And remarriage, he said, is adulterous. 'Anyone who divorces his wife and marries another woman commits adultery against her' (Mark 10:11). That is a hard saying. But Jesus said it.

His teaching was revolutionary. The liberal Rabbis allowed divorce and remarriage for trivial reasons, the strict Rabbis only for adultery. But Jesus said there should be no divorce and no remarriage. This was the final stage of God's revelation on sex and marriage. The Old Testament set out the ideal in Genesis, but some Old Testament behaviours clearly fell short of this, not least through polygamy. Here, with second marriages being declared adulterous, Jesus by implication was ending polygamy.

Jesus' teaching was consistent. A married man and woman are to be seen as 'no longer two, but one' (Mark 10:8). A second marriage with a former married partner still living is therefore a form of adultery in respect of that first married partner, with whom there is still 'oneness'. True, the marriage may be terminated according to law, but not in the sight of God.

*Secondly*, Jesus taught that marriage is a *gift* from God (Matthew 19:11). Paul the apostle echoes that teaching (1 Corinthians 7:7). This gift is given when, first, a man (or woman) *leaves* his (or her) father and mother. Then, secondly, there is a free, decisive, definite and socially recognized act of *mutual commitment*. In our Western culture this commitment is verified by vows publicly made and registered. It promises a *cleaving* in marriage to a new partner and means a permanent, lifelong and exclusive relationship. This is to be consummated in, thirdly, a sexual union, a *becoming one flesh*. When these three things take place, there is more than human action involved – God is doing something. God himself is joining two people together (Mark 10:9). And this is God's gift.

People outside the Church find it difficult to think of marriage as 'given'. Rather, they think of it as something to be 'achieved', but to their cost. If you believe that marriage is God-provided and not something you and your partner are striving to achieve, the living out of the relationship is so much easier. You know you are indeed in a new lifelong relationship that cannot be broken. Like any kinship relationship (e.g. being brother and sister), you may sometimes be at a distance from each other, but you do not cease to be related. From the security of that knowledge in marriage you can work out your relationship; and you can do so with a freedom which is emotionally releasing. To realize this at the start of a marriage brings release from false expectations. Tensions are easier to deal with. You are not forever thinking you must excel, otherwise the marriage will end. In this way the marriage – which is a 'structure', an 'institution' or a 'state' – creates the relationship, not the relationship the marriage. The strict teaching of Jesus is part of this understanding of marriage.

## EXCEPTIONS – MATTHEW 19:9

What about the 'Matthean exception', however? In Matthew 19:9 Jesus says, 'I tell you that anyone who divorces his wife, *except for marital unfaithfulness*, and marries another woman commits adultery' (italics mine). Is Jesus' teaching so strict after all?

Matthew's Gospel appears to be in contrast to those of Mark and Luke, where there is no such exception mentioned. And that exception has been a cause of problems since the Reformation. The way some have interpreted it has undoubtedly been part of the development of the divorce culture in the West. That is why the correct interpretation of these texts is of more than academic interest. There is a wider social significance.

How, then, are we to explain these apparent divergences? You can say one of two things. *Either* you say that Mark and Luke give the understanding of Jesus' teaching that was common in the early Church. This was the precise teaching of Jesus, at least in summary form, that the early Christians remembered. It was clear and simple. Matthew, however, was giving that same teaching but with a qualification for one particular technical problem. *Or* you say that Matthew is the one who gives the understanding of Jesus' teaching that was passed on in the early Church, but, in fact, when you look at it carefully it is still an absolutist position and so is really no different from Mark and Luke.

Let me explain further. Take the first of the two answers above, where you say that the passages without an exception in Mark (10:11–12) and Luke (16:18) control our interpretation of Matthew. The argument is this: the specific teaching of Jesus that was generally remembered and handed down in the early Church contained no exception. That is to say, it was more like Mark and Luke than Matthew. And the proof is provided by Paul in 1 Corinthians 7:10, where he seems to be referring to this (absolute) tradition when he says, 'To the married I give this command (not I, *but the Lord* [i.e. this is verbatim from Jesus]): A wife must not separate from her husband' (italics mine).

If that is the case, what do we say about Matthew? Is Matthew putting words into Jesus' mouth for later pastoral purposes, to make life easier in the early Church, as some suggest? I do not think so. Rather, when Matthew records the words translated as 'except for marital unfaithfulness', it is too readily assumed that Jesus was talking about adultery. That is actually unlikely, for if he had meant adultery he would have used another Greek word – *moicheia*. It is more likely that he was referring to 'marriage within the forbidden degrees', or incestuous relationships. He used a wide term – *porneia* – which has all sorts of meanings, including 'marriage within the forbidden degrees'. This was a burning issue in the early Church. On this understanding Jesus is, therefore, talking about a 'nullity' in modern terms. Such incestuous relationships seem to have been an issue in Antioch, Syria and Cilicia (see Acts 15:23,29, where the same word is used). They were certainly an issue in Corinth (see 1 Corinthians 5:1, where again the same word is used).

More important for our understanding of what this word means in Matthew 19:9, however, is the very public scandal that everyone was talking about at the time – the case of Herod and Herodias. The Jews were outraged by Herodias. She had divorced her husband, Herod Philip, so as to marry *his brother*, Herod the tetrarch of Galilee. This, indeed, was 'marriage within the forbidden degrees'. And because John the Baptist challenged this incestuous marriage, he was beheaded.

If this is correct, the 'Matthean exception' is a qualifier on Jesus' strict teaching, to show he did not mean that incestuous unions have to continue. Herod *should* get rid of Herodias and Herodias *should* quit Herod, for there is a 'nullity'. The exception is a logical qualifier against the complaint, probably being raised by some Jews, that Jesus' strict teaching – as commonly understood and as recorded in Mark and Luke – would mean that Herodias should *not* separate from Herod. Jesus was saying, in effect, 'Nonsense! Of course, my teaching must not be misapplied like that.' We know Jesus' enemies were often trying to trip him up in this sort of way. According to this interpretation Matthew 19:9 is *not*, therefore, an exception allowing either divorce or remarriage after divorce.

If that is so, how do we understand Paul's teaching in 1 Corinthians 7:11 when he says, 'but if she [a wife] does [separate], she must remain unmarried or else be reconciled to her husband'? Presumably Paul is referring to a pastoral situation where there is, for example, violence, abuse or other danger and there has to be a practical separation. He is reminding the Christian woman that, in such a case, she must not remarry; she must remain single or else be reconciled.

It is because of this verse in 1 Corinthians 7, however, that some give an alternative interpretation and say that Matthew's version of Jesus' teaching with the exception – 'except for *porneia*' – was the tradition widely remembered in the early Church rather than the version given in Mark and Luke. Paul himself, they say, is alluding to this Matthean tradition here in 1 Corinthians 7:11.

If that is so, it *certainly* means that the Matthean exception does not allow remarriage. For Paul clearly understood it to mean that the separated wife 'must remain single'. Verse 11 proves that. What the exception did positively allow (though not of course require), on this understanding, was separation or divorce in certain circumstances – but without remarriage in any circumstance. Those who take this view would say that *porneia* was not 'marriage within the forbidden degrees' but probably 'major sexual wrongs and violations'. Personally I am less convinced by this interpretation, preferring the former.

Either way, however, Jesus' teaching is absolutist and so Matthew is really no different from Mark and Luke. There is to be no divorce and no remarriage. Nonetheless, common sense dictates that in dire cases there may have to be a physical separation for safety's sake.

There is one final point to make. Some people will say, 'All that may be true, but didn't Paul himself relax Jesus' teaching later on in 1 Corinthians 7, so why can't we?' They cite verse 15 of that chapter where Paul says, 'If the unbeliever leaves, let him do so. A believing man or woman *is not bound* in such circumstances; God has called us to live in peace' (italics mine).

What is happening here, however, is that an unbelieving partner is wanting to divorce a believer. But does this verse with the words 'is not bound' imply a permission to remarry? That is unlikely in the light of verse 11, as we saw above. Paul seems to be saying that in such situations the believing partner is to allow their (pagan) partner to leave. The Christian partner is 'not bound' to move heaven and earth to stop them going, so they need not feel guilty.

We must not be misled either, as some are, by 1 Corinthians 7:39 where Paul goes on to say, 'A woman is *bound* to her husband as long as he lives. But if her husband dies, she is free to marry anyone she wishes, but he must belong to the Lord.' The word 'bound' in verse 39 is translated from a completely different word in the original from the word translated as 'bound' in verse 15.

Paul is clear. He teaches that death, not divorce, alone releases the marriage bond. And we need to remember that at Corinth some people wanted to get out of marriage not so that they could remarry, but so that they could go into some 'superspiritual' celibate state. Paul is fighting a false asceticism as much as a desire for new unions.

## HARD TEACHING

That, in short, is the teaching of Jesus as presented in the Gospels and as understood by the apostle Paul. It is hard. That is what the disciples said when Jesus gave this teaching in Matthew 19:10: 'The disciples said to him, "If this is the situation between a husband and wife, it is better not to marry."'

In the current divorce culture, many Christians have the same reaction to Jesus' strict ruling, but down the centuries faithful Christians have sought to live by it. In the first five centuries all the evidence is that the early Church understood Jesus' teaching as follows: 'It is wrong to divorce, but if there is a divorce initiated by a nonbelieving partner or for some other circumstance, it is wrong to remarry.' Twenty-five individual writers during those early centuries are known to have forbidden remarriage, and so did two Church Councils. There was only one exception, Ambrosiaster, who was writing in the late fourth century.[5] As we have seen, the Church of England still understands Jesus' teaching in a way which is in line with the majority in the early Church.

During the time that I have been vicar of Jesmond in Newcastle upon Tyne, we have always had a tight policy on marriage, divorce and remarriage at the church. For a few it has been hard, but we believe this is the way of Christian obedience. It is no more than the current marriage discipline of the Church of England, as we have seen. We follow it, however, whereas many do not. My conviction that this discipline is right has, as a matter of fact, firmed up as time has passed.

When I was a student in the early 1960s, a number of my Christian contemporaries were becoming more liberal about marriage, divorce and remarriage as the moral revolution gathered speed. I, however, went the other way. I felt uneasy with the relaxed line on divorce that I found in a number of Evangelical churches. The problem for me, fundamentally, was the texts that I have just outlined. I could not get round the fact that the disciples reacted so strongly to Jesus' teaching in Matthew 19:10. If Jesus was *no more strict* than the stricter Rabbis, such as those of the school of Shammai who allowed divorce for adultery and then remarriage, why should they have been surprised or shocked by Jesus? If the disciples' reaction was anything to go by, Jesus was in fact teaching something far harder.

Then there were the problems I had with the non-Anglican Reformed tradition. This was (and is) the root of the Evangelical validation of divorce, and so the validation of the divorce tradition in the US which comes more from the dissenting and Presbyterian traditions than the Episcopal or Roman traditions.

---

[5] William A. Heth and Gordon Wenham, *Jesus and Divorce*, London, Hodder and Stoughton, 1984, p. 38.

At the time of the sixteenth-century Reformation, in contrast to the discipline of the Roman Church, the French–Swiss Presbyterian John Calvin and the Scottish Presbyterian John Knox both accepted adultery as a ground for divorce, *and* they allowed the remarriage of the innocent party. I found their reasons unconvincing.[6]

Their starting point was the Old Testament death penalty for adultery. They argued that the adulterer or adulteress was to be *reckoned as a dead man or woman*. Death, they said, dissolves the marriage bond. If the guilty party was not punished but was allowed to go on living, that was the fault of the *civil* authority. The Church could not be held to ransom by the State failing to do its duty. This Calvinistic position is reflected in the teaching of the famous seventeenth-century Presbyterian Westminster Confession (Chapter XXIV.5): 'In the case of adultery after marriage, it is lawful for the innocent party to sue out a divorce, and, after the divorce, to marry another, *as if the offending party were dead*.'

I had real sympathy for those Presbyterian Reformers. Marriage was in such a mess at the time because of Roman indiscipline and immorality. But whatever fiction was going on amongst sexually active 'celibate' Roman clergy, I did not believe that one fiction deserved another. I have a huge regard for Calvin, and for Knox. But as the former Bishop of Liverpool, J.C. Ryle, argued in his tract *The Fallibility of Ministers*, 'The Reformers were honoured instruments in the hand of God ... yet hardly one of them can be named who did not make some great mistake.'[7]

My convictions have firmed up not only because of biblical and theological considerations. These have been fundamental. As I have already indicated, however, sociological considerations have also been important. Divorce simply is not good for the individual or for society. Adhering to the sanctity of marriage most certainly is.

[6] Rudolf J. Ehrlich, 'The Indissolubility of Marriage as a Theological Problem', *Scottish Journal of Theology*, vol. 23, no. 3, August 1970, pp. 305–6.

[7] J.C. Ryle, *Warnings to the Churches*, Edinburgh, Banner of Truth Trust, 1967, p. 68.

## THE DIVORCE CULTURE

How have we developed a culture that is so harmful? In part it has been due to a loss of faith in God and his standards. In the second half of the twentieth century there were fewer people interested in the biblical texts and God's purposes for marriage than in earlier times. Instead there was a growing idolization of the 'self' as the judge of all things and a concern to make the self 'feel good'.

Barbara Dafoe Whitehead, the author of *The Divorce Culture*,[8] argues that

*a key element [in the divorce revolution] was the introduction of a new psychotherapeutic ethic governing family life. According to this ethic, individuals had a primary obligation to pursue their own emotional well-being in family relationships and especially marriage ... This ethic created a new way of thinking about the meaning and purpose of divorce as well. Once considered a last resort remedy for an irretrievably broken marriage, divorce became the psychologically healthy response to marital discontents.*[9]

Whitehead's own strategy for reinstitutionalizing marriage and defeating the divorce culture is, first, 'to encourage those who have been the traditional teachers and norm-setters in marriage – women and clergy among them – to return to the side of marriage. In the past thirty years many have defected to the divorce culture and become the leading teachers and norm-setters in divorce.' She is particularly concerned about the clergy. She claims there has been a 'retreat from preaching and teaching about marriage, especially among liberal Protestant denominations', and this 'has been one of the more remarkable and unremarked-upon changes in American religious life in recent years. Many churches are simply afraid to upset the divorced faithful.' This does not apply only to the situation in the US.

Secondly, she sees the importance of changes in approaches to psychotherapy. These need to be further encouraged. Leading

[8] Barbara Dafoe Whitehead, *The Divorce Culture*, New York, Alfred A. Knopf, 1996.
[9] Barbara Dafoe Whitehead, 'End No-Fault Divorce?', *First Things*, no. 75, August/September 1997, p. 28.

practitioners are now criticizing the bias against marriage evident in many marital therapists. They are also condemning the language of individual self-interest which has pervaded therapeutic practice. Mary Pipher, a best-selling author and therapist, writes,

> *In the late 1970s I believed that children were better off with happy single parents rather than unhappy married parents. I thought divorce was a better option than struggling with a bad marriage. Now I realize that, in many families, children may not notice if their parents are unhappy or happy. On the other hand, divorce shatters many children.*[10]

Another therapist writes, 'If we stay in denial [about divorce's effect on children] and refuse to recognize divorce's cancerous effect on society, we may experience a shredding of the social fabric that may take decades to repair.'[11]

Whitehead summarizes the growing consensus: 'Divorce is not a positive or liberating experience for everyone involved, many therapists now acknowledge. It may improve the well-being of the spouse who seeks it, but it does damage to others: the spouse who does not want to divorce, parents, grandparents and other relatives, and especially dependent children.'[12]

The growing consensus may also be seen in some interesting statistics from the American Enterprise Institute. Children born when the moral revolution and the new morality were being established – that is to say, born 1965–77, known as 'Generation Xers', and aged 21–33 at the start of the new millennium – are more likely than any other adult group to say that 'divorce should be harder [rather than easier] to obtain'. This is significant because it deviates from previous generational trends. In the past the younger generation has typically been more liberal. This was certainly true of the 'Baby Boomers' – those who are 34–50 years old at the start of the twenty-first century and who provide much of today's leadership. Twenty years ago they said divorce should be easier, while their elders disagreed.

[10] Ibid., p. 29.
[11] Ibid.
[12] Ibid.

What is the explanation for this? Some have said it is simply that this younger generation does not understand how complex marriage is – they need to be exposed to its hardships! More compelling is the argument that, far from being ignorant of the hardships of marriage, Generation Xers have personally experienced the devastating effects of divorce more than any other generation, and they do not like it. It is estimated that more than 40 per cent of Generation Xers have spent at least some time in a single-parent family by the age of 16.

## DIVORCE AVOIDANCE

What, then, are the practical steps which can be taken to foster divorce avoidance? One is to oppose cohabitation. The Family Research Council reports evidence that cohabiting women are more than twice as likely to be the victims of domestic violence than married women; and they have rates of depression that are three times higher than married women and more than twice as high as other unmarried women. Yet another study of 13,000 adults found that couples who had cohabited prior to marriage reported 'greater marital conflict and poorer communication' than married couples who had never cohabited.[13]

Also saving sex for marriage is not only better for sex, as we have seen (see Chapter 1), it is also better for the stability of marriage and so for divorce avoidance. Another study following the same people over a period of time (a longitudinal study) in the *Journal of Marriage and the Family* found that women who save sex for marriage have lower divorce rates than those who are sexually active prior to marriage. This finding apparently holds true even after taking into consideration differences in maternal education, parents' marital status, religion and other measures of family background. That is why 'abstinence programmes' of sex education need to be publicly funded in the UK as they are in the US. They are not just there to

---

[13] Elizabeth Thomson and Ugo Colella, 'Cohabitation and Marital Stability: Quality or Commitment', *Journal of Marriage and the Family*, vol. 54, 1992, pp. 259–67.

reduce teenage pregnancies but are also vital for the long-term health of marriage.[14]

In addition, people must no longer hear that the Church wants to ease up on divorce and remarriage. This is a crucial point. People need to be reminded that God hates divorce. Deep down they know we are talking about sin when we talk about divorce and remarriage. Too many have experienced the trauma involved. Divorce is always a tragedy; and a high percentage of remarriages end in divorce, causing further tragedy.

However, people also need to be hearing the message of forgiveness. 'If we confess our sins, God is faithful and just and will forgive us our sins and purify us from all unrighteousness' (1 John 1:9). It is one thing to be divorced and remarried and then to say, 'We are in a mess, but God can forgive, help and use us.' It is quite another thing to say that divorce and remarriage is a way of solving marriage difficulties. The distinction must be made.

Even one of the architects of modern permissiveness, the anthropologist Margaret Mead, saw the problems of buying into 'a divorcing society'. She describes

> the emotional strain in a divorcing society where husbands and wives nevertheless hope they can maintain their marriage. When divorce is a fairly open door, enormous care to satisfy the other partner and not to arouse his or her suspicions, is required. An emotional clutchingness which is very wearing, 'an endless incitement to anxious effort', has to do duty for what in former generations was performed by the unshakeable conviction that marriage was permanent. 'It was safe to be romantic when there was no real danger that new romances could tempt away.'[15]

We should be working as hard as we can to encourage marriage stability and the avoidance of divorce. But how, in a pastoral sense, should churches help those who *are* divorced or remarried?

[14] Joan R. Kahn and Kathryn A. London, 'Premarital Sex and the Risk of Divorce', *Journal of Marriage and the Family*, vol. 53, 1991, pp. 845–55.

[15] Quoted in Demant, *An Exposition of Christian Sex Ethics*, op. cit., p. 118.

## PASTORAL CARE

Christian fellowships must be especially conscious of the needs of divorced people who remain unmarried. Coming to terms with divorce and a celibate life on your own is doubly difficult today, and there are two factors which a programme of pastoral care for the divorced must address.

First, within the Church too many people seem to assume that the married state is for all *eternity*. Jesus taught otherwise. He said, 'When the dead rise, they will neither marry nor be given in marriage; they will be like the angels in heaven' (Mark 12:25). This suggests that, whatever the future state will turn out to be like, the married state will be transcended. It will be better than being in the best of marriages and the divorced will not be disadvantaged.

Secondly, outside the Church too many assume that to be human you *must* be sexually active. But Jesus, the most truly human person ever, was sexually *inactive*, as we noted earlier. We cannot say he was not tempted. He was 'tempted in every way just as we are – yet without sin' (Hebrews 4:15). Those who are divorced can go to him to 'receive mercy and find grace to help us in our time of need' (Hebrews 4:16).

What, though, do you say to someone who was married, then divorced because his or her spouse committed adultery, and then remarried? That question was asked by a Christian who had relied on the 'Matthean exception' for his remarriage. He was listening to a distinguished clergyman who writes on marriage matters, as he expounded Matthew 19 along similar lines to those given earlier in this chapter. The reply given by the clergyman was something like this:

> *Christ is not asking you to say my present marriage is a disaster. We frequently get into situations which we were mistaken in getting into, and yet which God meets us in and blesses us in. So God is not saying to you that you are to regard your marriage, your second marriage, as a disaster. Rather thank him for how he has blessed you in your new wife, and in the way that he has used you together. Yes, some things are closed to you, when you are divorced and remarried. But you should not renege on your second marriage. To say, 'I shouldn't have*

*married in the first place;' therefore, I should now separate from my second wife,' is wrong. You have new commitments to your second wife. It would be adding insult to injury and committing a second evil, to repudiate a wife to whom you have made solemn vows.*

*However, the logic of Christ's position is, first, that you need to admit your remarriage was something which at the time, had you understood Jesus' teaching, you should not have entered. Secondly, you need to admit that you have a continuing relationship with your first wife. You should not invite her to live in your marital home; but you do have, in God's eyes, a continuing relationship with her, which is a marital relationship, though it cannot be expressed fully. It is therefore required of you to be reconciled to her to the extent that that is possible, in terms of forgiveness, of re-establishing communication if necessary and possible, and of fulfilling any financial responsibilities. Particularly all this is important for any children of an earlier marriage and your commitment to them. But, of course, you must, at the same time, take account of your commitment to your second wife.[16]*

These things are difficult. And certainly to come to terms not only with Jesus' teaching but also to reinstitutionalize marriage in our society is going to require considerable effort.

Can permissiveness be reversed? Yes it can. In addition to prayer for God's help, there needs to be a multidimensional strategy. One area where permissiveness has already been reversed is smoking. The anti-smoking lobby has been highly successful. The result has been that not only have individuals changed their own behaviour, but there has also been support for legislation to modify the behaviour of others. Smoking is now seen to be very damaging. Many strategies have been employed to reach this outcome. There has been careful research into health risks. There has been media persuasion and health education in schools. There has been a systematic pursuit of incremental changes in public policy (for example, in respect of advertising). And there has been ongoing provision to help people wanting to make behavioural changes.

[16] Andrew Cornes at 'Divorce and Remarriage', a Christian Institute conference, 10 June 1995.

The result is that the smoking culture has been rolled back to a considerable extent. We must work for the same result with the divorce culture. It will not happen overnight. As in so many areas of life, however, many overestimate what they can achieve in one year, but underestimate what they can achieve in five years (and certainly ten). Persistence is the key.

Divorce and remarriage are not good news. Why do we not oppose divorce and remarriage more vigorously? Perhaps it is a subject too near for comfort. For many Christian people the issue of homosexuality is usually a case of 'them' and 'us': it does not apply directly and personally. Divorce is often directly applicable to 'us' – to our own families and our own churches.

# CHAPTER TWELVE

# THE VIRGIN BIRTH, THE EMPTY TOMB AND THEIR RELEVANCE

## HERESY

On London Weekend Television's religious affairs programme, *Credo*, on 29 April 1984 there was an interview with a little known Professor of Theology from Leeds University. The discussion turned to the doctrines of the Virgin Birth and the Empty Tomb. 'The Virgin Birth, I'm pretty clear,' said the Professor in answer to his interviewer Philip Whitehead, 'is a story told after the event in order to express and symbolize a faith that this Jesus was a unique event from God ... I wouldn't put it past God to arrange a Virgin Birth if he wanted to, but I very much doubt if he would.'

'So,' continued the interviewer, '[the birth narratives] don't amount to a historical record and shouldn't be seen as such, but as a series of stories to emphasize the unique importance of Jesus?'

'Yes...' replied the Professor.

'Could we move on then, now,' asked Philip Whitehead, 'to the most important miracle in the whole story of Jesus, the story of the Resurrection? Do you hold the view that Jesus rose from the dead and ascended into heaven?'

'Well,' said the Professor, 'I hold the view that he rose from the dead. The question is what that means, isn't it? I think I should like to say that it doesn't seem to me, reading the records as they remain in both the Gospels and what Paul says in 1 Corinthians, that there was any one event which you could identify with the Resurrection. What seems to me to have happened is that there were a series of experiences which gradually convinced a growing number of the people who became apostles that Jesus had certainly been dead, certainly buried and he wasn't finished. And what is more he wasn't just not finished but he was "raised up", that is to say, the very life and power and purpose and personality which was in him was actually continuing and was continuing both in the sphere of God and in the sphere of history so that he was a risen and living presence and possibility.' The Professor seemed to be talking about a spiritual resurrection without an empty tomb.

There was an immediate outcry over these views because the Professor had just been chosen to be Bishop of Durham, the fourth most important bishopric in the Church of England. Here was a prospective bishop publicly denying or doubting fundamental tenets of the faith. The *Church of England Newspaper* declared that Professor David Jenkins was not a Christian believer in the New Testament sense. Others joined that paper in saying that he should not be allowed to take up his appointment. The reaction from around the country was, indeed, remarkable. But the protesters did not include *any* members of the General Synod of the Church of England. Why not?

That was a question I had to ask myself, having by then been a Synod member for nine years. Had we – particularly those of us who were Evangelicals – not got involved in the Synod in order to bring the Church of England back to its biblical roots? Why were we doing nothing? What was the point of being a member if you then kept quiet at such a time and did not stand up for the truth and denounce error?

It was only then that I realized how hard it was to do that. The pressure from the ecclesiastical institution to conform to the ascendant liberal leadership, the subtle temptation of fearing for your career (certainly that was true for clergy on the Synod), the concern not to be classed as an 'extremist', and the simple desire for the quiet life, all conspired to induce a state of passivity when confronted by plain heresy. But in the end I decided to act, and took the modest step of writing a letter to *The Times*. That this was a significant step indicates the scale of the problem. 'Going with the flow' had become a virtue not a vice in the Church of England. I was so nervous about writing that letter! Being in London on church business at the time, I took my letter round on foot to Gray's Inn Road, where the newspaper's offices used to be. I must have walked up and down outside the building three or four times before going in to give the letter to the receptionist. When I walked out, a huge sense of freedom came over me.

## BREAKING RANKS

The die was cast. I had broken ranks. And for simply standing up for obvious Christian truth I would be considered a fundamentalist, an 'arch-conservative' and a 'turbulent priest'. So what had I written? Nothing more daring than this relatively innocent letter which appeared in *The Times* on 19 June 1984:

*Sir,*

*Clifford Longley [the then Religious Affairs Correspondent] has written (June 4) very perceptively about the views of Professor Jenkins, the Bishop-elect of Durham.*

*The nub of the problem relates to 'history'. On BBC Radio 4 recently David Jenkins said: 'No single historical fact can be certain ... historical facts are a matter of probability and doubt and uncertainty ... there is absolutely no certainty in the New Testament about anything of importance.'*

*But all this is sheer nonsense! There are commonly agreed criteria that can give us sufficient certainty about the past. It is not 'probable' that D-Day took place on June 6, 1944; it certainly did. Nor is it 'probable' that Julius Caesar had an expedition to Britain in the first century before Christ; he certainly did.*

*Professor Jenkins, in his* Credo *television broadcast, denied that there was 'any one event which you could identify with the Resurrection'. But in the duplicated letter he has sent out to critics he said: 'I believe in the Resurrection in exactly the same sense as St Paul believed in the Resurrection (i.e. on the basis of the accumulated testimony of the first disciples and personal experience).'*

*This is confused. David Jenkins is confusing how he (and St Paul) came to faith with what he (and St Paul) believe. They came, he says, to faith in the same way. But David Jenkins' subsequent belief in the Resurrection and St Paul's are poles apart.*

*Paul believed that there was 'a datable event'. And Paul believed in the empty tomb: 'He was buried, he was raised on the third day' (1 Corinthians 15:4).*

*Of that verse, C.H. Dodd, one of the greatest of English New Testament scholars, has written this: 'The natural implication would be that the Resurrection was (so to speak) the reversal of the entombment.' And he adds: 'When (the early Christians) said, "He rose from the dead," they took it for granted that his body was no longer in the tomb; if the tomb had been visited it would have been found empty. The gospels supplement this by saying, it was visited and it was found empty.'*

*For these reasons is it right that David Jenkins should allow himself to go forward for consecration? We can't have bishops whose teaching undermines the truth of the Resurrection.*

*This is not to question for a moment David Jenkins' personal faith, or to deny that he has a real experience of the risen Christ. But a bishop has to be a person who can communicate the faith. He also has to lead with the good will and agreement of the Church.*

*At Professor Jenkins' consecration the Archbishop would have to say: 'Is it your will that he should be ordained?'*

*The people are to respond: 'It is.' What if a significant proportion were to say, 'It is not'?*

*Yours faithfully,*
*DAVID HOLLOWAY*

Believe it or not, to write like this *was* to break ranks. In the Church of England in the early to mid-1980s you did not challenge the episcopate and you certainly did not do such a thing as write to a newspaper about it. The culture of centralism had produced spineless and passive clergy. And I was – or had been – one of them.

## FOLLOW-UP

When people from around the country wrote or telephoned messages of support, my confidence grew. It seemed that I had done the right thing after all. And it also seemed that something more should be done. The first step was to organize a group of clergy on the General Synod from the northern Province of York to request the then Archbishop of York to defer the consecration of the new Bishop of Durham. At least the move would introduce this very serious matter to the General Synod's agenda. The Archbishop refused the request. Perhaps he thought the matter would go away. It did not. Too much was at stake.

The story of the Durham saga has been told elsewhere.[1] The aftermath is still with us at the start of the twenty-first century. The significant point was this: here, for the first time in the modern world, a man was being consecrated bishop in the full light of his very public doubts and denials of the Virgin Birth and the Empty Tomb of Jesus, and without any demand for retractions or recantations. True, there was no hypocrisy – the doubts were out in the open. But it showed in a high-profile way how the leadership of the Church of England had drifted from the apostolic faith and its theological roots in the Bible, the Thirty-nine Articles and the Book of Common Prayer, and how a number of its leaders and clergy were awash in a sea of old-fashioned theological liberalism and the new relativism.

The aftermath started with the House of Bishops' response to the Bishop of Durham's statements. In their official report, *The Nature of Christian Belief*, the bishops made it clear that it was acceptable to deny the Empty Tomb of Jesus.[2] The doctrines of the Virgin Birth and the Empty Tomb were only *expressions* of the faith of the Church of England. Therefore, denials and doubts of the Virgin Birth and Empty Tomb were also legitimate *expressions* of the belief of the Church. The bishops were saying, in effect, that the real truth lies *behind* those 'symbols'.

Happily, being by this time on the Standing Committee of the General Synod, I helped to ensure that two further debates on this issue took place, one in the House of Clergy and the other in the House of Laity. Unlike the House of Bishops, both Clergy and Laity were emphatic that the doctrine of the Church of England was not that the Virgin Birth and the Empty Tomb were just *expressions* of the faith of the Church but that they *were* the faith of the Church.[3]

[1] See David Holloway, *The Church of England – Where Is It Going?*, Eastbourne, Kingsway Publications, 1985.

[2] *The Nature of Christian Belief*, London, Church House Publishing, 1986, pp. 26, 33.

[3] 10 November 1986, *House of Clergy Report of Proceedings*, London, General Synod of the Church of England, p. 44.

David Jenkins was soon rehabilitated, however, despite all the opposition to his theological views. That occurred when the whole General Synod debated the House of Bishops' report, *The Nature of Christian Belief.* In an emotional, clever and impassioned speech the Bishop of Durham alluded to the Gospel miracles as 'divine laser beam type of miracles', and he implied that those of us who believed in a miracle-working God as the Bible revealed him were worshipping 'a cultic idol' or 'the very devil'.[4] This was near blasphemy. Nonetheless, such is the way things are in the Church of England, at the end of his speech there was great applause. Undoubtedly it was a psychological, not a rational, moment. Some people began to rise as they applauded. One Evangelical bishop was on his feet clapping away and seeming to lead the applause. Hundreds of members – bishops, clergy and laity – joined in the standing ovation. I certainly did not.

In fact, I was already at the microphone because I was called upon to speak immediately after David Jenkins. I decided to stick to what I had prepared and not to improvise any kind of response. I reckoned that in such a hysterical atmosphere there was no way of countering the tide of irrationality. I was aware as never before of the power of group pressure within the Church. It was frightening.

Leaving that aside, the basic and simple question being raised during this saga was a substantive one, and it is still being asked: 'Can you really believe in the Virgin Birth and the Empty Tomb in the twenty-first century?' Apparently one-third of Anglican clergy 'believe that the Virgin Birth is a legend or are unsure if it is true', according to a study by Clive Field of Birmingham University.[5] Surely the question should not be, 'What is plausible in today's world?' Rather we should be asking the same questions there have always been, namely, 'What *actually* happened? What is *true*? Is the Bible correct or in error?' And the answers we give to these questions have public significance. They affect the sort of public society we are creating.

[4] General Synod July Group of Sessions 1986, *Report of Proceedings*, London, Church House Publishing, p. 466.

[5] *The Times*, 17 July 1999.

## THE IMPORTANCE OF FACTS

There is an assumption in the current climate of relativism and multifaithism that truth claims can be ignored as irrelevant. But, of course, that is incorrect. A person's religious heritage and education may well be relevant to the beliefs they hold. They are, however, irrelevant to the question, 'Are those beliefs true or false?'

Many people in the West never consider the truth claims of the Christian faith in a serious way. They have a view that the word 'Christian' just refers to types of moral behaviour of which they approve; it does not relate to definite matters of fact or to a personal faith in Jesus Christ. So for them a 'Christian' or a 'Christian society' is a person or a society marked by kindness and altruism – the opposite of what they consider 'un-Christian'. But is that what it really means to be a Christian? Is that what it really means to be a Christian society? Given such views, it is not surprising that there is confusion over whether countries in the West like Britain have a 'Christian' culture or not.

A 'culture' should mean a social way of life rooted in a tradition, which has evolved institutions and given rise to certain moral standards. Britain and most of the West, on that understanding, both do and do not have Christian cultures. A truly Christian culture depends on a social way of life that is based on the Christian faith – the faith of the Bible. Men and women are changed in themselves as they believe, and they then change the society around them. Yes, there is a time lag. The spiritual achievements of the present are embodied in the social life of tomorrow. And today's world reflects the spiritual achievements (or lack of them) of yesterday.

Without doubt the Christian faith has shaped the Western way of life. But as we enter the twenty-first century many are drifting away from that faith. This is having social consequences – and these will be negative unless there is a Christian revival or renewal. A Christian culture is never guaranteed. The Christian faith as it relates to moral standards and social institutions has to be 'renewed in every generation and every generation is faced by the responsibility of making decisions, each of which may be an act of Christian faith or an act of apostasy'. So writes Christopher Dawson.[6]

How, though, are these decisions to be made? Surely they must be made in the light of the truth, according to the facts, and by individuals. In spite of the totalitarian tendencies of modern governments, it is still individuals and individual minds, hearts and wills that determine social and civic realities. The great battle, therefore, for the transformation or the renewal of a culture or a society has to be fought in the mind:

> *Today the intellectual factor has become more vital than it ever was in the past. The great obstacle to the conversion of the modern world is the belief that religion has no intellectual significance; that it may be good for morals and satisfying to man's emotional needs, but that it corresponds to no objective reality. This is a pre-theological difficulty, for it is impossible to teach men even the simplest theological truths if they believe that the creeds and the catechism are nothing but words and that religious knowledge has no foundation in fact.*[7]

We cannot ignore these cardinal issues of the Virgin Birth and the Empty Tomb of Jesus. There will eventually be social consequences if they are rejected. Beliefs do affect behaviour and societies.

If the foundations of the Christian faith are myths, albeit elegant myths, with no real substance in history or fact, why believe Jesus' teaching on marriage and divorce, or any of his teaching that has so influenced Christian understanding of other social issues? These foundations therefore *have* to be explored and evaluated.

## THE VIRGIN BIRTH

The texts about Jesus' birth in the Bible could not be clearer:

> *This is how the birth of Jesus Christ came about: His mother Mary was pledged to be married to Joseph, but before they came together, she*

---

[6] Dawson, *The Historic Reality of Christian Culture*, op. cit., p. 17.
[7] Ibid., p. 89.

> *was found to be with child through the Holy Spirit ... All this took*
> *place to fulfil what the Lord had said through the prophet: 'The virgin*
> *will be with child and will give birth to a son, and they will call him*
> *Immanuel' – which means, 'God with us' (Matthew 1:18, 22–3).*

> *In the sixth month, God sent the angel Gabriel to Nazareth, a town in*
> *Galilee, to a virgin pledged to be married to a man named Joseph, a*
> *descendant of David. The virgin's name was Mary.*
> *...the angel said to her, 'Do not be afraid, Mary, you have found*
> *favour with God. You will be with child and give birth to a son, and*
> *you are to give him the name Jesus...'*
> *'How will this be,' Mary asked the angel, 'since I am a virgin?'*
> *The angel answered, 'The Holy Spirit will come upon you, and the*
> *power of the Most High will overshadow you. So the holy one to be*
> *born will be called the Son of God ... For nothing is impossible with*
> *God' (Luke 1:26–7, 30–31, 34–5, 37).*

How, then, can thoughtful people affirm all this? There are six key considerations to be kept in mind.

*First*, the starting point is these Gospel narratives themselves. Matthew and Luke both have the same central core – namely that Mary remained bodily a virgin in the conception of Jesus and did not have intercourse with Joseph. Yet both evangelists were drawing on very different sources for their information. Few, therefore, would deny the following claim of the New Testament scholar Raymond E. Brown, 'that a virginal conception through the power of the Holy Spirit is one of the few points on which they agree and that this tradition antedated both accounts'.[8]

The story of the Virgin Birth goes right back to the earliest period. Indeed, the infancy narratives in Matthew and Luke are clearly of Palestinian origin. They reflect Jewish fears of Herod the Great and Jewish piety centred on temple worship in Jerusalem. The traditional view is that the ultimate source of the narratives is the holy family – Joseph for Matthew and Mary for Luke. This is not at all unreasonable. We know that Luke spent two and a half years

---

[8] Raymond E. Brown, *The Virginal Conception and Bodily Resurrection of Jesus*, London, Geoffrey Chapman, 1974, p. 62.

in Palestine while Paul was in prison there. He could easily have obtained his story from Mary direct – and he was a medical doctor. Whether it was through direct or indirect reports, it is still perfectly believable to suggest that Luke's account goes back to Mary, and Matthew's to Joseph. We must also remember that James, Jesus' brother, became head of the church at Jerusalem. He was therefore in a position to correct any Palestinian traditions which were obviously untrue.

*Secondly*, the claim that 'virgin births' – or, as we should more correctly call them, 'virginal conceptions' – are common in other religious literature has to be challenged. Other religious literature mostly has accounts of 'holy marriage'. Here a 'god' in human or superhuman form impregnates a woman through sexual intercourse. But that is quite unlike the accounts of the virginal conception in the Gospels.

## HISTORICAL FACTS

*Thirdly*, the story of the Virgin Birth cannot simply be dismissed as a *midrash*. In Judaism a *midrash* was essentially a commentary on a passage of Old Testament Scripture which then 'took off'. The *midrashist* had a text in front of him which he elaborated and embellished, often in a most fanciful way. But the text was always the starting point.

Matthew, however, is clearly not starting with a text. He has a series of traditions about the birth and childhood of Jesus to narrate, and into these he weaves scriptural references. He is not adapting the narratives to fit Old Testament Scripture. If anything he is adapting Scripture to fit the narratives. The quotation in Matthew 2:23 ('he will be called a Nazarene') is a very drastic adaptation – it has no known reference in earlier Scripture!

Matthew is not, therefore, taking Old Testament texts and then writing myths to fit. If he were doing that, he surely would have chosen more evocative sections of the Old Testament. In addition, we know from other contemporary Jewish practice that basic events were never concocted out of texts. The Dead Sea Scrolls from Qumran show how texts were made to fit contemporary events, not vice versa. There was always a substratum of fact. Even the critic must admit that Matthew started with the basic factual outline of the infancy narrative.

*Fourthly,* Luke himself tells us that he was interested in the truth – 'it seemed good also to me to write an orderly account ... so that you may know the certainty of the things you have been taught' (Luke 1:3–4). Even if contemporary Jews had a more cavalier approach to history writing, there is every reason for thinking that the early Christians had a very different attitude.

Other Jews located the saving events of God in the distant past, or, if they were of an apocalyptic turn of mind, in the future; but the early Christians said they were located in the *recent* past. Hence we must presuppose that they had an interest in relating what *actually* happened.

*Fifthly,* the Old Testament said the Messiah would be born of David's line. The New Testament makes it clear that Jesus was believed to be the Messiah. Why then *invent* a story that separates Joseph (who was of David's line) from the process of conception?

*Sixthly,* if Mary had not been a virgin, no one would have created a myth to suggest that she was a great example of obedience. The strict moral climate of the day would have classed her fornication as highly disobedient.

These considerations mean that it is not feasible simply to reject the New Testament evidence on the Virgin Birth because to do so is 'modern'. The early Church had to face denials of the virginal conception by heretics such as Cerdo, Cerinthus, Saturninus, Carpocrates, Marcion and the Manicheans. The early Church heard what they said but judged them as simply wrong. We too need to judge these denials as wrong today. Much in modern scholarship gives us great confidence in the New Testament, and in the teaching of Christians down the centuries as it is summarized in the Creeds. As we say so regularly, 'He [Jesus] was conceived by the power of the Holy Spirit and born of the Virgin Mary.' The virginal conception *was* a supernatural miracle. As such it confirmed the fact that Jesus was, indeed, God incarnate – fully man, but without sin and also divine.

## THE EMPTY TOMB

The Resurrection – the New Testament doctrine of the Resurrection, not a postmodern reconstruction of it – lies at the heart of the Christian faith. 'If you confess with your mouth, "Jesus is Lord," and believe in your heart that God raised him from the dead, you will be saved' (Romans 10:9). But was it not just a 'spiritual' resurrection rather than a 'physical' resurrection?

Of course, the Resurrection of Jesus was not a crude resuscitation of a corpse; it was a glorious transformation. In that sense his old 'flesh and blood' (to use Paul's phrase) did not inherit the new order of 'the Kingdom of God' (1 Corinthians 15:50). But what Paul implies and the New Testament elsewhere makes quite clear is that on the first Easter morning Jesus' tomb was found empty; and it was found empty because Jesus had risen. To suggest that it does not matter if the bones of Jesus are still in the soil of Palestine is clearly contrary to the plain meaning of the texts and is, therefore, dangerous heresy and should be strongly opposed.

People who still want to use the language of 'resurrection' while denying the Empty Tomb have to say that the Empty Tomb is a myth. That is to say, they present it as a story concocted to illustrate the meaning of 'resurrection'. But that is not what the Bible teaches. According to the text of the Bible, the Empty Tomb is clearly not just an *illustration of the meaning* of the Resurrection; it is the *evidence for* the Resurrection itself.

If you believe the Empty Tomb is merely a visual aid, it will be of no essential significance. Belief in it, even though well grounded, will be held to be secondary or optional. That is the view of the former Bishop of Durham, David Jenkins. He argued that the Empty Tomb is a symbol of 'the assertion, made by God and received by faith, that in this world, through this world and beyond this world we may be sure that in the end, love succeeds, love brings it off, love has the last word. Jesus, the flesh and blood expression of down-to-earth love is at the very "right hand of God".'[9]

But that is to destroy meanings. The words sound so good (if you can understand them), yet they reduce the Resurrection to a

[9] Durham Diocesan Newsletter, *Durham Lamp*, April 1985.

platitude about love. Yes, love is vital. Yes, God is love. But the Resurrection of Jesus is saying more than just that – true though it is.

It was the philosopher Wittgenstein who said that you could trace the breakdown in religious belief to a 'credit rating decline' in the concepts that we use. The kind of reductionism expressed by the former Bishop of Durham has been and still is destroying the credit rating of the Resurrection.

This 'new theology' is not the position of the Christian Church down the centuries. It is not the faith for which countless men and women have lived and died. They knew that, had the tomb *not* been empty, everything they affirmed would have been falsified. If Jesus' remains had still been in the tomb, only the extremes of Gnosticism could have believed that death had lost its sting and the grave had lost its victory.

## THE NEW TESTAMENT

How, though, can we be sure that the tomb *was* empty? Is the evidence of the texts not rather weak? The main textual evidence for the Empty Tomb is there in the Gospel narratives – the Gospels of Matthew, Mark, Luke and John. But the argument is sometimes put forward that the Resurrection accounts are all so different and therefore cannot be reliable. What do we say to this?

It is true that the Resurrection narratives are different in the four Gospels. But the basic difference lies in the accounts of the appearances of Jesus to the disciples, not in the accounts of how the women (and others) found the tomb of Jesus empty. It is not at all strange, in any case, that the Gospel writers have different accounts of the appearances of Jesus to his disciples. Different apostles most probably reported different appearances on different occasions. On the other hand, it is quite remarkable how similar the accounts of the Empty Tomb are in all four Gospels. There is an amazing unanimity.

The three Synoptic Gospels (Matthew, Mark and Luke) all agree on three things:

1  that some women, including Mary Magdalene, went to the tomb of Jesus on the first day of the week and found the stone rolled away from the tomb's entrance;

2  that a young man (or some angelic presence) explained what had happened, saying, 'He is risen; he is not here';

3  that the women were frightened and left the tomb.

When we look at John 20:1–2 we find that the fourth Gospel also fits in with this outline. The only difference there is that the angelic interpreter is not mentioned – but two angels are mentioned in verses 11–13, when Mary is back at the tomb.

It is quite clear that the Gospel writers were drawing on different sources and different accounts of the Resurrection, but *these sources all agree about the Empty Tomb*. Mark's Gospel is generally reckoned to have been written in the 60s of the first century AD. But the information he (and the others) drew on was preached, remembered and probably recorded much earlier. As late as AD 56 when Paul was writing 1 Corinthians, we are told that many of the disciples who had seen Jesus after the Resurrection 'are still alive' (1 Corinthians 15:6). It is unthinkable that any eyewitnesses would have allowed an Empty Tomb tradition to develop so uniformly if it was fiction.

Paul, however, as someone is bound to point out, does not mention the Empty Tomb. True, but he implies it. In 1 Corinthians 15:3–8 he speaks about the basic core of the Gospel: 'that Christ died ... that he was buried, that he was raised on the third day ... and that he appeared to [various disciples].'

This early 'creed' thus focused on the burial as well as the death of Christ. As Professor F.F. Bruce says, 'Burial emphasizes the reality of the resurrection which followed, as a divine act which reversed the act of men.'[10] It points to the Empty Tomb. We have to say that what was raised was what was buried – i.e. the body of Jesus.

Note, also, that Paul specifies that the Resurrection happened on the 'third day'. What could give rise to this specific date except the discovery of the Empty Tomb? Had there been no Empty Tomb but only visionary experiences, there would be no possible reason for such an emphasis on the 'third day'.

More importantly, this 'basic core' or 'creed' of belief made it clear that Christians believed and must still believe *both* 'that he was raised on the third day' *and* 'that he appeared'. The appearances

[10] F.F. Bruce, *I and 2 Corinthians*, London, Oliphants, 1971, p. 139.

by themselves are not the gospel or good news. Some of the early disciples thought they were just having a psychic experience (Luke 24:37). But together with the Empty Tomb – a resurrection that reversed the burial – the appearances pointed to the true nature of Jesus' Resurrection: it was a 'bodily' resurrection. Certainly Paul presupposes 'bodily change' in 1 Corinthians 15:51: 'We will not all sleep, but we will all be changed.' He may not explicitly have mentioned the Empty Tomb – instead he took it for granted, as any Jew would have done in talk of 'resurrection'. Unlike the Greeks, the Jews did not see a person as a soul entrapped in a body awaiting release at death. Rather, they saw a person more as 'body and soul' together. The great hope then was for a resurrection that included the body.

There are two further questions we must ask about the Empty Tomb. First, a very simple question: Why did the Jewish authorities never produce the remains of Christ to silence the Christian movement once and for all, if in fact Christ's body was still in the tomb or had been removed? The only explanation which has maintained its credibility over the centuries is that there was no body for them to produce, because of Jesus' bodily Resurrection.

Secondly, if the Resurrection does *not* encompass the transformation of the physical body, what do we say in the final analysis about this material universe? What ultimately happens to this universe of space and time? Is it all just some great mistake that God tries to forget? That was the Gnostic heresy – to say that 'matter is bad or mistaken'.

John Polkinghorne, formerly Professor of Mathematical Physics at Cambridge, subsequently ordained and then President of Queens' College, Cambridge, says, 'No! It is not a mistake.' And the key is the Empty Tomb. 'The Empty Tomb,' he writes, 'says to me that matter has a destiny, a transformed and transmuted destiny, no doubt, but a destiny nevertheless. The material creation is not a transient, even mistaken episode.'[11] That was Paul's view also. He saw Christ's Resurrection as the 'first fruits'. Ultimately, he said, the creative power of God will transform the whole material universe:

[11] John Polkinghorne, *The Way the World Is*, London, SPCK, 1983, p. 86.

'The creation itself will be set free from its bondage to decay and obtain the glorious liberty of the children of God' (Romans 8:21).

If the Virgin Birth and the Empty Tomb are established as facts, what next? If this is indeed the case, then the most awesome of claims, that Christ is divine, becomes believable (which is not necessarily the same as imaginable).

## THE INCARNATION AND THE TRINITY

The deity of Christ is, in a real sense, what the Christian faith is all about – that God himself came into the world as a man, to show us what he is like; to show us what we should be like; and by his death and then his Resurrection, to save us from the mess we are in.

Again, however, there are some people, even within the churches, who try to say that the Bible does not really teach that Jesus *is* God incarnate. That belief, together with the doctrine of the Trinity, they say, came from the influence of Greek thinking on the early Church.

What can be said in reply to such a suggestion? Very simply, it can be said that the suggestion is not true. The Bible *does* teach the unique deity of Jesus. He was most certainly a man – the man of Nazareth. But the Bible also teaches that he most certainly was 'God come in the flesh' – God incarnate.

Jehovah (or Yahweh) is the traditional translation of the Hebrew consonants *YHWH* – the special name for the one true God in the Old Testament. The Jews said that this name was too sacred to be pronounced. So they replaced it by a variety of names – such as 'Lord' or 'the Name'.

From Exodus 3:14 it seems that *YHWH* was derived from the verb 'to be': 'God said to Moses, "I AM WHO I AM. This is what you are to say to the Israelites: 'I AM has sent me to you.'"' The remarkable fact is that on a number of occasions in the New Testament Jesus refers to himself by using the words 'I am'. In John 8:58, for example, he says during a dispute with the Jews, 'I tell you the truth ... before Abraham was born, I am!'

Had he merely been saying that he was pre-existent, he would have said, 'Before Abraham was born, I *was*.' The Jews realized the blasphemous implications of what Jesus was saying. 'They picked up stones to stone him,' we are told (v. 59). Stoning was the Jewish penalty for blasphemy (Leviticus 24:16).

At the time of his trial, Jesus was asked by the high priest if he was the Messiah, the Son of God. He replied, 'I am ... And you will see the Son of Man sitting at the right hand of the Mighty One and coming on the clouds of heaven' (Mark 14:62). The violent reaction from the high priest, who 'tore his clothes', can only be explained if this was also understood as a claim to deity. The high priest said, 'You have heard the blasphemy...' (v. 64).

There are also other descriptions, titles or roles of Jehovah from the Old Testament used of and by Jesus in the New Testament. He is the author of eternal law, the light, the rock, the bridegroom, the shepherd, the forgiver of sins, the redeemer, the saviour and the judge. A very significant example comes from Isaiah 45:23, where God says of himself, 'Before me every knee will bow; by me every tongue will swear.' In Philippians 2:10 Paul says, 'At the name of Jesus every knee should bow ... and every tongue confess that Jesus Christ is Lord.'

Jesus had indeed been 'making himself equal with God' (John 5:18), and others were likewise ascribing that equality to him. He was also beginning to teach that the 'unity' of God involved a true uniting of three 'persons' in the Godhead or in the divine nature; and he was claiming to be one of them (John 17:21).

The New Testament never put into systematic doctrinal form the many statements made by Jesus and his apostles about his relationship to the Father. This only happened years later in the early Church. The word 'Trinity' never appears in the New Testament – but the reality is there. In the last book of the Bible, Revelation, there is a vision of the Lamb (Jesus) sitting on the *one* throne with God. It is 'the throne of God and of the Lamb' (Revelation 22:3). There was an essential oneness.

'Trinity' means 'three in one' and 'one in three' – 'trinity in unity' and 'unity in trinity'. This is not the same as 'tri-theism' or 'three Gods'; nor is it simply three aspects of God. Rather, there are three 'persons', where the word 'person' applies to the three distinctions within the one Godhead – 'Father', 'Son' and 'Holy Spirit'. Within the 'oneness' there is communication, fellowship and identity.

This Trinity is clear in the baptismal formula which the risen Jesus tells his disciples to use in Matthew 28:19: 'Therefore go and make disciples of all nations, baptising them into the name of the Father and of the Son and of the Holy Spirit.'

At the end of 2 Corinthians Paul pronounces a benediction in which the three persons of the Trinity are named as partners with co-equal power to bless: 'May the grace of the Lord Jesus Christ, and the love of God, and the communion of the Holy Spirit be with you all' (2 Corinthians 13:14).

The Trinitarian pattern also appears elsewhere in the New Testament, as do claims of Christ's deity. In Romans 9:5, for example, Paul is quite explicit about the deity of Christ: 'From them [the Jewish nation] is traced the human ancestry of Christ, who is God over all, for ever praised! Amen.' Then in Colossians 2:9 Paul writes, 'In Christ all the fullness of the Deity lives in bodily form.' In Titus 2:13 he writes, 'We wait for the blessed hope – the glorious appearing of our great God and Saviour, Jesus Christ.'

## CONCLUSION

With all this in mind, therefore, the conclusion has to be that the Bible clearly teaches the deity of Jesus Christ; and the doctrinal formulas of the early centuries were simply systematic reaffirmations of the Bible in the face of similar denials to those being made today. There is nothing new under the sun.

At the time of the Reformation in the sixteenth century, Martin Luther said, 'He [Jesus] ate, drank, slept, waked; was weary, sorrowful, rejoicing; he wept and he laughed; he knew hunger and thirst and sweat; he talked, he toiled, he prayed ... so that there was no difference between him and other men, save only this, that he was God and had no sin.'

In the twentieth century the great Archbishop of Canterbury, William Temple, said, 'It is now recognised that the one Christ for whose existence there is any evidence at all is a miraculous Figure making stupendous claims.'[12] The political implication of that is

---

[12] Quoted in David Watson, *My God is Real*, London, Falcon Books, 1970, p. 18.

expressed in the British Coronation Service. At one point in the Coronation the Archbishop presents the Orb to the monarch with these solemn words: 'Receive this Orb set under the Cross and remember that the whole world is subject to the Power and Empire of Christ our Redeemer.'[13]

[13] *The Music with the Form and Order of the Service to be performed at the Coronation of Her Most Excellent Majesty Queen Elizabeth II*, op. cit., p. 67.

# CHAPTER THIRTEEN

# THE CHANGING WORLD AND THE CHANGING CHURCH

## STARTING OUT

In late 1972 I was asked by Jim Hickinbottom, the Principal of Wycliffe Hall, Oxford, where I had been on the staff as a tutor and lecturer in doctrine and ethics for a short period, if I would be willing to look at Jesmond Parish Church in Newcastle upon Tyne as a possibility for future ministry. I was willing, and I accepted the invitation to become vicar of Jesmond. I was instituted in January 1973 and have been there ever since.

When I accepted the invitation I was fairly certain it would be for a long haul. I was told that there was a need, as Jim Hickinbottom put it, to work with graduates who lived in the area. On looking at the church, it was obvious to me that it also needed to develop a significant *under*graduate student ministry. With parts of the University of Newcastle in its parish, as well as the Polytechnic (now the University of Northumbria) and three top schools, along with BBC Radio Newcastle, the Civic Centre, Trades Union Headquarters and Mansion House, it clearly *could* be what its founders had intended it to be when it was consecrated in 1861: a church 'in which evangelical truth shall be declared [and which would] form a central point for the maintenance and promulgation of sound scriptural and evangelical truth in a large and populous town'.

The church seemed to have lost its way earlier in the twentieth century.[1] It became, as someone put it, 'the most exclusive club in Northumberland'. It had a great musical tradition; it was also a centre for Freemasonry, but this had put a spiritual ceiling on the church. The church was, therefore, hardly Evangelical. It was a 'low' church – hostile to ritualism but not too concerned with the Bible.

All that changed with my predecessor, Roger Frith. A decided Evangelical, he preached the basic fundamentals of the faith. The result was a 'backdoor revival' – that is, many people left. It was spiritually too 'hot' for them. You could not find a more gentle man than Roger, but the clear and simple presentation of Christian truth meant that people were challenged and some did not like it. Others, however, were converted and younger people started coming to the church. Overtly Christian youth work started, and students began to attend.

When I arrived at the church in 1973 all the spadework had, therefore, been carried out. True, the numbers were small; true, much still had to be done. But I was not only convinced that God had called me to work in Newcastle and at Jesmond – I was also convinced that the church could grow.

How was it best to start? Everything I learnt from my curacy at St George's, Leeds, where I was privileged to work under Raymond Turvey, was learnt by osmosis. He told me bluntly that he had no time to teach me anything; my colleague, the other curate, could teach me what was necessary. But the mere experience of working as minister to students in that large, city-centre church in Leeds, with hundreds in the congregation and more visiting its Crypt social work centre, was far more beneficial than any formal instruction. It taught me the importance of having a big vision and simple faith in God, for this was what Raymond Turvey had. For all his disclaimers, however, he did teach me three things, at least, about starting off in a new church.

The first lesson was that you must begin with prayer. The second, that you must then preach and teach the whole gospel. From day one, therefore, the Sunday preaching programme at Jesmond was of primary importance. Now, with the church having grown significantly, every sermon is published as a booklet, and is also on audio

[1] Alan Munden, *Jesmond Parish Church*, Newcastle upon Tyne, Clayton Publications, 1981.

and video cassette, and on the Jesmond Parish Church website.[2] The third lesson was that you must establish a crèche. My wife, a paediatrician, was soon put in charge of the crèche at Jesmond, where she has been responsible for hundreds of babies over the years since then. If you have a crèche run to professional standards (or better), young married couples will feel secure in leaving their babies there. Not only do you then have new sources of leadership potential, but you also have a 'young' church. Change becomes easier and the church relates more naturally to changes in the wider culture.

## DEVELOPMENTS

In 1973 that was all I knew about 'church growth'. Common sense dictated a number of other things, including the need for more staff. I knew that the ministry of any church is not just that of the vicar or other paid church employees (at Jesmond at the time there was one curate and a verger who occupied the church flat). Other, non-full-time people were therefore asked to lead in the various groups that were developing. But such growth as we were beginning to experience also required more full-time workers. There is a myth that the more you use lay people the less you need professionals or full-timers. The reverse is the case. You need more full-time staff to facilitate the work of non-full-time lay people. We started to employ extra staff.

In view of the centralism that was developing in the Church of England during the 1970s, we decided to operate independently. This was necessary in terms of both economy and efficiency. We therefore set up the Jesmond Trust, to which congregational members could give and which could hold property and, when necessary, fund staff. The result, under God, of what we did and are doing is church growth. At the time of writing there are now over 20 people on the church staff, including some working part time and with only two 'official' Anglican staff (myself and one of my clerical colleagues). These minister to a congregation now

[2] The Jesmond Parish Church website address is: http://www.church.org.uk

averaging over 900 different people on a Sunday, from babies to the elderly. Our regular congregation – people who genuinely treat Jesmond Parish Church as their spiritual home – is in excess of 1,000.

In the early years at Jesmond, however, life was very different and difficult. Many changes were required. It was also clear that preaching and teaching the Bible had to be a top priority. It was something that urgently had to be recovered nationally in every church in the light of the serious drift following the 1960s. I was also clear that biblical preaching alone was not sufficient. There are some words of the Anglican Reformer, Richard Hooker, which I have long believed to be important. He said that the Church is 'a society and a society supernatural'.[3]

What does that mean? Simply this: the normal dynamics of human interaction do not cease for church groups or Christian churches. A church is still 'a society', for all that it is also 'a society supernatural'. The theological axiom that grace does not deny nature but perfects it is self-evidently true. Human management skills are required of congregational leaders as well as spiritual maturity and gifts. Too many good Christian leaders, however, only concentrate on the Church being a 'society supernatural'. They preach the Bible; they pray; they care for individuals – but they have little idea how to lead and help manage 'groups', whether large or small.

In my early days at Jesmond there was no one to help me learn how to manage a growing church. For most of the time I was flying blind and using a mixture of common sense and help from secular management teaching. Secular management teaching, however, is often inadequate because a church is not a business or a government agency. It is a voluntary non-profit organization where *motivation* is everything in terms of getting things done. That contrasts with a voluntary for-profit organization (a business) where financial considerations are everything; or a non-voluntary non-profit organization (like the State and its agencies), where penal sanctions can be applied.

[3] Richard Hooker, *Of the Laws of Ecclesiastical Polity Vol. I*, London, J.M. Dent, 1954, p. 221.

In 1979 I went to Fuller Seminary in Pasadena, California, to their School of World Mission and their department of Church Growth, in order to 'audit' the Doctor of Ministry programme.[4] It was stimulating. I was introduced to a whole range of thinking that was only common sense, but in the light of my six years' experience at Jesmond, too easily ignored. I was also introduced to some authors whose writings on church management I have read avidly ever since.

All of this has led to our mission statement at Jesmond: 'Godly living, Church Growth and Changing Britain.' That is to say, there is a need for individual conversion and growth of faith in Christ. But an individual also needs to be in a lively, supportive fellowship. And then there is a duty towards the State, to see God's standards met as far as possible in the public arena.

A commitment to evangelism should mean all of this, but so often the neglected factor is a commitment to church growth. That is so necessary if the goal is not decisions but *disciples*. Of course, there must be no artificial creation of growth by underhand means. If there is no truth in a church, if the apostolic faith is not being taught, numerical growth will normally not occur. It is a fact, established years ago by Dean Kelley in *Why Conservative Churches Are Growing*, that theologically liberal churches which deny or drift from the basics of the faith are usually *not* growing.[5] Occasionally they do. A notorious case in Britain in 1995 was the Anglican 'Nine O'clock Service' in Sheffield, which the Archbishop of Canterbury described as 'a blow to the entire church'.[6] These 'creation rock' services with a New Age theology attracted many, but were accompanied by abuse and a cult structure. Generally, however, it is the biblically orthodox churches which grow.

At Jesmond there has been growth which has been encouraging and, happily, more healthy. Over the last quarter of the twentieth century we saw hundreds upon hundreds of students built up in the Christian faith and then going out to other parts of the country

---

[4] 'To audit' means to take the courses, but not the degree, for a fraction of the normal fee.

[5] Dean M. Kelley, *Why Conservative Churches Are Growing*, New York, Harper and Row, 1977.

[6] *The Times*, 14 September 1995.

(and the world) to work and witness for Christ. Over the last five years of the century the congregation grew by one-third. This in turn helped support the student and youth work. It has been a privilege to work at Jesmond. There has been, and is, a wonderful staff team and very supportive lay leaders and congregational members. There is much to thank God for. But we cannot take the future for granted at Jesmond. There is opposition as a result of us being so firmly biblical, and this comes even from within Anglicanism. That is why, when I look out at the wider Church, particularly the Church of England, far from finding similar encouragement, there is so much that is discouraging. In fact there is a crisis in the Church at the very time when the Church should be ready for a great future and could be growing.

## THE TWENTY-FIRST CENTURY

Just before he died in 1976 André Malraux, the French novelist and politician, said, 'The twenty-first century will be religious or it will not be at all.'[7] This is a rather cryptic but, I believe, important remark.

Richard Neuhaus, the ex-Lutheran Roman Catholic sociologist, has this view of the future:

> *At the threshold to the Third Millennium, it seems that the alternatives to religion have exhausted themselves. That is true of the materialistically cramped rationalisms of the Enlightenment encyclopaedists, which along with ideological utopianisms, both romantic and allegedly scientific, have been consigned, as Marxists used to say, to the dustbin of history. The perversity of the human mind will no doubt produce other ideological madnesses, but at the moment it seems the historical stage has been swept clean, with only the religious proposition left standing.*[8]

[7] Quoted in Richard Neuhaus, 'The Approaching Century of Religion', *First Things*, no. 76, October 1997, p. 75.
[8] Ibid., p. 75.

In a similar vein, the distinguished Harvard political scientist Samuel Huntington has written a major work on the future entitled *The Clash of Civilizations and the Remaking of World Order*. Henry Kissinger calls this 'one of the most important books to have emerged since the end of the Cold War'. Huntington's thesis is that world affairs in the nineteenth century were chiefly determined by the nation-state, and in the twentieth century by ideology, but in the twenty-first century they will be dominated by religion – by the conflict of civilizations, with civilizations being defined by cultures and cultures defined by religion. The collapse of communism does not, therefore, point to a simple worldwide embrace of democratic capitalism and Western values and vices. Rather, he sees an era of conflict that will be deep seated and endemic. And the West will be at a great disadvantage, with its Christian culture having disintegrated under an elitist imposition of a noncohesive relativism and pluralism. 'Peoples and countries with similar cultures are coming together,' writes Huntington. 'Peoples and countries with different cultures are coming apart.'[9]

Who can deny that? You only have to look at the Balkans, the Sudan and the Indian subcontinent. It is quite frightening. Huntington's thesis is that culture is eclipsing both nationalism and ideology as the nexus of politics. And at the heart of culture, he argues, is religion: 'In the modern world religion is a central, perhaps *the* central force that motivates and mobilizes people.'

The eight distinctive civilizations, according to Huntington, are Islamic, Sinic (with China the core), the West (with the US the core), Orthodox (with Russia the core), Japanese, Hindu, Latin American and African. The most dangerous clashes of the future are likely to arise from the interaction of Western arrogance, Islamic intolerance and Sinic assertiveness.

That is the picture for the international, worldwide scene. What about the future of Western society, and society in the UK in particular? If this worldwide scenario is correct, there will be a significant process of desecularization. There will be a new consciousness regarding culture and religion. For the State this will reduce the

---

[9] Samuel P. Huntington, *The Clash of Civilizations and the Remaking of World Order*, New York, Simon and Schuster, 1997, p. 125.

significance of what is currently understood as the 'political' and the 'structural', and heighten the importance of the 'cultural' and the 'religious'.

David Martin, the Anglican English sociologist, seems to echo this new analysis in his study, *Forbidden Revolutions*. He argues against the 'misleading polarity ... between culture and structure, where the former is seen as derivative and passive and the latter as the arena of effective power and political action'.[10] His point is that, for the past hundred years, religion and culture (and so, we may add, personal behaviour and belief) have been progressively considered as marginal and part of people's *private* lives. The real action of life, it is said, takes place in 'the structures' and so in 'the politics of society'. But what we saw in the second half of the twentieth century, he says, was a contradiction of that. The cultural and religious margins around the world changed the so-called centre and structures – certainly in Latin America and Eastern Europe.

Martin is surely correct. Structures are subordinate; beliefs are primary. That has huge implications not just for our national corporate life but also for institutional churches, or churches with developed structures. At the end of the day, biblical and apostolic belief, prayer and straightforward evangelism – bringing men and women to faith in Christ – *are* central, while the structures (such as parliamentary and synodical life) are marginal.

## THE CRISIS IN THE WEST

But can the West meet this new challenge? The process of secularization has so weakened the West, not only in terms of social coherence but also in terms of spiritual discernment. A public creative response to this new and emerging situation will be difficult. Secularization is not just the product of a loss of faith. It is the product of thinking that the Church and State have no relationship to each other. It has come from thinking that the Christian faith is irrelevant to everyday life and that society has no need for the truths expressed in the Bible and the Christian tradition. The effect

[10] David Martin, *Forbidden Revolutions*, London, SPCK, 1996, p. 15.

of such secularization is ultimately to de-moralize society. It leads to the assertion that the Christian faith has nothing to say about the goals that men and women should aim for in life, or about the way they should conduct their lives once they are clear about their goals.

Secularization means that the West is ill prepared for a 'religious' twenty-first century. Calvin's claim in the sixteenth century is now not looking so foolish after all. He argued, presumably referring to Greek and Roman authors, that we could learn 'from the pagan writers'. He said,

> There is not one of them who, when dealing with the duties of magistrates, law-making and the civil order, did not begin with religion and divine worship. By so doing, they all acknowledged that no polity can be well constituted, unless it makes duties owed to God its first concern, and that for laws to attend only to the well-being of men, while disregarding what is owed to God, is an absurdity.[11]

While governments cannot legislate for faith, they can legislate to protect believers and to maintain moral standards. You cannot legislate to make people good; but you can legislate to stop the worst effects of their wrongdoing. The fact that Western governments were not always doing this in the twentieth century means that in the twenty-first century there will need to be significant spiritual renewal for the West to maintain a recognizable form of civilization. Nor should we be expecting a 'perfect' civilization from such renewal. What is wanted is simply a civilization where the majority not only admit that the Christian way of life is right and normal but also seek to shape its institutions accordingly. This will only happen as the Christian Church seeks to widen the frontiers of the kingdom of God. It can do that by increasing the number of Christians through evangelism, and by involving itself more thoroughly in all aspects of human life and society. But is the Church at present able to do that?

[11] John Calvin, 'On Civil Government – Institutes, Book IV, Chapter 20', in Höpfl, *Luther and Calvin on Secular Authority*, op. cit., p. 58.

## Spiritual Decline

Let us turn our attention, then, to the Church of England and the serious crisis it is in. A similar crisis is troubling other denominations and Churches, and not only in England but in other parts of the West. Nevertheless, I can best speak about the Church of which I have personal experience and knowledge.

In the UK we are witnessing spiritual degeneration. There is a decline in numbers of people attending church. In the Church of England the decline in terms of Sunday attendances is about 1 per cent per year. That is not huge, but it *is* inexorable. Over the 11-year period from 1984 (the year David Jenkins was consecrated bishop) to 1995, the usual Sunday attendances in Anglican churches went down from 1,182,000 to 1,045,000 (a 12 per cent decline).[12] Only about 2 per cent of the population are now in an Anglican church on any given Sunday (with 10 per cent plus in church overall).[13] The situation is no better generally in other denominations. One study shows growth in house churches, Pentecostal churches and the Orthodox Church, but together these represent a very small percentage of the whole. Globally over the last two decades of the twentieth century UK church membership, it said, would have decreased by 21 per cent.[14]

We must not, however, confuse beliefs and commitments with the *institutional expression* of those beliefs and commitments. What continues to be significant is the overall self-identification of the people of Britain. As we have seen, according to the last Independent Television Commission's survey, *Seeing is Believing*, just over 71 per cent of the population identify themselves as Christian. Only 3 per cent say they are of other faiths. Just over 22 per cent say they are nothing (see Chapters 1 and 3).

If that is the spiritual profile of British public life, what can we say about the interface of this public life and the Church of England itself? That is best seen in the self-identification of individuals as

[12] *Church Statistics*, London, The Central Board of Finance, 1997, p. 23.

[13] According to the *Sunday Times*, 11 July 1999, the figures are now lower than 2 per cent.

[14] See Peter Brierley (ed.), *UK Christian Handbook, Religious Trends 1998/99*, No. 1, London, Christian Research, 1997, p. 2.6.

revealed by opinion polls. A Gallup survey from 1982, published by the Bible Society in 1983, found that 64 per cent identified themselves with the Church of England.[15] In the 1987 survey from the old Independent Broadcasting Authority's religious department, published as *God Watching*, the figure was 50 per cent.[16] In the latest broadcasting survey from the new Independent Television Commission in 1993 the figure is 40 per cent.[17] And a 1996 survey shows 32 per cent.[18] That is a decline in people's self-perception as Anglican of 10 per cent every few years. In the year 2010 we could expect 10 per cent of the population to claim to be Anglican, and by the year 2020 the sense of belonging might be limited to the tiny percentage who attend regularly. That would be very serious. In no way would the Church of England then be 'the Church of the nation'. It would be irrelevant whether or not there were bishops in the House of Lords. In terms of social strength, the Church would be a mere 'sect'. For many of us that would create great problems.

Anglicans are committed by their history (and most Anglican Evangelicals by conviction) to what is called the 'magisterial' Reformation (*magister* is the Latin for the 'secular ruler'). The more radical Reformers wanted to establish Christian ghettos of pure churches. By contrast, the magisterial Reformers like Luther, Calvin, Cranmer and the other great Reformers of the Church of England (including Hooker) wanted to relate the teaching of Christ to the wider realities of life which came under the authority of the 'magistrate' – to the secular (or in their jargon 'the temporal') as well as the spiritual.

We believe our task is to share the gospel with all the people who live in our area. But if in the year 2020 the shell that some would call the 'Church of England' is simply a tiny sect, and if – as indicated by present trends – it becomes also a theologically liberal sect, will it be appropriate to be fully identified with that shell? That is a

[15] Jan Harrison, *Attitudes to the Bible, God and the Church*, London, Bible Society, 1983, p. 23.

[16] M. Svennevig, I. Haldane, S. Spiers and B. Gunter, *God Watching*, London, John Libbey, 1988, p. 19.

[17] Gunter and Viney, *Seeing is Believing*, op. cit., p. 12.

[18] R. Jowel, J. Curtice, A. Park, L. Brook and K. Thomson, *British Social Attitudes, the 13th report*, Aldershot, Dartmouth Publishing Company, 1996, p. 261.

question some are beginning to ask, for that shell would not be significantly part of the Western Reformed Catholic tradition. It would have lost the gospel; it would have lost its 'magisterial' significance; and it would not in any meaningful sense be the biblical Church that was defined by our Reformers, by the Thirty-nine Articles, by the 1662 Book of Common Prayer, by the Ordinal, and by the Church of England (Worship and Doctrine) Measure 1974, section 5 (1), which establishes *at law* the Church of England as a biblical Church.

In practical terms that shell, or the structured Church of England, would be rather like some of the ancient churches in other parts of the world – just elegant buildings, not very well kept, attended by only a few, mostly elderly people. In England under such a hypothetical scenario, this Church of England shell would survive, but it would be of historical rather than spiritual interest to the majority of people. The clergy would merely be glorified vergers, taking a service from whatever politically correct prayer book was then in fashion in a side chapel for any who happened to attend.

In response to this scenario some will no doubt say, 'This is all just based on opinion polls and surveys. It's scaremongering.' No – it is most certainly for real. Take the official infant baptism figures available from the Central Board of Finance's official *Church Statistics*. These are black-and-white matters of fact, not mere opinion or prediction. The loss of the pull of the Church of England is mirrored in our infant baptism figures.

In 1950, 67 per cent of infants in England were baptized in the Church of England.[19] That means that only 33 per cent were not so baptized. That is to say, the great majority of people over 50 years of age at the start of the new millennium were baptized in an Anglican church. In 1960, 55 per cent of infants were baptized in the Church of England. In 1970 it was 47 per cent; in 1980 it was 36 per cent; in 1990 it was 27 per cent. The figures for 1995 are 24 per cent baptized Anglican, with 76 per cent not so baptized. That is a huge difference from 1950, when the split was 67 per cent baptized and

---

[19] *Church Statistics*, op. cit., p. 22.

33 per cent not. Nor do minor differences in collecting the statistics before and after 1978 much affect the result.

The fact is that *in the year 2020 the vast majority of 25-year-olds – in fact over three-quarters of them – are unlikely to feel any personal attachment to the Church of England*. The point is surely made, and it is based on simple facts. Unless something happens to change the situation, the Church of England as we know it will become marginal as far as public loyalty is concerned. A process of marginalization is already underway. It is down to some of us to take action today. Remember, however, that people are still identifying as Christian – 71 per cent of them, according to that Independent Television Commission survey. No doubt that will be lower in 2020 if things continue as they are, but not necessarily much lower. So what is happening?

One significant point to note is that we are now in a period of postdenominationalism. People born after 1960 do not choose a church because of its denominational label. They are in a particular church because that is where they were converted, or because the music is good, the preaching is good, the crèche is good, the youth work is good, the small group system is good, or something else is good.

## THE DENOMINATIONS

Denominations as we know them are probably going to become things of the past. At the time of the sixteenth-century Elizabethan Settlement when the Church of England was being established there were really no denominations as such. In terms of its social structure, the Church of England was evolving into a federation of churches connected together by the Crown, the episcopate, the Prayer Book and the Articles. The Act of Uniformity of 1662 and the ejection of 2,000 Presbyterian ministers from their livings meant that by the beginning of the eighteenth century denominations would inevitably have evolved. The Act of Toleration of 1689, at the accession of William and Mary, saw their formal beginning. Originally these denominations were also federations of churches linked together by whatever made them distinctive – presbyteries, independency, baptismal practice, or the Quaker ethic.

In the nineteenth century, however, with the growth of Evangelicalism and the missionary movements, there was further change. The denominations became 'corporations' rather than 'federations'. That is to say, they operated 'corporately' together in an ever-increasing number of activities. So came the formation of the Baptist Missionary Society, the Methodist Missionary Society, the Church Missionary Society and the like. There were other agencies for moral and social welfare work, for education and administration. This form – the denomination as a 'corporation' where a central agency acted on behalf of the whole denomination (or that part of it that had an interest) – lasted until the 1960s.

The growth of denominational activity in the nineteenth century – by the denominations acting as corporations – meant that there were inevitably clashes and the wrong sort of competition, especially on the mission field. This led to the famous Edinburgh World Missionary Conference of 1910. It aimed to set forward an agenda for world-evangelization. Its main achievement was the beginning of the ecumenical movement and what became the World Council of Churches.

Far from lessening the denominational distinctives, however, the ecumenical movement gave encouragement to a new denominational self-consciousness. By the late 1950s and early 1960s the high point of denominationalism had probably been reached, with people paying intense attention to 'their denomination' and arguing that sound ecclesiology was all-important. It was during this time that many in the recent and current leadership of the Church, including the Church of England, were in training and being formed in ministerial norms and ideals – people such as George Carey and David Hope, the Archbishops of Canterbury and York, and also lesser clergy such as myself. These people were, and still are, thoroughly denominational. Today they find it difficult to think in terms other than that of 'the denomination' when they think about 'the Church'. In the Church of England this was also the period of canon law revision and the debates about setting up synodical government.

At the same time during the 1960s something else was happening. Extreme liberal and permissive theology was taking root, centred (in England) at Cambridge and on the south bank of the Thames in Southwark, London.

Michael Ramsey was then Archbishop of Canterbury. In part the present erosion of the Church goes back to him. A brilliant and godly man, he was nonetheless among the first in a high-profile position to espouse the principle of affirming truth *without outlawing serious error*. He would not condemn heresy, while being himself personally and often helpfully orthodox.[20] This comprehensiveness was new in the Anglican tradition. Richard Hooker, the Reformer and Anglican theologian of the Elizabethan Settlement, would only allow comprehensiveness in matters of church order, never in matters of fundamental doctrine. There had always been latitudinarianism and a 'broad church' party – but nothing like the 'anything goes' approach which Ramsey tolerated.

At this time, in the words of the former Dean of Salisbury, Fenton Morley, 'the heart was taken out of the Church of England'; and there were parallel situations in other denominations. These radical theological innovations meant the evaporation of the old consensus from which the denominations 'as corporations' could work on behalf of those they represented.

No longer able to work in the way they had before, the denominations now had to change into something else, and they did just that. From starting as federations and then becoming corporations, the denominations – and this was true of most of them, not just the Church of England – now became 'regulatory agencies'.[21] This meant that they became more centralized and their function became mainly holding budgets and trying to tell people what they could or could not do. The result of this change into regulatory agencies has been a significant denominational breakdown.

[20] See Michael Ramsey's 7 May 1993 Convocation of Canterbury address and the description in Owen Chadwick, *Michael Ramsey – a Life*, Oxford, Clarendon Press, 1990, p. 371. See also Michael Ramsey, *Image Old and New*, London, SPCK, 1963, and J.I. Packer, *Keep Yourselves from Idols*, London, Church Book Room Press, 1963.
[21] Craig Dykstra and James Hudnut-Beumler, 'The National Organizational Structures of Protestant Denominations: an Invitation to a Conversation', in M.J. Coalter, J.M. Mulder and L.B. Weeks, *The Organizational Revolution*, Louisville, Westminster/John Knox Press, 1992, pp. 318ff.

## DENOMINATIONAL BREAKDOWN

If churches are 'voluntary non-profit organizations' they have no sanctions and no power – certainly as far as the laity are concerned. Motivation is everything. The new denominations – or the denominations in their new form as regulatory agencies – therefore have a problem. They cannot motivate. Lay people who are Bible-believing and can administer multimillion-pound companies, perform sophisticated surgical operations, or lead modern educational institutions do not take kindly to less than brilliant clergy (even if they are bishops or moderators) or clericalized lay people telling them, from denominational headquarters, what to believe or how much to give in support of causes of which they disapprove.

This has led to the denominations becoming quite dysfunctional. With the erosion of the doctrinal consensus their future is secured only so long as there are certain functions they still control and on which the clergy are dependent. Fundamentally this means matters of stipend and pension – hence the near panic about 'quota-capping' (withholding some central payments) or about the suggestion that the local congregation should be formally responsible, as it once was, for stipend and pension or even the parsonage house.

In the aftermath of the denominational high point of the 1960s, while the pervasive Church consciousness was still denominational, there was massive centralization taking place. Synodical government facilitated this process. In particular it related to stipends in the Church of England, with the setting up of the Central Stipends Authority in the 1970s, initially on the grounds that this would be more convenient for everyone. But with the devaluation of central subsidies – de facto, if not de jure – clergy stipends are once again the responsibility of the local congregation. And now, certainly in the Church of England, pensions are also the responsibility of the local congregation.

What, then, is the function of the central organization now? Many would say it holds responsibility for training the next generation of ministers. But that training itself has become dysfunctional. Originally, ordination training was pluralistic: in the Church of England in the last century and until the Second World War it operated as a 'free market'. This was particularly because the different traditions – Anglo-Catholic and Evangelical – insisted on training their own clergy in their own way. In terms of output, it was successful. Now, however, even when numbers are artificially maintained or improved, the quality is often weak. According to Andrew Brown, 'The claim that the number of ordinands is rising ... means the number of stipendiary priests is shrinking more slowly than it would otherwise do.'[22] Whatever the figures, it is a fact that some, if not many, good young men and women have problems with the way in which the denominational Churches are evolving, and this affects recruitment and therefore the 'quality' of the recruits.

Is this too pessimistic a picture? No. Here is the distinguished German theologian, Wolfhart Pannenberg, to prove that my analysis is not unique:

> It is quite possible that in the early part of the third millennium only the Roman Catholic and Orthodox Churches, on the one hand, and evangelical Protestantism, on the other, will survive as ecclesial communions. What used to be called the Protestant Mainline Churches are in acute danger of disappearing. I expect they will disappear if they continue neither to resist the spirit of a progressively secularist culture nor to try to transform it.[23]

And here is the American, William Willimon, Dean of Chapel and Professor of Christian ministry at Duke University:

> One of the big stories we are witnessing is the dismantling of national denominations. We have been slashing national staffs due to huge budgetary problems. Some of our concern about the national denominations will dissipate due to this dismantling of bureaucracies. We're seeing a move to the local, to the congregational ... We've seen the end of denominationalism as we know it, although not the end of some kind of chastened denominationalism. It may be a stripping down for service. I don't meet any young adults interested in feeding national organizations.[24]

[22] *Church Times*, 16 July 1999.
[23] Wolfhart Pannenberg, 'Christianity and the West: Ambiguous Past, Uncertain Future', *First Things*, no. 48, December 1994, p. 23.
[24] William H. Willimon, 'The Spirit hasn't left the Mainline', *Christianity Today*, vol. 41, no. 9, 11 August 1997, p. 16.

## CONCLUSION

What, then, can we do? First, we must face the facts. Then at a structural level, among other things, we must see in the West the rise of large, seven-day-a-week churches in urban areas, which can provide a range of ministries adequate to modern needs. That will mean teams of leaders working from one base. David Martin writes,

> At the cutting edge of modernity the megacity may well be complemented by the megachurch, which (in the range of functions it includes) almost harbingers a return to the medieval Church. Megachurches are emerging in Latin America as well as in North America (and Korea) and are even to be found in Eastern Europe. Only Western Europe so far lacks them.[25]

Large or small, *all* churches must preach the Bible and structure themselves for growth. Our concern must be not to keep other clergy happy, but to save souls. Where there is heresy we must note what the Evangelicals of ECUSA (the Episcopal Church of the USA) have recently said:

> We will not be bound, in the exercise of our presbyteral or diaconal ministries, by the legal or geographical boundaries of any parish or diocese, if those boundaries are being invoked to prevent the preaching and teaching of 'the doctrine, discipline, and worship of Christ as this Church has received them'.[26]

At a theological level we need to recover the biblical doctrine of sin. It was Bishop Ryle who said, 'Dim or indistinct views of sin are the origin of most of the errors, heresies, and false doctrines.'[27]

Communion with bishops and other clergy must inevitably be impaired where there is heresy over the fundamentals – not over secondary matters but over primary matters. Nor must we be

[25] Martin, *Forbidden Revolutions*, op. cit., p. 24.

[26] ECUSA, *First Promise Statement*, 9 September 1997. The words 'the doctrine, discipline, and worship of Christ as this Church has received them' is a quote from the American Ordinal.

[27] J.C. Ryle, *Holiness*, London, James Clarke, 1956, p. 1.

intimidated by the word 'schism'. As Hooker said, 'What they call schism we call our reasonable service unto God.'[28] In classical theology, 'schism' is defined as division where there is no reason for it. In classical theology, heresy was deemed *good* reason for such a division. It was Cyprian, the great proponent of unity in the Church, who said in the third century, 'A people obedient to the precepts of the Lord and fearing God is bound to separate itself from a sinful Prelate.'[29]

Finally, at a practical level all Christians, but especially Church leaders, should heed Paul's words in Colossians 1:28–9:

> *We proclaim him [Jesus], admonishing [saying things are wrong when they are wrong] and teaching everyone with all [not 'some'] wisdom, so that we may present everyone perfect [or 'mature'] in Christ. To this end I labour [it will be hard work], struggling [it will involve conflict] with all his energy, which so powerfully works in me [we need the power of God's Holy Spirit].*

Many Church leaders are wanting to serve the State effectively in the twenty-first century and to work for the national spiritual renewal which is needed. At the very least, those words can provide a starting point.

[28] John Keble (ed.), *The Works of Mr Richard Hooker Vol. III*, Oxford University Press, 1851, p. 675.

[29] *Epistles* 67.3 – on the refusal of the Spanish churches to communicate with their Bishops Basilides and Martial.

# CHAPTER FOURTEEN

# REFORMING
# THE CHURCH

## BACKGROUND

On 10 December 1992 I was asked to convene a group of parochial clergy from across England, mainly from larger mainstream Anglican Evangelical churches. We met in London to discuss financial issues in the Church of England, including the right way forward for 'net-givers' in responding to ever larger financial demands for central Church funds through 'the quota'. The quota in the Church of England is a voluntary payment, but it is treated quite improperly by the Anglican diocesan centres as an enforceable demand or tax. This has meant that huge sums of money, often from Evangelical churches, are subsidizing work that the donors believe is frustrating the gospel or downright heretical. A number are saying that they cannot and will not agree to these demands, and they are 'capping' their quotas.

The problem is on the one hand theological liberalism in the Church at large, and on the other hand bureaucratic centralism – i.e. there is both a doctrinal and a practical problem. At Jesmond Parish Church in the early 1980s, we were requested out of the blue to pay immediately an increase of 300 per cent in our 'quota'. The sum even then ran into thousands of pounds. At the very same time, however, a neighbouring clergyman had decided he should bless lesbian couples; the then Canon Missioner of Newcastle Diocese, Peter Selby (at the time of writing, the Bishop of Worcester), had said regarding gay relationships that 'most of the biblical statements about homosexuality seem to me to be unaccept-able', and his thinking on heterosexual marriage was equally idio-syncratic;[1] and the Bishop's Council had appointed a high-profile gay campaigner to our diocesan Board for Social Responsibility.

None of this commended itself to our Finance Committee or the Parochial Church Council. In fact they were appalled. So there was little problem over deciding how to deal with this request for more money. In business terms it was seen to be foolish. If it had been right and reasonable, it would still have needed phasing in. Even a large church like Jesmond cannot just find great extra sums of unbudgeted money. We have no reserves or surpluses. All our income comes from congregational giving. Had there been a city-wide mission with Billy Graham, or some other cause that warranted a great effort for that amount, we would have tried to help for the sake of the gospel. But in the context of such local immorality, which we should not be funding even indirectly or minimally, we simply said, 'No! Not with our money you don't.'

It was the obvious and appropriate response, and we have 'capped' these voluntary quota payments ever since. We want to give to the wider Church. We give a great percentage of the entire sum for home mission, overseas mission and Third World relief which goes out from the churches in the Newcastle Diocese – but the donors at Jesmond decide where their giving goes, not the diocese. We also have a duty to make provision for the opportu-nities for evangelism at Jesmond.[2]

With the new centralized structures in the Church, the quota is a way of paying stipends. The money goes into the central fund and then goes out again, back to the parishes. Morally speaking, a parish church can therefore only cap its quota when it is a net-giver – when it is paying in more than it receives back from the centre. At Jesmond we currently cap at the costs we are to our diocesan centre in terms of stipends and housing, plus 15 per cent for central costs, plus the cost of pensions. When we do that, it means we are not making any use of the huge Church Commissioners' subsidy that

[1] Peter Selby, 'Our Authority Problem', *Christian Action*, Autumn 1979, p. 7.
[2] On the negative effect of financial subsidies for the growth of churches receiving long-term subsidies see David Holloway, *Ready, Steady, Grow*, Eastbourne, Kingsway Publications, 1989, p. 84ff.

still comes into Newcastle Diocese: it is all available for 'poorer' churches. A significant amount of the Church Commissioners' Assets, which we now never see, is money originally deposited by Evangelical Christians for Jesmond Parish Church in 1861, for its own mission and ministry. It is now helping to fund, without distinction, any bishops, bureaucracies and churches that need subsidizing.

There were three reasons why I was asked to convene the meeting in London of leaders from such 'net-giving' churches. One, I had many years' experience of the Newcastle Diocesan Board of Finance, so I knew exactly how the financing of a diocese worked. Two, I had also been a member of the Joint Budget Committee of the General Synod (1986–90), so I knew how financing the General Synod worked. Both these experiences had shown me how bureaucracies, either intentionally or unintentionally, so elaborate funding procedures that outsiders find it hard to discover the facts. And, three, I was from a larger church that had not only already capped its quota but had also experienced the vitriol which such an action attracts. Such a response is to be expected. Any attempt at reformation is bound to involve money at some point, as history teaches, and then all hell is let loose. John Wycliffe's fourteenth-century attempts at reformation involved telling people not to pay tithes to support a 'notoriously negligent' curate: they should not foster 'such wickedness'.[3] Luther's sixteenth-century attempts at reformation involved attacking the system of indulgences so that money dried up for the building of St Peter's in Rome. People can ignore appeals to obey the Bible, but money talks in the Church just as it does in the world.

This finance meeting at the end of 1992 coincided with a sense of 'profound crisis' in the Church of England – at least that was how a non-Anglican journalist described it in *The Times* on 18 January 1993. Things were coming to a head.

Anglican Evangelicals had been aware of the crisis for some time. Once the consecration of David Jenkins as Bishop of Durham in 1984 had institutionalized fundamental doubts regarding the virginal conception of Jesus and his bodily Resurrection, they saw the writing on the wall. This was followed by official uncertainty

[3] Matthew Spinka (ed.), *Advocates of Reform*, London, SCM Press, 1953, p. 38.

with regard to homosexual practice because of the Bishops' report *Issues in Human Sexuality*. Then the holding of multifaith worship in a number of churches, including Westminster Abbey, made many question Anglican commitment to belief in the uniqueness and finality of Christ.[4]

For Anglican Catholics the crisis was finally confirmed with the vote to ordain women to the presbyterate in November 1992. They realized then what Anglican Evangelicals had known since much earlier, namely that the Church of England was losing touch with its apostolic roots.

## EVANGELICALS AND REFORM

After the finance meeting in December 1992, I was invited to another meeting for parochial clergy that Dick Lucas, of St Helen's, Bishopsgate, was convening on 20–21 January 1993. This was a small conference to hear how Philip Jensen, an Australian Anglican and rector of St Matthias, Sydney, saw the situation from his perspective.

The problem was clear. The Church of England seemed to be drifting from the gospel of Jesus Christ as proclaimed in our Anglican tradition at the Reformation, as enshrined in our historic formularies, and as restored in Evangelical revivals. Being English, however, this was a slow and polite process. At the same time similar problems were being experienced around the world, and it was even worse in America. ECUSA (the Episcopal Church of the United States of America) was being more brash in its apostasy.

The parochial clergy who met in January 1993 saw that action was needed. The need was not to secure a place for Evangelicals in a steadily declining Church, but to enable men and women throughout the parishes of England to come to a living faith in Jesus Christ, to be built up in the fellowship of his Church and then to be effective for him in his world.

4 In September 1991 an open letter 'To the leadership of the Church of England', signed by hundreds of clergy, protested against 'gatherings for interfaith worship and prayer involving Christian people. These include the Interfaith Commonwealth Day Observance in Westminster Abbey.'

The clergy who were present would have been described as 'mainstream Evangelicals'. The 1989 *English Church Census* by MARC Europe distinguished between 'broad', 'mainstream' and 'charismatic' Evangelicals. While there is some overlap in these categories, the survey shows that the only significant adult growth in the Church of England is of mainstream Evangelicals.[5] This group, therefore, felt a responsibility for asking the question, 'How can we help the nation and the Church?' They saw three options.

The first was to opt out, to ignore the wider Church, and simply to engage in a caring, intelligent and thorough local parochial ministry. This was a strategy employed by Anglican Evangelicals earlier in the twentieth century. The result, however, was an unchallenged Liberal–Catholic leadership and the current situation.

The second option was to work for evolution and to follow the strategy adopted since the Evangelical Congress at Keele in 1967. At that time Evangelicals decided to enter the structures of the Church at every level and participate fully so as to 'capture the Church of England' for an Evangelical gospel. By the 1990s, however, it was clear to many that this strategy had resulted in a number of Evangelicals being captured *by* the Church of England and consequently being ineffective.

I saw this myself on the General Synod. I also saw that even if you tried very hard not to compromise, you still did not achieve a great deal. A former colleague of mine described the work that I did, and the work of others concerned to uphold the apostolic faith at the centre, as little more than 'stopping other people pulling the plug out'. But we never managed to fill the bath with water. Nonetheless, that effort of stopping what was negative was not unimportant. It was, I am sure, a vital holding activity. But this would not win the nation for Christ. Something more was needed – a third option.

That third option was to work for reform – not through the centre but through the parishes and congregations – the grass roots – committed together and helping each other. The policy proposed was one of deliberate and, where necessary, revolutionary change from the bottom upwards. It was for the parishes to take back responsibility for the Church of England from the

[5] Peter Brierley (ed.), *Prospects for the Nineties*, London, MARC Europe, 1991, p. 42.

centralizing bureaucracies, whether of bishops or synods. Those of us who met in January 1993 were convinced that the only hope for the Church of England was in such reform. Canon Marriott once wrote, 'History offers few examples of an institution which effects its own revival. In the majority of cases that is brought about by a minority movement within its borders. Christianity was itself such a movement, so was Franciscanism, so was Wesleyanism, so was Tractarianism.'[6] We agreed.

There was yet another conference on 1–2 February 1993, also convened in an ad hoc manner. This was at Swanwick in Derbyshire. It was held for mainstream Evangelicals to discuss the November 1992 vote in the General Synod on the ordination of women and its consequences for Evangelicals opposed to women's ordination. Some of the clergy present at the previous two meetings were also present at this conference. Again it was clear that the issue of women's ordination was only a presenting problem – the real crisis was something far deeper. One of the results of the conference was a vote for 'an association of reforming Evangelicals to evangelize the nation and for the biblical reform of the Church of England'.

Following these three meetings, a group of us – mostly from larger churches around the country and from the mainstream Evangelical tradition – met together in London on 22 February 1993 to consider further action. We needed a network and we needed a name. We set up a council to coordinate the network and I suggested the name 'Reform'. This found general acceptance. But how does this relate to issues of Church and State?

It is very simple. A society needs, like that three-legged stool described in Chapter 1, a healthy political order and a healthy economic order, but also a healthy spiritual order. So for the Church to fall sick is a serious social pathology, and for the established Church to fall sick is particularly serious. Other public institutions formally look to it for spiritual and moral leadership and guidance. The reform of the Church is therefore necessary as an act of social responsibility.

---

[6] S.J. Marriott, 'The Soul of Man', in *Towards a Christian Order*, London, Eyre and Spottiswoode, 1942, p. 28.

## GOALS AND BASIS

What was to be the primary goal of Reform? The primary goal was and is obedience to the great commission of Jesus Christ:

> *All authority in heaven and on earth has been given to me. Therefore go and make disciples of all nations, baptizing them in the name of the Father and of the Son and of the Holy Spirit, and teaching them to obey everything I have commanded you. And surely I am with you always, to the very end of the age (Matthew 28:18–20).*

The great objective is to evangelize the nation and see others become Christians. What is the basis for this objective? Our basis of faith is found in Canon A5, *Of the Doctrine of the Church of England*:

> *The Doctrine of the Church of England is grounded in the Holy Scriptures, and in such teaching of the Ancient Fathers and Councils of the Church as are agreeable to the said Scriptures. In particular such doctrine is to be found in the Thirty-nine Articles of Religion, the Book of Common Prayer, and the Ordinal.*

This, by law, is the doctrine of the Church of England as established in the Church of England (Worship and Doctrine) Measure 1994 (5.1). It reflects the moderate Reformed tradition of our Anglican forefathers – a tradition that we believe is a faithful exposition of the apostolic faith. It sees the Bible as the supreme authority. It agrees that the Bible, to avoid wrong private interpretation, is to be read through the lens of the first four General Councils and the interpretation of the early Fathers; but if the reading of the Bible challenges those Fathers or Councils, the scriptural truth rather than the patristic interpretation is to be accepted. So the Church is to be subordinate to the Bible and the Bible has to be interpreted as a whole. Article XX says, 'It is not lawful for the church to ordain any thing that is contrary to God's Word written, neither may it so expound one place of Scripture that it be repugnant to another.'

Some will ask, however, 'Is the Bible clear enough?' The answer is, 'Yes.' In terms of its broad outline and in terms of fundamental issues, it is not difficult to see what the Bible is teaching. There is a 'perspicuity' to it. This is the Anglican understanding of scriptural hermeneutics (or interpretation). In his *Prologue or Preface to the Bible* Thomas Cranmer quotes John Chrysostom with approval when he says of the Bible:

> For the Holy Ghost hath so ordered and attempered the scriptures that in them as well publicans, fishers and shepherds may find their edification, as great doctors their erudition. For those books were not made to vain-glory like as were the writing of the Gentile philosophers and rhetoricians, to the intent the makers should be had in admiration for their high styles and obscure manner of writing, whereof nothing can be understand without a master or an expositor. But the apostles and prophets wrote their books so that their special intent and purpose might be understood and perceived of every reader, which was nothing but the edification or amendment of the life of them that readeth or heareth it.[7]

The Church of England is fundamentally a biblical Church. Tradition and reason are important but not equal partners. Although this biblical tradition is the authentic Anglican tradition, however, it has now been rejected by many in the leadership of the Church. The grounding of the Church of England is no longer for them in the Holy Scriptures but in the episcopate (or the synods). So the bishops rather than the Bible become the ultimate authority. The Church historian R.A. Norris has written:

> Originally [in classical Anglicanism] episcopacy had been defended as the normative, divinely ordained or approved ordering of the Church; but the one absolutely indispensable mark of a Church was taken to be its continuance in apostolic and scriptural teaching. Now, however, episcopacy has come to count as a factor that grounds the identity of the Church.[8]

This Catholic element is now united with a general doctrinal liberalism, as we have seen. Reform is concerned that this Liberal–Catholic

[7] Carl S. Meyer (ed.), *Cranmer's Selected Writings*, London, SPCK, 1961, pp. 4–5.
[8] R.A. Norris, 'Episcopacy', in Stephen Sykes and John Booty (eds), *The Study of Anglicanism*, London, SPCK, 1988, p. 306.

drift is destroying the Church of England. What is to be done about it as we enter the twenty-first century?

## CHARLES SIMEON

One of the greatest figures in the history of the Church of England was Charles Simeon. As much as any, under God, Simeon was remarkably used in the nineteenth-century Evangelical revival in England and around the world. He was the vicar of Holy Trinity, Cambridge, at the end of the eighteenth and the beginning of the nineteenth centuries. Macaulay said of Simeon after his death: 'As to Simeon, if you knew what his authority and influence were, and how they extended from Cambridge to the most remote corners of England, you would allow that his real sway was far greater than that of any primate.'[9]

What would Simeon have said to help reform the Church as we enter the twenty-first century? There were six points which he might well have made.

The first is clear from his life's goal, inscribed on his monument. His goal was for the whole Church 'to know nothing "but Jesus Christ, and him crucified"'. He also tells us that his aim was to vindicate 'the great doctrines of *salvation by grace through faith in Christ*' and to ensure that all should 'uniformly tend *to humble the sinner, to exalt the Saviour [and] to promote holiness*'.[10] His first concern for the twenty-first century would, therefore, be to re-establish those Evangelical fundamentals in the Church.

Secondly, he would be concerned to see the Bible back in its rightful place and people maintaining the proportion and balance of the Bible. He put it like this:

> *The author [Simeon] is disposed to think that the Scripture system is of a broader and more comprehensive character than some very dogmatical theologians are inclined to allow; and that, as wheels in a*

[9] In Hugh Evan Hopkins, *Charles Simeon of Cambridge*, London, Hodder and Stoughton, 1977, p. 118.

[10] Arthur Pollard (ed.), *Let Wisdom Judge – University Addresses and Sermon Outlines by Charles Simeon*, London, Inter-Varsity Fellowship, 1959, p. 13.

*complicated machine may move in opposite directions and yet subserve one common end, so may truths apparently opposite be perfectly reconcilable with each other and equally subserve the purposes of God in the accomplishment of man's salvation. The author feels it impossible to avow too distinctly that it is an invariable rule with him to endeavour to give to every portion of the Word of God its full and proper force, without considering what scheme it favours, or whose system it is likely to advance [he was referring to decided Calvinists or Arminians].*

He concludes this passage: 'He [Simeon] is content to sit as a learner at the feet of the holy Apostles, and has no ambition to teach them how they ought to have spoken.'[11]

For Christians to take this approach on board at the start of the new millennium is vital. Formulas of inerrancy, infallibility or final authority with respect to the Bible at the end of the twentieth century could mean almost anything. But the distinction made by Simeon is key. Christian believers can have fellowship with almost *anyone* of whatever Christian persuasion or denomination who is genuinely 'content to sit as a learner at the feet of the holy Apostles'. People who claim to agree to the formulas but then want to 'teach the Apostles how they should have spoken', by contrast, are hard to live with.

Simeon would have had that 'back to the Bible' vision right up front for the twenty-first century – and so must we. He probably knew of Luther's comment, 'The word of God is seldom retained in its purity in any one place beyond the period of twenty or at best forty years. The people become accustomed to it, grow cold in their Christian love, and regard God's gift of grace with indifference.'[12]

## FIGHTING THE WOLF

Thirdly, Simeon would have wanted a Church where there were more good shepherds than hired hands. What is the difference between the good shepherd and the hired hand? It is not that the

---

[11] H.C.G. Moule, *Charles Simeon*, London, Inter-Varsity Fellowship, 1956, p. 79.

[12] Quoted in S.M. Houghton, *Sketches from Church History*, Edinburgh, Banner of Truth Trust, 1995, p. 174.

hired hand does not feed the sheep. He does. No; the answer is that the hired hand *does not fight the wolf.* Jesus says, 'The hired hand is not the shepherd who owns the sheep. So when he sees the wolf coming, he abandons the sheep and runs away. Then the wolf attacks the flock and scatters it' (John 10:12).

Simeon knew all about fighting the wolf – those that would seek to frustrate, destroy or distort the gospel. Originally the churchwardens tried to lock him out of Holy Trinity Church, and then tried to lock the congregation out of the pews – so he preached to people as they stood in the aisles. When there was rowdyism, on the other hand, he took stern action. On one occasion he made a student read out a public apology for his behaviour. Later in life he had to fight the bishops who would not ordain his men because they were too evangelical or Calvinist. That meant circumventing systems and getting the men ordained irregularly by other bishops who were willing to play ball. Certainly this happened to Church Missionary Society ordinands.[13]

Fourthly, related to the above, Simeon was always concerned to train up men for the ministry, men who would be faithful and effective leaders. Simeon did that through his 'sermon classes' and his 'conversation parties'. So at the start of the new century, he would have said that we must review and expand our training, and where necessary develop new models of training. People must learn the Bible and how to teach it; but they must also learn how to manage and lead growing churches.

Fifthly, he would be concerned to see the establishment of large churches with effective evangelical ministries in urban areas. Through acquiring advowsons (the right to appoint to a living) in the Church of England he managed to achieve that goal in his own day. He tells us that his aim was always 'the securing of a faithful ministry in influential places'.[14] He saw how important it was to have faithful workers in key locations.

A number of strategic Evangelical churches in England owe their existence (in human terms) to Simeon. Acquiring the right to

---

[13] I am grateful to the Rev. Dr Alan Munden, formerly on the staff at Jesmond, for his research on this.

[14] Hopkins, *Charles Simeon of Cambridge,* op. cit., p. 218.

appoint to a living is no longer possible, however, so we must try other methods. With the establishment of alternative episcopal oversight to which Reform is committed, there are a number of possibilities.

We still need more large churches 'in influential places', however. Larger churches are important for re-evangelizing the nation. The larger church is where teams of full-time workers are able to function together. They have economies of scale, usually a thriving music ministry and a strong youth work (children tend to prefer larger groups where they can find friends), more social effectiveness, more media involvement and (contrary to some suggestions) a healthy effect on smaller churches. Also most people seem to prefer larger churches. In the Church of England two-thirds of the worshippers attend one-third of the churches, half attend one-fifth of them, while well over one-third attend just one-tenth of the churches.[15] That is to say, the majority are found in larger not smaller churches. If our concern is with people and not with keeping clergy and central bureaucracies happy, we ought to be thinking about encouraging the development of such churches. Sadly, the present centralism in the Church of England militates against this sort of development.

Sixthly, and connected to the subject of worshippers, Simeon would be concerned that there should be men and women of both prayer and action. Simeon not only prayed – and he did that more faithfully than many – he also acted. It was Simeon who was the one who really got the Church Missionary Society going in 1799. Simeon asked, 'What shall we do? When shall we do it? How shall we do it?' And he provided his own answers: 'We require something more than resolutions ... Directly ... It is hopeless to wait for missionaries ... Send out Catechists.'[16] Thus in April 1799, within a month of the meeting at which he said those words, the Church Missionary Society was founded – and has been going for over 200 years.

Simeon set a great example of walking the tightrope. He wanted Evangelical unity. He did not want the secession of Evangelicals

[15] See Holloway, *The Church of England – Where Is It Going?*, op. cit., p. 168; see also Holloway, *Ready, Steady, Grow*, op. cit., p. 106ff.

[16] Pollard (ed.), *Let Wisdom Judge*, op. cit., p. 12.

from the Church of England. But he knew that unless he took firm action, of the sort which some other people might not like, there would be even greater disunity.

To sum up, then, Simeon's prescription for the twenty-first century would be as follows:

1  To re-establish Evangelical fundamentals
2  To maintain biblical truth and the whole of biblical truth
3  To ensure that we have good shepherds and not hired hands (i.e. people who can and will fight the wolf)
4  To train men and women for their appropriate ministries
5  To have a concern for larger Evangelical churches in all urban areas
6  To be firm in taking action as well as praying

## ECCLESIOLOGY

One other essential as we enter the twenty-first century is to have a renewed confidence in the Reformed doctrine of the Church, or a Reformed ecclesiology. This, I submit, is more biblical than others.

The Reformed doctrine of the Church can be summed up using the Creed, and in particular those four words 'one, holy, catholic and apostolic', and by referring to Christ's high-priestly prayer in John 17.

First, the Church is *one* not because of external organization but essentially because it is one 'as the Father is in Christ and Christ is in the Father' (John 17:21). As Archbishop William Temple said, 'The way to the union of Christendom does not lie through committee-rooms, though there is a task of formulation to be done there. It lies through personal union with the Lord so deep and real as to be comparable to his union with the Father.'[17]

Secondly, the Church is *holy* not by being withdrawn from the world but as God 'protect[s] it from the evil one' (John 17:15). And the means to holiness is God's Word. So Jesus prays for his disciples, 'Sanctify them by the truth; your word is truth' (John 17:17).

[17] William Temple, *Readings in St John's Gospel*, London, Macmillan, 1950, p. 327.

Thirdly, the Church is *catholic* (*katholikos* is the Greek word for 'universal'), on the one hand, in so far as it is missionary minded and its members go into all the world: 'As you sent me into the world,' says Jesus, 'I have sent them into the world' (John 17:18). Catholicity comes about by being obedient in evangelism.

On the other hand, the Church is also catholic or universal when it meets a certain test. How do you test for catholicity? The old Vincentian Canon, 'what has been believed everywhere, always and by all' (*quod ubique, quod semper, quod ab omnibus creditum est*) will not do after the East–West break and the Reformation. But of course, there was another vital Canon in the early Church, the Canon of the Old and New Testaments, with the New Testament as we know it certainly fixed by AD 367 and Athanasius' *Festal Letter*. That Canon gives you the teaching of Christ and his apostles, and is now the true test for catholicity.

Fourthly, the Church is *apostolic* in so far as its members, 'those who will believe in [Christ] through their message', are in unity with the apostles of Christ. Jesus prays 'that all of them [believers and apostles] may be one' (John 17:20–21). Subsequent believers relate to the apostles not by an apostolic succession of bishops (before the Canon of Scripture existed, that succession was better than nothing), but through the Bible where they find apostolic teaching, and as they follow the example of the apostles and go out into the world to witness to Christ. 'Apostolicity' basically means 'sentness'.

In addition to those credal marks of the Church, the Reformers stressed the importance of the 'invisible' Church or, as the Book of Common Prayer puts it, the Church 'mystical'. Richard Hooker, for example, wrote, 'For lack of diligent observing the difference, first between the Church of God mystical and visible, then between the visible sound and corrupted, sometimes more, sometimes less, the oversights are neither few nor light that have been committed.'[18]

The denominations, of which the Church of England is one, are forms of scaffolding supporting the true Church of Christ – the true covenant community of believers which God has called out

---

[18] Richard Hooker, *Of the Laws of Ecclesiastical Polity Vol. I*, op. cit., p. 289.

down the ages and across the world. The Church of England is part of the visible Church. And we must have no illusions about the visible Church, as Hooker implied. That is why we have to work for its reform.

The Reformed summary of the doctrine of the Church in the Thirty-nine Articles is very simple, but profound. Article XIX states, 'The visible Church of Christ is a congregation of faithful men, in the which the pure Word of God is preached, and the Sacraments be duly ministered according to Christ's ordinance in all those things that of necessity are requisite to the same.'

You have there four *essentials* for the Church:

1 An actual body of believers, a congregation (not some denominational superstructure)
2 Sound preaching
3 The proper administration of the sacraments
4 Sufficient discipline which ensures that you have 'faithful' men and women making up the body of believers

Our Reformers were committed to the concept of 'essentials'. The Reformed doctrine of the Church, therefore, presupposes the Pauline distinction between fundamentals and secondary issues (Romans 14). In the sixteenth century Bishop Davenant said, 'Brotherly communion between Churches Evangelical is not to be cut asunder because of divers opinions about questions controversial ... This is to be premised; the bonds of the brotherly communion of Christian Churches ought not to be dissolved upon every difference of opinion, but only for the denying of opposing fundamentals.'[19]

## UNITY

It is in the context of 'essentials' and 'secondary issues' that believing Christians, of whatever denomination, surely need to work together for as much unity as is possible in the twenty-first

[19] Quoted in Jeremiah Burroughs (1599–1649), 'What we are to bear with in others', in Iain M. Murray (ed.), *The Reformation of the Church*, Edinburgh, Banner of Truth Trust, 1987, pp. 327–8.

century. Among the denominations 'episcopacy' has been one crucial issue. Evangelicals in the Church of England are now re-evaluating what they believe about ministry, order and oversight.

Members of Reform are planning alternative episcopal oversight for early in the new millennium.[20] Sadly, some bishops are now denying what are clearly biblical fundamentals. But surely the New Testament categories of 'idolatry' (with multifaith religion being a subset of idolatry) and 'fornication' (with homosexual sex being a subset of fornication) have to be seen as fundamentally sinful. To tolerate these is sinful in itself, and to promote them is particularly wicked. There have to be lines in the sand. If crossed, there must be some break of communion. Clear markers are given in Revelation 2.20, which reads, 'Nevertheless, I have this against you: You tolerate that woman Jezebel, who calls herself a prophetess. By her teaching she misleads my servants into sexual immorality and the eating of food sacrificed to idols.' Some bishops are already transgressing these lines, and in areas of public significance. There are extreme examples, including the bishop (prominent in ordaining women, a supporter of the gay agenda and now retired) in the following story of

> an Episcopalian priest who wanted a baby but definitely not a husband. She invited three friends over (two of them priests) to masturbate for her, and she then impregnated herself with the mixture of their sperm. The purpose of having several sperm sources, she explained on national television, was to avoid knowing who the father was, and thus to make sure that the child would have an intimate bond to no one but herself. The child is now three years old, and the mother has declared that she intends to have another baby by the same procedure. The Washington Post described her as the first artificially inseminated priest in history, which is probably true. Her bishop, Paul Moore of New York, appeared with her on television and gave his unqualified blessing to this undertaking, citing the need for the church to come to terms with the modern world.[21]

[20] See David Holloway, *Alternative Episcopal Oversight*, Sheffield, Reform, 1999.
[21] Neuhaus, *Guaranteeing the Good Life*, op. cit., p. 3.

But there are more moderate bishops who are also crossing these lines. 'Conservative moderates' say that they accept the Bible and that its doctrinal and moral teaching is clear, but for pastoral reasons they ignore it and can end up on the same side of the line as Paul Moore. 'Liberal moderates' ignore or reject the Bible as liberals, but as moderates they say the Church is not *ready yet* for their new doctrines or morality. They would support Paul Moore in principle but say that he is moving too fast. With such men in the hierarchy, there is, indeed, a need for alternative episcopal oversight.

Perhaps a new form of 'episcopate' or oversight could embrace some Evangelicals outside the Church of England. Why should there not be an interchangeability of ministries between Anglican Evangelicals and Free Church Evangelicals – other things being equal? This in turn might lead to a wider unity of believers. It is a huge task, of course. In simple terms, if Anglican Evangelicals could develop a polity that would allow two integrities over baptism and some Free Church Evangelicals could accept a genuinely reformed episcopacy (unlike the present unreformed 'prelacy' that the Church of England has inherited), we might be some way to getting there.

There must be no illusions over unity, however. Three rules of thumb are be kept in mind. One – a principle already touched on – do not overestimate what you can achieve in one year, or underestimate what you can achieve in five years. Two, with regard to the life of institutions, as with human life, it is usually easier to give birth than to raise the dead. And three, relevant for any thinking about unity (small or large, deep or shallow, formal or informal), if you put one corpse next to the other, normally neither of them comes alive!

Nevertheless, is it so implausible that we could aim to develop structures for the twenty-first century to allow this interchangeablity of ministries? Ministers might start out in an Anglican church, and then move to be in a Free church, and vice versa.

The ecumenical movement has run into the ground not only because of its self-defeating theological liberalism, but because we now live in a post-denominational age. People under 40 years old do not, on average, choose churches according to denominational labels. Many are not concerned with structures. But it is a time for radical political restructuring in the British nation, as determined by New Labour. Maybe this is a good time – as it is part of the public mood – to think about restructuring in the Church also. We need minimal structures and minimal institutions. My dream is not for anybody to leave their denominations or affiliations, but to take on board 'dual citizenship'. Already the Church of England has done this with its electoral rolls. You can be on the books of a Baptist church and also on the electoral roll of an Anglican parish, and so potentially a member of the General Synod.

The Church has to think about all these things in the context of the wider world, where there are not only problems but also, as we should keep in mind, possibilities.

## THE FUTURE

There are two stories to tell of what is going on in the world. Like Dickens and his *Tale of Two Cities*, we can say, 'It was the best of times, it was the worst of times.' It is like that today in the West and in the UK. At the moment things are not good, but in the US, as we have seen, there are accounts of change happening at the grass roots – at least morally. And what happens in the US often comes to the UK, albeit later.

In the January 1999 edition of *Christianity Today* Charles Colson wrote an article entitled 'The Sky Isn't Falling'. He was writing against Christian doom-merchants, pointing out that in America now the divorce rate is down, the birthrate for unmarried teenagers is down; abortion is down; even crime is down. He then wrote about 'the gods that failed': 'The twentieth century was the age of ideology, of the great "isms" – communism, socialism, nazism, liberalism, humanism, scientism.' But these idols, he said, have now sunk.

> *Nazism was forever disgraced by the horrors of its concentration camps. The Soviet Union crumbled with the Berlin Wall ... Liberalism, while still powerful, has lost its lustre ... Even science often seems a Frankenstein's monster turning on its creators.*
> *This is the most significant fact at the end of the twentieth century.*

*All the major ideological constructions have failed, tossed on the ash heap of history...*

*The only remaining 'ism' is Post-modernism, which is not an ideology but a repudiation of all ideologies. Its relativism is the admission that every attempt to construct a comprehensive, utopian world-view has failed. It is a formalized expression of despair.*

*Only one compelling claim to transcendent truth remains, one secure hope: Christianity. The church has stood unshaken through the ebb and flow of two millennia. It has survived both the barbarian invasions of the Middle Ages and the intellectual assaults of the modern era.*

*The dawn of the new millennium is a time for Christians to celebrate, to blow trumpets and fly the flag high. To desert the field of battle now would be historical blindness, betraying our heritage just when we have the greatest opportunity ... This is the time to make a compelling case that Christianity offers the only rational and realistic hope for both personal redemption and social renewal.*

As Paul says in 1 Corinthians 16:9, 'A great door for effective work has opened to me, and there are many who oppose me.' That is going to be the story for Christians at the start of the new millennium. The spiritual health of the nation will depend on the response of the Church to that opening.

# CHAPTER FIFTEEN

# CONCLUSION

## AFRICA

It may well be, as the 1998 Lambeth Conference of Anglican Bishops from all over the world indicated, that the Christian moral and spiritual centre of gravity is moving to the Third World, not least to Africa.

I have been very grateful for the contacts I have had with Africa over the years, in the Sudan and in Kenya. From the Sudan I learnt the fact that God calls his people to suffer, and something of how they can endure that suffering. I remember Bishop Oliver Allison preaching at a confirmation service in a packed Khartoum Cathedral to many Sudanese, mostly southerners who had lost loved ones, homes, money and security. Theirs was, and still is, a terrible condition, as bad as that of any suffering people in any part of the world, but without cameramen or reporters to relay their plight every night on the BBC nine o'clock news or on CNN. The text the Bishop preached on was Hebrews 13:5–6:

> *Keep your lives free from the love of money and be content with what you have, because God has said,*
> > *'Never will I leave you;*
> > *never will I forsake you.'*
> *So we say with confidence,*
> > *'The Lord is my helper; I will not be afraid.*
> > *What can man do to me?'*

The text preached itself. It was while in the Sudan that I became aware of the wisdom of Paul and Barnabas, who were 'strengthening the disciples and encouraging them to remain true to the faith. "We must go through many hardships to enter the kingdom of God," they said' (Acts 14:22).

On average, evidence from the West shows that a Christian's life chances and quality are better than a non-Christian's, as we have seen. But even if *on average* that were also true globally – and comparing like with like – God seems to let his people, and sometimes whole regions where there are many Christians, go through times of extreme difficulty. Indeed, the twentieth century probably saw more persecution of Christians than any previous century. 'In general we can say,' reported Paul Marshall in 1997, 'that, currently, two hundred to two hundred fifty million Christians are persecuted for their faith, and a further four hundred million live under non-trivial restrictions on religious liberty.'[1] Hebrews says, 'The Lord disciplines those he loves' (12:6). On that basis you are to 'endure hardship as discipline; [for] God is treating you as sons' (12:7). These are lessons not only for Africa but for the West as well.

If I learnt about suffering from the Sudan, I learnt about the joy of straightforward faith from Kenya. Jesmond Parish Church has had a partnership with St Philip's Church, Mburi, Ngiriambu Parish, in the Diocese of Kirinyaga in rural Kenya since the mid-1980s. Through a link with David Gitari, the Archbishop of Kenya, we have been able to help with the building and development of the church centre at St Philip's, with a small clinic, laboratory, school, technical workshop and the main auditorium. We have had reciprocal visits too. I have been able to visit St Philip's on several occasions, and I always come back spiritually refreshed.

If it can be said of Britain and the West in general that we live 'in relative physical and economic splendour but in a spiritual and psychological slum', the situation is reversed with many of the Christians I have met in Kenya. Many of them have to live in material slums but are in spiritual splendour. What is their secret? They understand the heart of the gospel. These Christians who have such uninhibited joy have not departed from the faith as many

---

[1] Paul Marshall, *Their Blood Cries Out*, Dallas, Word, 1997, p. 255.

have in the West. That departure is our number one problem – a spiritual problem with social consequences.

## DIFFERENT GOSPELS

Some, however, would say that our problem in the relationship between the Church and State is that of passivity. The West, they say, has become secularized largely because Christian people have been passive and allowed cultural and social leadership to pass to a non-Christian minority. On this reading of the situation the key is to defeat the social inertia of Christians. Overcome that, it is said, and there will be desecularization and the possibility of restoring a Christian society.

There is undoubtedly truth in this analysis. It takes seriously the reality of a Christian culture. It recognizes that wherever there is a sufficient number of faithful Christians there will sooner or later be a Christian society to some degree. In time social traditions and institutions will develop or change. The State will be affected because these will be traditions and institutions based on biblical principles and insights rather than secular ones.

Nevertheless, behind passivity, which is an undoubted problem, there is a basic spiritual drift. And that is the number one problem in the Church–State equation. The apostle Paul wrote to the church at Galatia, 'I am astonished that you are so quickly deserting the one who called you by the grace of Christ and are turning to a different gospel – which is really no gospel at all' (1:6–7). Later he said, 'It is for freedom that Christ has set us free. Stand firm...' (5:1). That could equally well be said to us in the West at the beginning of the twenty-first century.

It was Peter Berger, the sociologist, who began his 1987 Erasmus Lecture with those very words from Galatians 1:6–7. His subject was 'Different Gospels: The Social Sources of Apostasy'. His thesis was the following:

> *Every age has a distinctive genius, for evil as well as good, and our age has produced evils that can safely be called unique. But apostasy – the substitution of different gospels for the gospel of Christ – has been*

*a constant in the history of the Church. It was there right from the beginning, as the letter to the Galatians (along with many other portions of the New Testament) serves to remind us. The essence of apostasy is always the same: seeking salvation not in the grace of Christ 'heard with faith' but rather in what Paul calls 'the works of the law'.*[2]

He argued powerfully that the mainline Protestant churches have substituted cultural (not least feminist) and political agendas for the gospel of faith in Christ. And he concluded, 'Serving the church today, I believe, must begin with an understanding of the specific forms of apostasy that confront us today; we must recall the true meaning of the gospel, church, and ministry, and then put our ecclesial houses in better order.'[3]

We have seen the confusion in the Church and in the wider world of the State. But judgement has to begin 'with the family of God' (1 Peter 4:17). Christians today should therefore pay special attention to this letter to the Galatians. Times have not changed so radically as some people think, either. More than 100 years ago Bishop J.C. Ryle could write these words:

*We cannot be too jealous in these days about the slightest departure from the 'faith once delivered to the saints'. We cannot be too careful to add nothing to, and take nothing away, from the simplicity of the Gospel...*

*Let us mark the testimony of Scripture on this subject. The Epistle to the Galatians is the inspired handbook for these times. Mark how in that Epistle St Paul declares, 'Though we, or an angel from heaven, preach any other Gospel unto you than that which we have preached unto you, let him be accursed' (Galatians 1:9).*[4]

One hundred and fifty years earlier than Ryle, Charles Wesley was reading Luther's Commentary on Galatians. He wrote:

[2] Peter Berger, 'Different Gospels: The Social Sources of Apostasy', in Richard John Neuhaus (ed.), *American Apostasy: the Triumph of 'Other' Gospels*, Grand Rapids, Eerdmans, 1989, pp. 1–2.

[3] Ibid., p. 14.

[4] J.C. Ryle, *Knots Untied*, London, Thyme, 1932, p. 15.

*I marvelled that we were so soon and so entirely removed from him that called us into the grace of Christ, unto another Gospel. Who would believe that our Church had been founded upon this important article of justification by faith alone? I am astonished I should ever think this a new doctrine; especially while our Articles and Homilies stand unrepealed, and the key of knowledge not yet taken away...*

*I spent some hours this evening in private with Martin Luther, who was greatly blessed to me, especially the conclusion of the second chapter. I laboured, waited and prayed to feel 'who loved me, and gave himself for me'.[5]*

Four days later, Charles Wesley's prayer was answered, when on Whit Sunday he experienced his 'evangelical conversion', as it was called. He knew then what it was to have not only the doctrine of justification by faith in the head but a consciousness in the heart of being justified and accepted.

Fifty years earlier than that, John Bunyan, the author of *Pilgrim's Progress*, wrote these words:

*The God in whose hands are all our days and ways, did cast into my hand, one day, a book of Martin Luther; it was his comment on the Galatians ... the which, when I had but a little way perused, I found my condition, in his experience, so largely and profoundly handled, as if his book had been written out of my own heart.[6]*

One hundred years before that, Luther himself was captured by the message of Galatians and wrote his famous commentary.[7]

## THE MESSAGE OF GALATIANS

What, then, does Paul's epistle to the Galatians have to say? It makes it clear that these issues are deadly serious. The Galatians were 'being bewitched' (3:1). They thought it was all so plausible

[5] Quoted in the editor's preface to Martin Luther, *The Commentary on St Paul's Epistle to the Galatians*, London, James Clarke, 1953, p. 3.

[6] Ibid., p. 14.

[7] First edition, 1535; second edition, 1538; first English edition, 1575.

and so spiritual, but in reality they were turning from a true life in the Spirit and a true life of faith to a life of works and human effort. What were the Galatian Christians doing? They were simply saying that people needed the extra experience of being circumcised. That identification with Judaism would be the real answer to all their problems and needs, so they alleged – it would be the key to religious success and God's approval.

'Works' then included more than the ritual of circumcision and other parts of the Jewish religious system. Then as now, they included anything that comes between believers and faith in Christ and love for him, even good things. Orthodox Christians can be so caught up with their 'religion' that they forget the one to whom all their religion is directed. That is the danger not only with Church machinery – its councils and committees – but also with the various Christian movements (even reform movements) that develop. Once these things are allowed to take centre stage, we are 'bewitched'.

Galatians makes clear, contrary to what many believe, that there is present *and* ultimate judgement and 'destruction' (6:8). God hates what is evil and loves what is good. There is a divine hostility against sin – against all human neglect of God. And all are at fault, whether by commission (what they positively do wrong) or by omission (the good they just fail to do). The good news is good news *only* when heard in this context. For it is about the grace of God in Christ who rescues from current and future judgement.

So comprehensive has been the indoctrination of a theologically liberal agenda in the West that such concepts as this seem quite alien in today's therapeutic culture. In its place is what is felt to be a more congenial gospel. But this is 'a different gospel – which is really no gospel at all'. This is the challenge that faces the Church in the new millennium. This false gospel came into the West from the Enlightenment, during the second half of the nineteenth century and the first half of the twentieth century, and has been undermining the Church, and then the State, ever since. Richard Niebuhr summarizes its message as follows. He calls it 'the romantic conception of the kingdom of God'.

*[It] involved no discontinuities, no crises, no tragedies, or sacrifice, no loss of all things, no cross and Resurrection. In ethics it reconciled*

*the interests of the individual with those of society by means of faith in
a natural identity of interests or in the benevolent, altruistic character
of man. In politics and economics it slurred over national and class
divisions, seeing only the growth of unity and ignoring the increase
of self-assertion and exploitation. In religion it reconciled God and
man by deifying the latter and humanizing the former ... Christ the
Redeemer became Jesus the teacher or spiritual genius in whom the
religious capacities of mankind were fully developed ... Evolution,
growth, development, the culture of the religious life, the nurture of
the kindly sentiments, the extension of humanitarian ideals, and the
progress of civilization took the place of the Christian revolution...*

*A God without wrath brought men without sin into a kingdom
without judgment through the ministrations of a Christ without a
cross.*[8]

But which is true? That, or the message of Galatians? The truth of
the Resurrection proves the latter, as Paul preached to the sophisticated Athenians: 'In the past God overlooked such ignorance, but
now he commands all people everywhere to repent. For he has set a
day when he will judge the world with justice by the man he has
appointed [Jesus]. He has given proof of this to all men by raising
him from the dead' (Acts 17:30–31).

The essential message of Galatians is summed up in verse 4 of
chapter 1: 'The Lord Jesus Christ ... gave himself for our sins to
rescue us from the present evil age, according to the will of our God
and Father.' That is what needs to be heard once again in the
public arena in the twenty-first century.

Jesus Christ did not primarily come to teach ethical maxims. He
did that, but fundamentally he came to die, or as Paul says here in
Galatians 1:4, to 'give himself for our sins'. And that, says Paul, is
the only way people can be 'rescued from the present evil age'.

It is not unfair to call today's public and political world 'the
present evil age'. There is much evil around, as any cursory inspec-
tion of the newspaper, television news, or television programming
in general makes crystal clear. But who will deliver us from it? Most

[8] Quoted in Alec Vidler, *The Church in an Age of Revolution*, London, Penguin
Books, 1965, pp. 212–13.

of the solutions we can offer ourselves are merely 'sticking-plaster' solutions. What is needed is major surgery.

That means we first have to teach that God's Word and will, if violated, sooner or later will bring judgement. And God's verdict is spelled out in Galatians 3:10: 'Cursed is everyone who does not continue to do everything written in the Book of the Law.' That includes all of us in some measure. But the gospel that people need to hear is in Galatians 3:13–14: 'Christ redeemed us from the curse of the law by becoming a curse for us, for it is written: "Cursed is everyone who is hung on a tree." He redeemed us in order that the blessing given to Abraham might come to the Gentiles through Christ Jesus, so that by faith we might receive the promise of the Spirit.'

## TWO WAYS

The implication of this is that there are two ways to live. One is the way of 'the law', and that covers our self-effort, attempts at religion, religious interests, charitable giving, social involvement, political campaigning, or whatever obscures Jesus Christ. Its destination is the 'curse' (or hell) – which is currently not an acceptable concept, but it is there in the Bible. The other is the way of 'faith'. Faith is simple trust in Christ, a confidence that on the Cross of Calvary wrong was righted, that Christ bore our sins, that he became a curse for us and so we are now free from guilt and condemnation. The destination of this road is 'blessing' (not cursing) and the 'promise of the Spirit' (Galatians 3:14). The challenge is this: which way or which road are we on?

The evidence and the proof of our choice will come through our lifestyle. The Bible teaches that although 'works' must not come first, they must come second. 'Faith' must always be accompanied by 'works' – by some effect or action. This may involve sacrifice.

More than ever today there is a need for the sacrifice of some-times standing alone – even in the Church – and being prepared to be in a minority of one if necessary. Evil prevails because good men and women do nothing. And 'works' must include seeking to exhibit those fruits of the Spirit given in Galatians 5:22: 'love, joy, peace, patience, kindness, goodness, faithfulness, gentleness and self-control'.

The message of Galatians needs to be taken on board. It is about faith in Christ from start to finish. That is the real way to reform the Church and then change the world. It may mean sometimes shaking the foundations to ensure that the Church is truly standing on the one and only true foundation, Jesus Christ. On the negative side there will inevitably be conflicts with those denying the gospel. Paul had a very open conflict with Peter (Galatians 2:11–21). On the positive side, however, there will be new opportunities for active obedience – 'the obedience that comes from faith' (Romans 1:5). Active obedience which changes societies and whole nations is not necessarily to be found in the great gesture, but in faithful acts of service which really count but which few notice. In conclusion, here is what Paul said to the Galatian Christians about such service:

> *Do not be deceived: God cannot be mocked. A man reaps what he sows. The one who sows to please his sinful nature, from that nature will reap destruction; the one who sows to please the Spirit, from the Spirit will reap eternal life. Let us not become weary in doing good, for at the proper time we will reap a harvest if we do not give up. Therefore, as we have opportunity, let us do good to all people, especially to those who belong to the family of believers (Galatians 6:7–10).*

Surely these words from the New Testament are still relevant for us in the twenty-first century. They echo the Old Testament proverb, 'Righteousness exalts a nation, but sin is a disgrace to any people' (Proverbs 14:34).

## SUMMARY

Certainly these words from the Old Testament would have been endorsed by the great thinkers and writers on the relationship between the Church and the State in previous generations.

The Anglican Reformer Richard Hooker was so clear. He supported not only the Bible but also Aristotle's contention that 'for every politic society' the aim should be not simply 'to provide for life as for means of living well'. He saw that the only way to 'live well' was to be obedient to God. So he argued that 'human societies are much more to care for that which tendeth properly unto the soul's estate than for such temporal things as this life doth stand in need of'.[9]

It is dangerous for States like the United Kingdom (and the United States) to attempt to direct society to 'live well' when it has lost that spiritual vision rooted in the assumptions, values and morality of the Judaeo-Christian tradition. It leads to the totalitarianisms witnessed in the twentieth century. It is leading, as we enter the twenty-first century, to a creeping totalitarianism where a new morality and a new paganism are being imposed under the cloak of liberal legislation.

We face a dilemma at the start of the twenty-first century. The alternative to an immorally interfering State is a morally *laissez-faire* State where anything goes. This was the ideal of John Stuart Mill in the nineteenth century and the reality for much of the West in the twentieth century. In the twentieth century such *laissez faire* was possible because of an inherited Christian culture, whose laws and institutions formed a framework within which 'living well' could freely be attempted. The situation is very different now, as that culture is eroding at the beginning of the twenty-first century.

In 1942 Christopher Dawson wrote, 'During the nineteenth century in the heyday of economic expansion and bourgeois prosperity, it seemed as though the world could get along very well if everybody looked after their own interests and agreed to differ on everything else.'[10] Alec Vidler commented on this observation,

> *The practical implications of this did not become clear in this country for a long time, because there was – indeed there still is – a protracted hang-over from the past of a diffused and diluted Christianity in the State, so that a condition of moral and spiritual chaos did not immediately appear. Is it not beginning to appear now?*[11]

Vidler's basic question is this: 'Is political well-being, and political unity, compatible in the long run with every degree of religious

[9] Richard Hooker, *Of the Laws of Ecclesiastical Polity*, Book VIII, 1.4, Cambridge University Press, 1989, pp. 131ff.

[10] Christopher Dawson, *Dublin Review*, April 1942, p. 113.

[11] Vidler, *The Orb and the Cross*, op. cit., p. 75.

diversity?'[12] The answer must be 'No!' if that religious diversity leads to a relativism that allows the State to defy fundamental moral law. The argument of this book has pointed to the State having a moral duty. Its duty is limited and must be limited, but it is vitally important.

Let the last words be from a former British Prime Minister and a Congregationalist clergyman, expressing their understanding of this 'duty' and the relationship between the Church and State. William Gladstone put it like this in the nineteenth century:

> *The State and the Church have both of them moral agencies. But the State aims at character through conduct: the Church at conduct through character; in harmony with which, the State forbids more than enjoins, the Church enjoins more than forbids. The Church brings down from heaven a divine principle of life, and plants it in the centre of the human heart to work outwards and to leaven the whole mass: the State out of the fragments of primeval virtue, and the powers of the external world, constructs a partial and elementary system, corrective from without, and subsidiary to the great process of redemption and spiritual recovery which advances towards it from within.*[13]

P.T. Forsyth put it more simply early in the twentieth century:

> *Both (Church and State) are divine agents for human perfection. But the one by way of the law and its evolution, the other by way of conscience and its redemption. The State does not exist to make men good, the Church does. The State exists to secure the conditions of goodness, the Church to create the thing itself ... The State is an agent of the Kingdom of God, the Church is the Kingdom of God in the making.*[14]

At the start of a new millennium many in the West are sympathetic to that understanding. The evidence of this book suggests that working towards a similar vision for the Church and State in the twenty-first century would be in the interests of social health and stability.

---

[12] Ibid., p. 77.

[13] William Gladstone, *The State in its relations with the Church*, vol. 1, p. 115ff, quoted in ibid., p. 45.

[14] P.T. Forsyth, *Theology in Church and State*, p. 255, quoted in ibid., p. 95.